FOR KING AND KANATA

For King and Kanata

Canadian Indians and the First World War

TIMOTHY C. WINEGARD

University of Manitoba Press

For King and Kanata : Canadian Indians and the First World War
© Timothy C. Winegard 2012

21   20   19   18   17   3   4   5   6   7

University of Manitoba Press
Winnipeg, Manitoba, Canada
Treaty 1 Territory
uofmpress.ca

Cataloguing data available from Library and Archives Canada
ISBN 978-0-88755-728-6 (PAPER)
ISBN 978-0-88755-418-6 (PDF)
ISBN 978-0-88755-417-9 (EPUB)

Cover design by Frank Reimer
Interior design by Jess Koroscil
Cover image: Ojibwa sniper Private Michael Ackabee,
Library and Archives Canada, e005176082.

Printed in Canada

The University of Manitoba Press acknowledges the financial support
for its publication program provided by the Government of Canada
through the Canada Book Fund, the Canada Council for the Arts, the
Manitoba Department of Sport, Culture, and Heritage,
the Manitoba Arts Council, and the Manitoba
Book Publishing Tax Credit.

Funded by the Government of Canada | Canadä

Contents

Acknowledgements

This book is the product of years of enquiry, deliberation, discussion, and (re)writing, during which time numerous people have given generously of their own research, insight, and time. For starters, I would like to thank Dr. P. Whitney Lackenbauer (and his wife Jennifer) for his indefatigable enthusiasm, his valuable comments and keen eye when reading the manuscript, his sharing of primary sources, and, most importantly, his limitless friendship. I would also like to extend a debt of gratitude to: Prof. Hew Strachan, Bruno and Katie Lamarre, Dr. Sean Maloney, Dr. David Murray, Dr. R. Scott Sheffield, Dr. Noah Honch, Dr. Julian de Hoog, Dr. Robert Johnson, Prof. Terry Copp, Jane Whalen, and the staff at the Laurier Centre for Military, Strategic and Disarmament Studies. Thanks also to Captains Edward Jun and Bryan Bereziuk in Ottawa, and Gregory Liedtke and Ed Wissian at the Royal Military College of Canada for their familiar hospitality and engaging conversation. Thanks to Alan Anderson and Jeff Obermeyer for their acceptance and selfless support, and for graciously inviting me into their families.

I would be remiss if I did not acknowledge the staffs at various archives, libraries, and museums, and the welcoming members and administrators of numerous First Nations for their help and time. Without their valuable knowledge this endeavour would not have been possible. As such, my appreciation must also be extended to my caring editors Jean Wilson and Glenn Bergen, and to David Carr and Cheryl Miki, at the University of Manitoba Press. I am also appreciative of the employees at the Camlachie post office for, not only their interest in my work, but also for handling a never-ending stream of boxes and packages. Life in rural Ontario is a blessing. This research was also made possible through a postdoctoral fellowship from the Security and Defence Forum of the Department of National Defence. In addition, a Social Sciences and Humanities Research Council of Canada postdoctoral fellowship facilitated the completion of this book and the procurement of photographs during 2010–11.

As always, my parents Charles and Marian deserve my utmost thanks and love for their brainstorming sessions, proofreading, and support. They have taught me the ways of the Force and continue to suffer through my endless stories and bouts of frustration without flinching, all the while grounding me to what is most important—our Longhouse. They are both, unquestionably, my heroes. To my siblings, Casey, Kelly, Tom, and Whitter—I love you all. Thanks to my grandparents and great-grandparents for providing such a proud, yet humble, history to which to belong. There are teachings to be heard through silence, and I hope I am listening.

Lastly, while I have enjoyed the generosity of colleagues, friends, and family in writing and preparing this work, any errors remain mine alone. Nine years as an officer in the Canadian Forces taught me to seek and accept responsibility.

Thank you all,
Tim

Camlachie, Ontario
June 2011

This book is to be neither an accusation nor a confession, and least of all an adventure, for death is not an adventure to those who stand face to face with it. It will try simply to tell of a generation of men who, even though they may have escaped shells, were destroyed by the war.

— Erich Maria Remarque,
    dedication to *All Quiet on the Western Front* (1928)

To the First Nations, Inuit, and Métis soldiers who served, and continue to serve, the shared interests of our national forces.

Notes on Sources

Documentation of the participation and contributions of the founding peoples of Canada during the First World War is, surprisingly, scant. Most of the literature dedicated to the wartime experiences of Indians exists within a national perspective permeated by a dominant thematic tradition that P. Whitney Lackenbauer and R. Scott Sheffield label the "Forgotten Warrior" genre.[1] Within this construct, historians and commentators have recently resurrected the exploits of Indian servicemen and -women in order to promote an agenda of recognition and commemoration akin to that bestowed upon their white comrades. The goal of these studies, which succumb to an interpretive orthodoxy based on recycled generalizations and anecdotal corroboration, is to ensure that Indian veterans receive acknowledgement for their forgotten sacrifice in increasingly reconciliatory and apologetic Canadian political and social environments. Fred Gaffen's *Forgotten Soldiers* (1985), *Pegahmagabow: Legendary Warrior, Forgotten Hero* (2003) by Adrian Hayes, and Janice Summerby's *Native Soldiers, Foreign Battlefields* (2005) adhere to this paradigm.[2] While this remembrance is certainly worthy, and extremely important, it is not representative of the broader transnational issues and Canadian-specific realities and policies surrounding Indian participation in the First World War.

In the last decade, however, academics have begun to deviate from this motif by engaging in more scholarly appraisals, represented by L. James Dempsey's *Warriors of the King: Prairie Indians in World War I* (1999).[3] Similarly, other detailed explorations of regional contributions and community-specific experiences have recently appeared.[4] Nevertheless, all accounts remain lodged in a national framework permeated by the "Forgotten Warrior" approach. Historians have not moved beyond blinding national affiliations and have completely disregarded the position of the British Colonial and War Offices in requesting, and promoting, Indian service. This investigation addresses this national component, along with the dominant international themes that directly influenced Indian participation, and the policies and administration surrounding their multi-faceted involvement in the Great War.

The most valuable sources of information for this investigation were archival records from the Library and Archives of Canada (Ottawa), the National Archives of the United Kingdom (Kew, London), the House of Lords Records Office/Parliamentary Archives (London), and small collections from the United States National Archives (Washington, DC). In addition, Colonial and War Office records, and those of certain secretaries, were consulted at various libraries in the United Kingdom, including the national British Library in London and the Bodleian Library at the University of Oxford. Select libraries, departments, and ministries in Canada, such as the Department of Indian Affairs, also provided valuable information. The annual reports of Indian Affairs, available online from Library and Archives Canada, are an excellent source of national and regional information. The *Canada Yearbook,* published annually by the former Office of Census and Statistics, also available online, contains an extremely detailed statistical database for Indian Affairs. This resource should certainly be taken advantage of by any student or scholar investigating Native-newcomer relations. The application of this raw data, in combination with information from other sources, has provided context for many aspects of the Indian war experience.

Maps, Tables, and Illustrations

Maps

Tables

Illustrations

Preface

Any author investigating aspects of First Nations history must, if by peer scrutiny alone, delineate approaches to descriptive nouns and chronological representations. Yet each label assigned to the original peoples who traversed the land mass known as Beringia to eventually populate "the Americas" is flawed in both proof and construct. Anthropologists, geneticists, and historians, not to mention the oral histories of the descendants of these original hunter-explorers, provide numerous, and often contradicting, explanations and theories for the settlement of what we now refer to as the Western hemisphere.

The name Beringia itself is proof enough of the endless cycle of deconstruction and reconstruction of terminology. The Bering Strait, over which a 1,000 mile-wide "bridge" joined Siberia to Alaska, between 60,000 and 16,500 years ago, was one passage by which peoples "globalized" (as some historians purport) the entire land mass approximately 12,000 years ago. When the Danish-born navigator of the Russian Navy, Vitus Jonassen Bering, travelled the coastal waters of the Arctic in 1741, he surely was not aware that the geographical namesakes bestowed upon him would ultimately lead to such political and academic discourse.

What follows is a detailed account of the involvement of Canadian (and at times American, by way of geographical, historical, and ethnological association)[1] First Nations, indigenous, Native, Aboriginal, and Indian populations during the First World War—all of these nomenclatures are flawed and debatable in perception and definition. A lifelong friend of the *Aamjiwnaang* Chippewa (Ojibwa) of Sarnia once told me, "Tim, I was born an Indian, raised an Indian, treated like an Indian, so I will die an Indian." I assumed he had heard this somewhere before or, perhaps, was misquoting Sioux activist Russell Means or Vine Deloria Jr's *Custer Died for Your Sins: An Indian Manifesto* (1969).[2] Nevertheless, he taught me much in that adolescent conversation about "Indianness" and I will use, for this work, his blunt and honest appraisal. J.R. Miller asserts, "Much of the language used in relation to aboriginal peoples is as likely to obscure as to clarify what and whom is under discussion....

Whatever term one uses, there will almost certainly be someone who takes exception to it."[3] The debate and deconstruction and reconstruction of lexis, therefore, will be left to those so inclined.

Indian will be used to describe those First Peoples of Canada, and of the United States when required for comparison. Some scholars choose to place the word *Indian* in quotation marks to affirm the flawed construction of the label; others simply replace the word with the more current *Aboriginal* or *First Nations*. Yet, to employ an alternative word or phrase, or to surround in quotation marks, is to impart a consciousness to policy makers and populations that did not exist at the time in which this history takes place. For the most part, both Indians and non-Indians used the word, exclusively, during the nineteenth and early twentieth centuries.

Given the multiplicity and diversity of Indian nations, however, Indians did not represent a monolithic, homogenous entity. Many Indians felt a stronger affiliation to their clans than to either their nations or (unknown prior to European contact) their Indian collective. Moreover, enduring animosities still existed between traditional enemies. Therefore, grouping them together as Canadian Indians is seemingly specious. Fundamentally, however, based on the dominant policies of the Canadian and British governments, this generalization is not only unavoidable but also indicative of the social and political environments in Canada during the years of, and surrounding, the First World War. Community-specific Indian actions and reactions, however, did not match blanketed and sweeping political and military policies of the government of Canada. Indian nations or tribal groupings, therefore, will be applied where they directly relate to the arguments and are imperative to underscore important regional differences and decisions.

Given the number of Indian languages represented within Canada, their use will be kept to a minimum unless central to explanation and understanding. European names for Indian nations will be adhered to, not out of ignorance or insensitivity but to enhance readability and, more importantly, to adhere to contemporary convention. For example, the term *Mohawk* will be used in place of their linguistic name, *Kanien'keha:ka,* and *Blood* in place of *Kainai.* The Indian name will only be used when it is synonymous with the European counterpart, which in most cases, not surprisingly, is rare. Indian letters and writings, however, will be originally quoted (without interpolation) where they are readily comprehensible.

Defining settlers from the British Isles is also problematic, since many considered themselves Scottish, Irish, Welsh, or English, not communally British, as history purports. Conversely, settlers in Canada from the British Isles did feel strong connections to the metropole, shared many of the same cultural and societal values, and increasingly identified themselves as British. Hence, in most instances the term *British* will be used to describe those settlers from the British Isles during the periods of association with Indians. In the years approaching the First World War, a national Canadian identity began to emerge and was solidified in myth by the war itself, ushering in a more ambivalent stance towards imperial associations and British collectivism.

The term *contact* represents the first encounters between Indians and Europeans. This is not to impart the idea that Indian nations do not have, based on archaeological evidence and scientific theory, arguably over 15,000 (or as many as 60,000) years of history and socio-cultural evolution before the Norse temporarily settled and made contact with peoples they dubbed *Skrealings* on Newfoundland at the dawn of the eleventh century. Contact implies that Indian nations underwent an unavoidable cataclysmic crisis, unparalleled in their known previous history, due to the introduction of disease and an adoption of killing potential through the use of European weapon systems. Indian populations were moribund within 300 years of the introduction of deadly disease, warfare, and contact with peoples of differing genetic dispositions and viral immunities.

The Dominion of Newfoundland, which included mainland Labrador, was independent of Canada; it did not join the confederation until 1949. During the First World War, the 1st Newfoundland Regiment/Royal Newfoundland Regiment was raised, and distinctly maintained, from Canadian divisions and the Canadian Corps. The unit fought at Gallipoli and on the Western Front independent of Canadian formations, and it was under the political control of the Newfoundland (and British) government. The government of Newfoundland was responsible, in partnership with the imperial government, for promulgating its own policies for all aspects of the war. In many instances these policies did not mirror those of neighbouring Canada. Although Newfoundland-Labrador's Indian and Eskimo history, including that of the First World War, is now generally allied to that of Canada, it will be excluded from this investigation. Given its diminutive and remote indigenous population (an estimated 1,700 in 1914), Newfoundland did not formulate any Indian/Eskimo-specific military policies. Through Canadian and Newfoundland-Labrador archival records, this author has confirmed only twenty-one men of indigenous heritage who served in Newfoundland forces during the war.

Likewise, there is no evidence to suggest that the scattered Eskimo populations of Canada, totalling roughly 3,450 in 1914, were given any consideration by either the Ministry of Militia or Indian Affairs as a source of military manpower. In fact, they were wholly ignored in both policy and practice. Accordingly, Eskimos are generally excluded from this study, as are the Métis. During the First World War, Métis were not legally bound to or defined by the tenets of the *Indian Act*, and they were able to enlist in the same manner as Euro-Canadians.[4] While the wartime contributions of Métis soldiers and communities were certainly unique, policy did not shape their participation. The Indian experience, therefore, is the focus of this book.

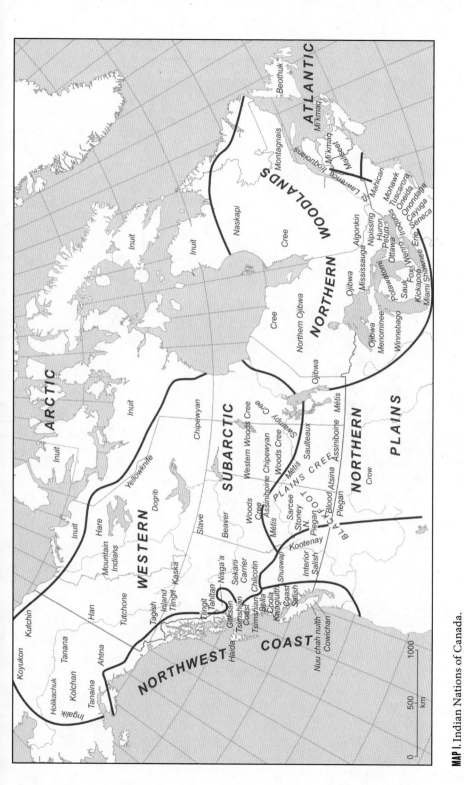

MAP I. Indian Nations of Canada.

Source: J.R. Miller, *Skyscrapers Hide the Heavens: A History of Indian-White Relations in Canada* (Toronto: University of Toronto Press, 2000), xvi. Reprinted with permission of the publisher.

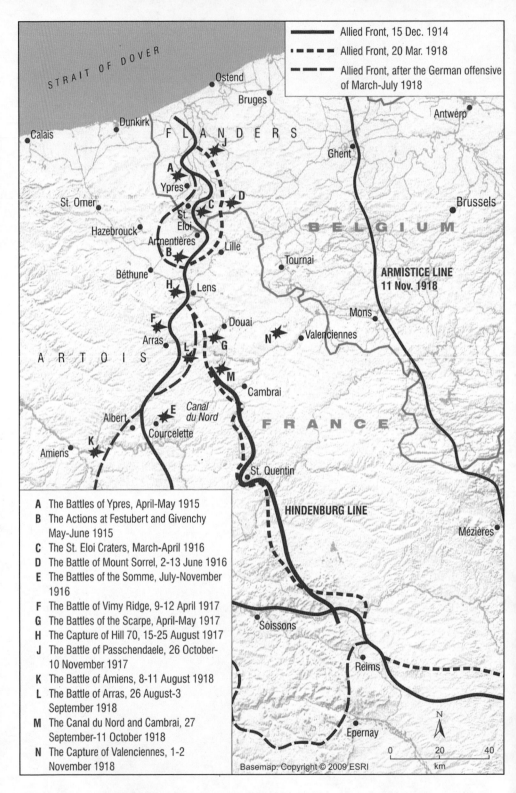

Legend:
- Allied Front, 15 Dec. 1914
- Allied Front, 20 Mar. 1918
- Allied Front, after the German offensive of March-July 1918

STRAIT OF DOVER

Ostend
Bruges
Antwerp
Dunkirk
Calais
F L A N D E R S
Ghent
J
A
Ypres
St. Omer
Brussels
D
C
B E L G I U M
St. Eloi
Hazebrouck
Armentières
Lille
B
Tournai
ARMISTICE LINE
11 Nov. 1918
Béthune
H
Lens
Mons
F
Douai
Valenciennes
Arras
L
G
N
A R T O I S
M
Cambrai
F R A N C E
E
Canal
du Nord
Albert
Courcelette
K
Amiens
St. Quentin

HINDENBURG LINE

Mézières

Soissons

Reims

Epernay

N

0   20   40
km

A The Battles of Ypres, April-May 1915
B The Actions at Festubert and Givenchy May-June 1915
C The St. Eloi Craters, March-April 1916
D The Battle of Mount Sorrel, 2-13 June 1916
E The Battles of the Somme, July-November 1916
F The Battle of Vimy Ridge, 9-12 April 1917
G The Battles of the Scarpe, April-May 1917
H The Capture of Hill 70, 15-25 August 1917
J The Battle of Passchendaele, 26 October-10 November 1917
K The Battle of Amiens, 8-11 August 1918
L The Battle of Arras, 26 August-3 September 1918
M The Canal du Nord and Cambrai, 27 September-11 October 1918
N The Capture of Valenciennes, 1-2 November 1918

Basemap: Copyright © 2009 ESRI

MAP 2. The Western Front, 1914–18: Canadian Operations.
Source: Department of National Defence.

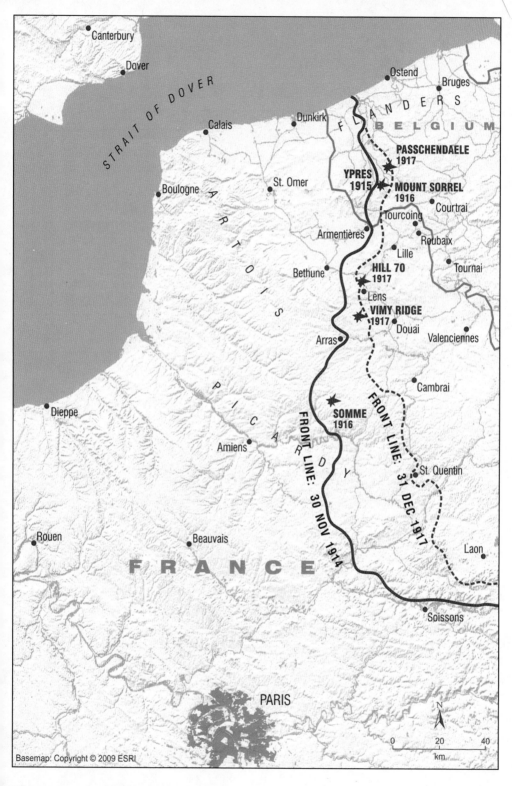

MAP 3. The Western Front: Topography and Battles.
Source: Department of National Defence.

FOR KING AND KANATA

Introduction

On Christmas Eve 1893, in customary Blood tradition, a medicine woman proclaimed the birth of Kukutosi-poota (Flying Star), or Albert Mountain Horse. His mother, Sikski, then offered her son to the Great Spirit: "The medicine women stood in dignified silence. She was not surprised by the baby for she knew her medicine was strong." The shower of "stars lighting the sky foretold that this boy would be a great man." Albert was fated to be an Indian-Canadian warrior-soldier and, by November 1915, a fatality in the "Great War for Civilization."[1]

During his childhood, Mountain Horse learned and practised the traditional customs and beliefs of the Blood, while being educated at the nearby Anglican St. Paul's Mission Boarding School. Like many young Indians of the time, Albert was torn between his traditional mores and the government's insistence on residential edification and assimilation. Nevertheless, Albert was described as "one of the brightest and most enlightened boys on the Reserve," and he thrived in St. Paul's cadet program.[2]

He volunteered for the militia summer training program in Calgary and, after completion, was commissioned a lieutenant in the Canadian Militia. At the outbreak of war in 1914, Albert was serving as a cadet instructor with the 23rd Alberta Rangers. He volunteered and was accepted into the Canadian Expeditionary Force (CEF) on 23 September 1914, taking a demotion to the rank of private to minimize further officer training and be deployed more quickly. Albert proudly exclaimed that he was "going forth to fight for my King and Country." He sailed with the 10th Battalion as part of the First Canadian Contingent in October 1914. Due to unofficial regulations excluding Indians from service, Albert was one of only a handful of Indians in the initial deployment of over 35,000 men: "I do not think the Germans will stand any chance when we get over there.... I am very anxious to get to the war."[3] For Albert, the war would be short-lived.

The sunny afternoon of 22 April 1915 was marked by a warm breeze blowing in the face of the Canadian battalions holding a portion of the line on

Gravenstafel Ridge in the Ypres Salient. Albert and the newly arrived 1st Division were enjoying a respite from the incessant German shelling. The warm wind, however, soon turned deadly. At 4:00 p.m., the Germans unleashed a sweeping bombardment on the Allied front. An hour later, a greyish-green cloud, six kilometres wide, slowly rolled over no man's land toward the 45th Algerian and 87th French Territorial Divisions occupying the Canadian left flank. This first gas attack of the war began the Second Battle of Ypres and the first major action for the inexperienced Canadian "civilian soldiers."[4]

This day also likely saw the death of the first Canadian Indian during the First World War. Private Angus Laforce, a Mohawk from Kahnawake, Quebec, went missing on the evening of 22 April. The following day, Lieutenant Cameron D. Brant of the Six Nations of the Grand River, great-great-grandson of Joseph Brant (Thayendanegea), was killed leading his men in a counterattack. His body was never recovered. His commanding officer, Lieutenant Colonel Arthur Birchall, a Briton on loan to the CEF, remarked that Brant was "quiet and unobtrusive [but] The Boys will follow him everywhere." Like his forefathers, Cameron was a worthy ally of the British Crown, prompting Six Nations elders to predict that "such nobility of purpose and sacrifice of life will go far to further cement the many units of our citizenship into one great unified front."[5]

At 4:00 a.m. on 24 April, the Germans launched a second gas attack, accompanied by an intense ten-minute artillery barrage aimed directly at Canadian forward positions. Albert Mountain Horse and his 10th Battalion, acting as a reserve unit, were pushed forward to close the gaps, preventing a German breakthrough. He wrote of this experience in a letter to his brother Mike:

> As I am writing this letter the shrapnel is bursting over our heads. I was in the thick of the fighting at Ypres and we had to get out of it. The Germans were using the poisonous gas on our men—oh it was awful—it is worse than anything I know of. I don't mind the rifle fire and the shells bursting around us, but this gas is the limit. I have a German helmet I want to give you … my it's a good one. I took it from a Prussian Guard. I gave him the steel through the mouth and then took his helmet.

Albert survived the fighting at Ypres only to be gassed twice more and was never able to give the souvenir helmet to his brother. He was hospitalized because of gas poisoning and, with acute respiratory distress, subsequently

contracted tuberculosis, a disease twenty times more prevalent among Indians than whites: "I told him [the doctor] I would sooner die like a man in the
trenches than have a grave dug for me." On 19 November 1915, only one day
after arriving in Canada, twenty-one-year-old Albert Mountain Horse died at
Quebec City. His body was shipped home to Macleod, Alberta, and Albert was
given a military funeral, presided over by his St. Paul's schoolmaster, the Reverend Samuel Henry Middleton, who described Albert as "One of the Empire's
greatest sons who fought to uphold the prestige and traditions of the British
race, and having gained all the honours and respect which can be shown to
a soldier and a man, has cast a brilliant reflection on the Blood Indians of
Alberta, proving to the world at large he was truly an Indian warrior."[6]

Shortly thereafter, Albert's older brothers Mike and Joe enlisted, as official
sanction to enrol Indians had been granted in December 1915. According to
Mike, "Reared in the environment of my forefathers, the spirit of revenge for
my brother's death manifested itself strongly in me as I gazed down on Albert
lying in his coffin that cold winter day in November 1915."[7] Joe was wounded
three times and survived the war. Mike was buried alive for four days at Cambrai in October 1917, leading to his hospitalization for shell shock. Upon
returning to action, he was twice wounded, attained the rank of sergeant, and
won the Distinguished Conduct Medal (DCM) for bravery. Following the war,
Mike became a translator for the Royal Canadian Mounted Police (RCMP), a
locomotive mechanic for the Canadian Pacific Railway (CPR), a journalist for
local newspapers, and a member of his band council.[8] His name now fittingly
adorns Mike Mountain Horse Elementary School in Lethbridge, Alberta.

More than 68,000 Canadian soldiers gave their lives during the First World
War, including approximately 300 Canadian Indians.[9] They lie in cemeteries
under white stones proudly bearing the maple leaf, or are simply remembered
by their names etched into a memorial, war having sequestered their bodies to
an unknown grave. (The names of Brant and Laforce adorn the Menin Gate in
Ypres.)[10] These cemeteries and memorials are scattered throughout Belgium
and France in towns whose names have become commonplace in Canadian
vocabulary. Ypres, Vimy, and Passchendaele are but a few that are emblazoned
on the cenotaphs of towns, cities, and Indian territories throughout Canada,
reflecting the shared sacrifice, and the inescapable impact, of the First World
War on all communities of the young nation.

From a population numbering 7.88 million, over 620,000 Canadians served in the Canadian Expeditionary Force (CEF) between 1914 and 1919. This number included over 4,000 Canadian Indians from a total 1914 population of 103,774 (excluding non-status Indians, Métis, and Eskimos). This enlistment figure represents 35 percent of the male Indian population of military age, roughly equal to the percentage of Euro-Canadians who enlisted. According to a 1919 Indian Affairs report of the Great War, "it must be remembered, moreover, that there were undoubtedly cases of Indian enlistment which were not reported to the department."[11] The exact number of Indians to serve in the First World War cannot be decisively tabulated. Most status Indians were not recorded as such upon enlistment, as attestation papers did not record race. Likewise, Indian Affairs lists compiled through the "Return of Indian Enlistments" form by Indian agents for individual reserves in 1917, and again in 1919, rarely included Indians from the Territories, and, most conspicuously, non-status Indians.[12] Nevertheless, through these lists, which are available for consultation at the Library and Archives of Canada, it is certain that at least 4,000 status Indians were enrolled in the CEF.

Although embarrassingly under-prepared at the outbreak of war, Canada was able to deploy an expeditionary force much larger than could have been imagined on 28 June 1914, when Austrian Archduke Ferdinand and his wife Sophie were assassinated by Gavrilo Princip in Sarajevo, an event that ignited the first major European war since the early nineteenth century. The outbreak of the First World War shattered almost 100 years of relative peace in Europe. Its nations had circumvented large-scale conflict since the defeat of Napoleon in 1815 through treaties, alliances, and an aspiration to maintain a balance of power in Europe and empire. In place of war, European armies were deployed to the fringes of empire to gain territorial acquisitions within the imperial scramble, or to quell indigenous rebellions in existing colonies.[13]

By 1914 the pan-European empire covered 84 percent of the globe, compared to 35 percent in 1800. The British Empire encompassed one-fourth of the world, and 445 million people lived under some form of British rule.[14] Within the social norms of this Victorian era and the ethnocentric ideologies of Social Darwinism, indigenous peoples were seen as an unfortunate component of the "white man's burden." Most were viewed as an inconvenient obstruction to imperial expansion driven by economic opportunity, religious agendas, and a desire to promote civilization, with its political and cultural appendages, to those deemed deficient, including Canadian Indians.

Crown-owned Indian reserves, incorporated into imperial protocol during the 1830s, served two strategic purposes: they opened up land for unhindered settlement and industry, and they established a framework by which Indians could be integrated or, alternatively, easily monitored. Reserves, however, were never intended to be a permanent solution to the "Indian Question." It was believed that the majority of Indians would die off (given the drastic decline in population since contact) and that those remaining would willingly enter Euro-Canadian society. The *Indian Act*, successive civilizing policies, and governmental programs, such as industrial and residential schools, were designed to abet this process to final assimilation.

Military service, however, was not generally viewed as a viable medium to achieve this end. At the dawn of the twentieth century, consolidation of the Canadian settler-state was ongoing, and the potential for armed Indian resistance still existed, most notably on the prairies. Training and arming Indians in a military capacity, therefore, would be dangerous to the domestic security of Canada.[15] In fact, at the onset of war no imperialist European state or overseas colony, save for France, regarded their indigenous populations as a source of military manpower for a European war.[16] Contemporary science, social biases, and public opinion accepted that certain identifiable ethnic groups lacked the intelligence and integrity to fight modern war. It was also believed that, since these groups were the subjects of vast European empires, prudence warned against allowing them to fight in a European war and thus forfeiting white racial supremacy.

Nevertheless, with Britain's declaration of war on 4 August 1914, most Indian communities and leaders openly declared their loyalty and sought avenues to exemplify their allegiance and worth to both Canada and the Crown. The majority of treaties and military alliances were fostered with Britain, not with Canada. Many communities offered support of men and money directly to the king, or the "Great White Father." Indian chiefs and leaders acted as "bridge people" between their cultures and repressive Canadian social and political systems. Linda Tuhiwai Smith asserts that "Their elite status came about through the alignment of their cultural and economic interests with the colonizing group rather than with those of their own society."[17] This interpretation, however, removes the dynamic and conscious participation of Indian peoples within the colonial experience and during the First World War.

Many believed that excelling, and showing themselves to be as capable as Euro-Canadians in so-called European civilized pursuits, was a means to prove their worth as Indians both individually and collectively—in other words, they embraced selective assimilation for the aims of equality and autonomy. This is not to say, however, that these Indians viewed themselves as assimilated, nor did it mean that they had rejected their culture. While certain commentators have criticized these chiefs and leaders for abandoning or becoming estranged from their traditional roots, given contemporary racial attitudes and socio-economic and political realities, this is unwarranted. The majority believed that by entering and engaging in Canadian society as Indians, they could participate on equal terms and win the respect of the dominant non-Indian society in order to gain rights for their own peoples. Accordingly, many viewed the First World War as an extension of this approach. Therefore, what follows is, by necessity, as much a socio-political and cultural investigation as it is a documentation of strictly military history.

In effect, just as the war stimulated and was used to promote nationalist attitudes and demands in Canada in relation to the imperial government, the same can be said for Indians in relation to Canada. Indians sought the same recognition from Canada (and to a certain extent the Crown) that Canada sought from the mother country—equality and autonomy. For both parties, significant participation in the war represented one avenue to achieve these ambitions. In this sense, the patriotic reactions of many Indian leaders in 1914, and their subsequent actions throughout the war, were no different from those of Prime Minister Sir Robert Borden and Canadian politicians. In an often overlooked premise, Canada did not cease to be an evolving settler society in light of the Great War.

Generally, Indians willingly participated in all aspects of the First World War. Four interwoven themes dominate this participation and the framework of this book. First, the calculated inclusion of Canadian Indians was not a departure from, but rather a continuation of, the pragmatic tradition of imperial and Canadian governments to use them in a military capacity only when it suited British-Canadian interests and the fulfilment of desiderata. This is exemplified by a catalogue of occurrences throughout the history of colonial warfare of North America and during imperial expeditionary campaigns.

Indians were employed as scouts during both the Red River (1869–70) and North-West (1885) Rebellions. They were specifically recruited as voyageurs by General Lord Wolseley for his 1884–85 Nile expedition to relieve Major General Charles Gordon at the besieged city of Khartoum. Conversely, Indians were officially excluded from the Canadian force raised for the Second Anglo-Boer War (1899–1902) and received no mention in the 1904 *Militia Act*. According to R. Scott Sheffield, "This was clearly differentiation in practice, meaning that Aboriginal individuals were specifically recruited for, and their service was defined by, culturally and/or racially defined skills and characteristics."[18] The progression of Indian participation during the First World War was an extension of this practice.

Second, based on collective imperial requirements and Canadian-specific necessities, primarily the need for manpower, this participation can be separated into three distinct phases. The period from the outbreak of war to December 1915 can generally be depicted by limited or restrictive policies regarding service. Although no official policy forbade the enlistment of Indians, the Ministry of Militia and Department of Indian Affairs actively discouraged enlistment and Indian-specific recruitment; thus, few were accepted for service. The war was expected to be short-lived, and the initial Canadian commitment of one infantry division was easily filled by men primarily of British stock, many with prior military service. Furthermore, the 1st Division did not deploy to the front until March 1915. The stage from December 1915 to the conclusion of 1916 saw restrictive policies relaxed and formal guidelines issued. By 1916 both ministries were advocating for, and lending support to, Indian recruitment, following the October 1915 British requests for their military employment. Coupled with the pressure provided by these appeals was the need for recruits to fuel the demand for manpower in a war of attrition. The 1st Division had suffered horrific casualties during the 1915 battles of Ypres, Festubert, and Givenchy. More importantly, on 1 January 1916 Borden raised the authorized strength of the CEF from 250,000 to 500,000 men. By August 1916 the Canadian Corps comprised four divisions, supported by auxiliary formations, and manpower was crucial in maintaining its fighting strength in the face of mounting casualties. In the final phase of Indian participation, from 1917 to the armistice, the government took a more active role in the recruitment of Indians to meet the increasing demand for replacements following the devastating losses sustained during the battles of St. Eloi Craters, the Somme, Vimy, and Passchendaele. Manpower concerns led to the contentious realization of conscription in August 1917, which initially included Indians. Mandatory service, however, led to a reassessment of their rights and those obligations of the Canadian government under treaties and laws.

Third, the abilities of Indians as soldiers and the perception of their martial prowess were measured against the colonial experience, including warfare and contemporary racial theories. Racial estimations were manifested in the function, role, and unit designation of Indians within the CEF. Some military recruiters believed Indians had enhanced martial proclivities and enrolled them as snipers and scouts, while others viewed them as little more than enlisted labourers and assigned them to non-combat service and support battalions. This dichotomy is the case in point to the pervasive concept of the noble savage that existed in the literature and racial discourse of British and Canadian societies.[19] For the Canadian government, however, military service was simply assimilation by other means, which mirrored the contemporary policies of the Department of Indian Affairs and the general consciousness of the Euro-Canadian social order. No unit composed solely of Indians was ever created, despite numerous proposals by senior officers and influential civilians. Borden and representatives from the Ministry of Militia and the Department of Indian Affairs refused to endorse these offers. Unlike blacks, both French Canadians (aside from the 22nd "Van Doos" Battalion) and Indians were scattered across CEF units to promote assimilation or—as Lieutenant General Sir Arthur Currie argued—equality with their peers.

Lastly, the vast Canadian Expeditionary Force, driven by the magnitude of the war and the incessant need for manpower, correspondingly led to a greater inclusion of Indians than had been previously required or witnessed. Britain and Canada called upon their subject peoples, in varying degrees, to defend the institutions of their subjugation.[20] The elevated Indian participation during the First World War, therefore, was the pivotal catalyst for their attainment of equal rights. For the first time in history they had been summoned, in unprecedented numbers, to fight and labour on foreign fields alongside Canadian, imperial, and other Allied soldiers for the common purpose of defending liberty and civilization.

Accordingly, Indian involvement in the war is inextricably coupled with that of Canada and Britain and, to some extent, linked to the evolution of the war in its entirety. The actions of the senior British government and military command, of its junior ally, Canada, and of Indian nations did not exist in isolation; rather, they formed a tripartite relationship that is the history of Canada's Indian populations during the Great War. Duncan Campbell Scott, deputy superintendent general of Indian Affairs from 1913 to 1932, rightly stated in 1919 that "The story of the part played by them at the front is, therefore, of necessity a series of disconnected incidents, rather, than a continuous narrative."[21]

Canadian histories of the First World War all too often depict Canadian contributions as if detached from the governing political and military structures of the imperial government. While the performance of the Canadian Corps was exemplary, and Prime Minister Sir Robert Borden and the corps commander (as of June 1917), Lieutenant General Sir Arthur Currie, achieved a semblance of autonomy for the CEF unparalleled by other dominions, Canadian formations were nevertheless part of the larger British Expeditionary Force (BEF). Correspondingly, the political influence of the British War and Colonial Offices in Canadian decisions surrounding the military service of Indians has been wholly and detrimentally overlooked.

At the outbreak of war in 1914, many Indian nations, or communities, felt a stronger allegiance to the Crown, under which treaties were signed and previous military alliances fostered, than to Canada, and they readily offered support of men and money directly to the king. Canadian Indians shared equally in the burdens of the war, both on the battlefields and on the home front, and voluntarily aided the empire in its time of need. As an Assiniboine elder remarked to his young men at the outbreak of war, "Don't die a woman's death in bed. Die the warrior's death at the end of the warpath trail, where a coup-feather awaits the brave."[22]

Chapter One

Indians and the Settler-State Experience

Canada progressed through a lengthy colonial experience, primarily under British sponsorship. It was a pioneer rather than a sojourner colony and was viewed as vacant for permanent European settlement. Land soon became the common currency, rapidly bringing settlers into conflict with Indian peoples after the inevitable shift from "beachhead settlements" to pastoral expansion into the hinterlands. In 1516, at the onset of British imperialism, Sir Thomas More's *Utopia* foreshadowed the pervasive themes of land acquisition, warfare, and assimilation that dominated European-Indian relations in Canada:

> If the natives wish to live with Utopians, they are taken in. Since they join the colony willingly, they quickly adopt the same institutions and customs. This is advantageous for both peoples. For by their policies and practices the Utopians make the land yield an abundance for all, which before seemed too small and barren for the natives alone. If the natives will not conform to their laws, they drive them out of the area they claim for themselves, waging war if they meet resistance. Indeed they account it a very just cause of war if a people possess land that they leave idle and uncultivated and refuse the use and occupancy of it to others who according to the law of nature ought to be supported from it.[1]

Despite the fact that North American Indian societies were less technologically developed than some Asian and European cultures, multifarious trade routes networking the entire continent had existed for millennia prior to contact. Complex political organizations, many very democratic, were strongly rooted in Indian ideologies, and great empires flourished. Warfare played an important role in the political, social, cultural, and genetic frameworks of Indian nations. Before contact, given the small population groupings, no standing warrior class could be maintained, as it was in European nations or princely states. Any substantial loss of men was detrimental to the overall welfare of these small bands of people. Additionally, the duration of any conflict was limited since participants, generally members of non-surplus-producing economies, were forced to cease hostilities to resume food gathering and hunting. During colonial warfare, these disadvantages accrued and left Indian populations incapable of fighting the more robust standing European or American forces.

In pre-contact warfare, raiding parties, which were led by proven war chiefs and usually numbered less than 200 warriors, were sent to settle scores, to acquire provisions, or to avenge the deaths of or replace deceased clan members (known as mourning wars).[2] The widespread practice of incorporating prisoners into the clan, often after a period of servitude or torture, ensured the exchange of cultural information, the configuration of alliances, enhanced trading opportunities, and the dissemination of broader genetic traits. Arranged marriages provided similar benefits. These practices perpetuated a chronic state of war, although protracted campaigns usually followed sowing and, subsequently, the harvest.[3] War chiefs were followed out of courage, respect, and experience, yet individual warriors had the prerogative to abandon campaigns if they lost confidence in their leaders. Tactics were based on "an impressive individual self-discipline grounded on personal honour, not fear of punishment."[4] Lawrence H. Keeley argues in his acclaimed work *War Before Civilization: The Myth of the Peaceful Savage* (1996), that pre-contact warfare in North America was far more prevalent than previously thought, and it was witness to large-scale massacres, including those of women and children. He concludes that population density had no correlation with either the frequency or intensity of war, and that those societies involved in dynamic trade also engaged more habitually in war.[5]

Nevertheless, there can be no doubt that for all the inhabitants of the Americas the arrival of Europeans was the most significant disturbance and threat to their populations, civilizations, and futures. The clash of mores encompassed many contradicting characteristics: a rapidly evolving modernity, stemming from the Reformation and the Age of Reason, set against indigenous tradition, relatively undisturbed by any equivalent social or intellectual revolution; Christianity versus a multiplicity of shamanistic and animistic rituals; European expansionism compared with relative isolation in the Americas.[6] Furthermore, the literate European society contrasted with an Indian oral tradition, which led to great misunderstandings and, at times, perfidious actions on the part of Europeans. Also, with the arrival of Europeans came modern weapons, deadly diseases, religion, and alcohol. Continental European wars were imported into North America, and Indians were enlisted to participate. These wars, in combination with trade, fractured long-standing Indian relations and altered the status quo. All had a profound impact on the shaping of North America.

Throughout the first two centuries of contact, the colonial wars that pitted the world's two most dominant powers, Britain and France, against one another in a struggle for imperial domination left Indian nations in the uncertain position of attempting to promote their own interests and agendas in the face of a cultural upheaval. J.R. Miller points out that "notions that one nation, or another took up arms to advance a commercial or strategical aim of the French or British were erroneous."[7] Indifferent to underlying motives, European settlers simply used Indians to satisfy their own needs.

European settlers and successive colonial and Canadian governments used an assortment of non-sequential strategies to subjugate Indian populations. These approaches included, but were not limited to: waging decisive military campaigns; destabilizing or banning political organizations and power structures; removing or inhibiting identifiable cultural traits and language; creating economic and trade dependency; drastically shifting demographics in Europeans' favour; and, most importantly and antagonistically, expropriating and limiting the land base of Indian nations, which was the foundation of their cultural fabric and livelihood.

However, early contact between Canadian Indians, who had a total population estimated between 300,000 and 350,000, and Europeans was, for the most part, peaceful and mutually beneficial through the medium of trade. During an encounter with the Mi'kmaq in 1534, Jacques Cartier observed that the Indians "set up a great clamour and made frequent signs to us to come on shore, holding up to us some furs on sticks," while the women remained hidden in the bush.[8] This description indicates that the coastal Indians of eastern Canada had interacted with European fishermen (with obvious inference to sexual exploitation) prior to Cartier's explorations. The disputation over land has existed in Canada since Cartier erected a cross at Pointe Penouille on 22 July 1534, to the strong objections of the St. Lawrence Iroquois: "We erected this cross on the point in their presence and they watched it being put together and set up.... And pointing to the cross he [the chief] made us a long harangue ... then he pointed to the land all around about, as if he wished to say that all this region belonged to him, and that we ought not to have set up this cross without his permission."[9] Arguably, this is the first land claim within the Canadian Native-newcomer relationship.

Europeans came to the Americas for fish, fur, exploration, riches comparable to those of the Inca and Aztec, and, finally, to promote Christianity. Originally, Indians tolerated the fishing, eagerly embraced the fur trade, cooperated with exploration if it did not interfere with their own interests, and, in certain Indian nations, most notably the Mi'kmaq and the Huron Confederacy, indulged evangelists.[10] Cross-cultural marriages and sexual relations were frequent, since Indians viewed these unions as representative of trade alliance. Most prevalent with the French fur traders in western Ontario and Manitoba, an area on the fringe of expansion, these partnerships produced the distinct French-Indian (and to a lesser extent Scottish-Indian) Métis population. European populations, however, remained small and were protected by their commodities' value. Europeans were eager for furs and required Indian knowledge, while Indians sought the prestige and practicability of European metals and commodities.[11]

The fur trade, however, in conjunction with the dissemination of European wars, weapons, and disease, and the increasing numbers of settlers, began to disrupt the balance among North American Indians. Furthermore, neither the 1763 Royal Proclamation nor Odawa chief Pontiac's short-lived, yet initially successful, rebellion (1763–66) deterred European settlement west of the Appalachian Mountains and, eventually, the Mississippi watershed. The Royal Proclamation forbade colonists from settling, selling, or buying land west of the Appalachian Mountains, giving the Crown sole jurisdiction in any transactions involving Indian lands.[12]

As the number of European settlements increased, Indian campaigns to secure access to hunting grounds, in order to attain furs to trade for European wares and firearms, transformed the traditional Indian landscape of North America. (Interpretations of these Indian campaigns, often referred to as the Beaver Wars, generally misinterpret Indian motives.) Those nations that secured furs, and in turn weapons, launched greater offensives against traditional enemies, resulting in the displacement or absorption of conquered tribes. The Iroquois Confederacy, or Six Nations (which include, from east to west: Mohawk, Oneida, Onondaga, Cayuga, Seneca and, as of 1722, the Tuscarora) was the most proficient Indian coalition in this cyclical pattern and quickly monopolized the fur-for-firearms exchange east of the Mississippi River. The

Iroquois used a combination of military might and skilled diplomacy to build an empire (albeit short-lived) that served the British as a protective buffer between British North America and the French, and later the Americans. The Confederacy was a powerful British ally throughout the colonial wars. For example, in 1784, in recognition of their service to the British during the American Revolution (1775–83), Mohawk Joseph Brant and 2,000 followers —predominantly Mohawk, Cayuga, and Onondaga, with smaller numbers of Oneida, Tuscarora, Seneca, Delaware, Tutelo, and Cherokee—were given land in Ontario known as the Six Nations of the Grand River. Other Mohawks, under John Deserontyon (or Deseronto) had been granted land the previous year at the Bay of Quinte (Tyendinaga), east of Belleville, Ontario.[13]

In this atmosphere of cooperation with the British, and as a result of treaties signed by the Crown, Indian nations, especially the Iroquois, regarded themselves (and still do) as autonomous nations within the confines of North America. The alliance between the British and the Iroquois Confederacy, represented by the Silver Covenant Chain, or Two Row Wampum Belt, was originally agreed to by the Confederacy and the Dutch in 1613 and was extended to the British, via the Covenant Chain, in 1677 (or arguably in 1664) and to the United States in 1794. The two parallel beaded purple rows (never touching) signify the mutual coexistence of two sovereign entities—the Iroquois and a European partner—in North America.[14]

Unlike other British settler states, such as New Zealand, Australia, and South Africa, or the Thirteen Colonies/United States, Canada did not experience protracted or incessantly violent frontier warfare, although it was not devoid of confrontation. The reason for this is simply that Indians were far too indispensable to the defence of British North America and were vital allies in the promotion of British strategic interests. The British government and those charged with Indian liaison, most notably Sir William Johnson (1715–74), had to pragmatically accommodate Indian demands in order to safeguard their military allegiance.[15] The United States, however, employed the opposite strategy, which undermined its military potency during the War of 1812. In effect, the Indian-British alliance, or the potential of partnership during that conflict, halted American aggression and incursion, and, ultimately, gratitude must be extended to Canadian (and northern American) Indians for their role in preventing future American threats and in fostering the environment for the confederation of *Kanata*—"our village."[16]

ILLUS. I. The Surviving Six Nations Reserve Veterans of the War of 1812. This studio portrait was taken in July 1882. Left to Right: Young Warner (born c. 1794); John Tutela (born c. 1797); John Smoke Johnson (Sakawaraton, born c. 1792). *Library and Archives Canada, C-085127.*

Following the War of 1812 (1812–15), the Rush-Bagot Treaty (1817) demilitarized the Great Lakes and nullified future American threats. As a result, Indians, including the Iroquois, lost their importance as military allies. They had been used as required and were no longer featured in British strategy. The British began to initiate policies of subjugation and assimilation rather than cooperation. In fact, in the 1820s the British Indian Department was transferred from military to civilian control—an obvious indication of this shift.[17] Indian nations east of Manitoba had decreased in population as a result of war and disease; they were relocated to reserves, by force or necessity, and left economically destitute after the expropriation of their hunting grounds and the collapse of the fur trade. Indian reserves, incorporated into Crown protocol during the 1830s, served two strategic purposes: they opened up land for unhindered settlement and industry, and they established a framework by which Indians could be integrated or, alternatively, easily monitored.[18] The tenets of prior treaties, and the Royal Proclamation of 1763, were never enforced, and the ensuing westward expansion of settlers, in conjunction with the disappearance of the buffalo, threatened the survival of the Plains Indians in both Canada and the United States. As westward settlement increased, construction of the Canadian Pacific Railway (1881–85) eased the passage for further settlement west of Ontario.

After the War of 1812, the United States continued its practice of Indian relocation and patterns of extermination, which reached a tragic nadir under President Andrew Jackson's "Indian Removal" policy (1828–36) and ultimately in the final subjugation of the Sioux at Wounded Knee in 1890. This massacre of Oglala Sioux concluded the American-Indian wars, which had been intermittent between 1622 and 1890.[19] These wars and the slaughtering of buffalo herds (in some instances under U.S. government initiative to starve out or compel the relocation of Indians to reservations) had a detrimental effect on the Plains Indians of Canada. Furthermore, the migration of American Indians, including Sitting Bull and his followers, north across the "Medicine Line" into Canada to escape the punitive expeditions of the U.S. Cavalry escalated existing tensions between the two governments.[20]

The influence of the United States in ushering in Canadian Confederation in 1867 was paramount. Fear of American interests in western Canada, coupled with the American ideology of manifest destiny and 25,000 residual troops stationed on the American plains following the American Civil War (1861–65), spurred the colonies of British North America eagerly to embrace British proposals for confederation. American incursions into western Canada had already taken the form of hunters and whisky traders, who frequently raped and pillaged Indian villages in the absence of any significant Canadian law enforcement. (The North West Mounted Police [NWMP] was not created until 1873.)[21] In addition, the Fenian Raids staged from the U.S. into the Niagara Peninsula in 1866 consolidated opinion both in the colonies of British North America and in the United Kingdom that confederation was essential for the protection of Canada. Lastly, the recent American Civil War had shown Canadian colonial leaders the vulnerability of a federation of dominant states with a weak federal foundation.[22]

The Indian Affairs portfolio was inherited from the British and remained under federal jurisdiction after Canadian Confederation. However, previous Crown policy, including over eighty treaties signed by the British prior to 1867, had predetermined the continuation of paternalistic authority over Indians. In

1869 the *Gradual Enfranchisement Act* placed traditional political practices of Indians under governmental scrutiny and further undermined Indian leaders. The act also removed "status" from any Indian female who married a non-Indian, a penalty inherited by offspring. The Department of Indian Affairs (DIA) was unofficially formed in conjunction with the 1876 *Indian Act*, which after several revisions remains in force today. The core features of this policy included the resettlement of Indians to federally controlled reserves owned by the Crown, federal supervision of Indian political organizations, and the banning of certain rituals, such as the Potlatch and Sundance.

The act also established the residential school system, whereby Indian children were removed from their communities for religious and agricultural instruction. Another component of the *Indian Act* was the assignment of Indian agents to reserves or districts; these agents were appointed by, and answerable to, the superintendent general of Indian Affairs, a sub-portfolio within varying ministries.[23] In 1880 the Department of Indian Affairs was formally established and gave the federal government powers to impose elected *Indian Act* band councils in place of traditional Indian forms of non-elected leadership, such as the Iroquois Longhouse/Great Law of Peace. The government only negotiated with, and recognized, the *Indian Act* councils. The *Indian Advancement Act* of 1884 added a clause whereby Ottawa had power to depose any chief who was considered unfit.[24]

These imposed *Indian Act* band councils were often installed—by the NWMP before 1920, and subsequently by the RCMP—through the arrests of traditional chiefs and the confiscation of wampum belts and other archival records. In the vast majority of cases this was done without Indian consultation and against their wishes. These so-called chiefs did not necessarily command the respect and support of the populations they purportedly represented. Many Indians viewed them as corrupt pawns, aides to the promulgation of Indian Affairs policy. The legacy of this arrangement is still evident today, and it is the root of internal factionalism on reserves, and of the convoluted and seemingly untenable politics between the governments of Canada and Indian nations and communities. Currently, many reserves, predominantly Iroquoian, have both an *Indian Act* elected council and a traditional council, with divided domestic support. This impasse and the enduring factionalism and political complications were created by the government of Canada via Indian Affairs, *not* by Indian peoples.

Not all Canadian Indians welcomed Confederation or the edicts of the *Indian Act*. The newly formed government immediately encountered insurrection in the form of the Red River Rebellion between November 1869 and August 1870, led by Métis Louis Riel. Although the resistance ended peacefully, Prime Minister Sir John A. Macdonald had ordered the deployment of an armed force, 1,200 strong, to Manitoba under the command of Colonel Garnet Wolseley.[25] The 1870 rebellion made the Canadian government attentive to the unrest in western Canada and to the problems associated with the influx of settlers to the vast prairies. To defuse the tensions among government, settlers, and Indians, and to safeguard the West from the United States, a series of "numbered treaties" (Treaties 1 to 10) were negotiated between 1871 and 1908 in an area covering the majority of western Ontario, Manitoba, Saskatchewan, and Alberta. These treaties were negotiated in haste to secure Indian lands in order to make way for the deluge of settlers and for the railway. Many treaties were initiated by chiefs to safeguard what remained of their land and livelihood after the vanishing of the buffalo and the unregulated encroachment of settlers onto their territories. During treaty discussions, promises were also made that Indians would not be called upon to fight in British ventures, that "the English never call Indians out of their country to fight their battles."[26]

On reserves, however, Indians were dissatisfied with static existence, increasing starvation, and the government's insistence on agricultural and religious education through its policy of the "Bible and the plough."[27] Portions of treaties were not honoured, and some Indians viewed confrontation as a means to secure treaty rights and promote their waning interests. In Saskatchewan, restless young Cree men, led by Wandering Sprit and Fine Day, were beyond the authority of traditional chiefs and elders. Blair Stonechild and Bill Waiser, in *Loyal Till Death: Indians and the North-West Rebellion* (1997), refute the idea of Métis-Indian collaboration in 1885, arguing instead that Indians acted independently of the Métis to promote their own interests. They also suggest that Indian actions during the rebellion were sporadic, if not accidental or Métis coerced, and unsupported by leaders such as Poundmaker and Big Bear.[28]

Nevertheless, the discontented Métis began to mobilize, summoning Riel, who was in exile in the Montana Territory, back to Canada in July 1884. Riel established the Provisional Government of Saskatchewan at Batoche on 19 March 1885, with 800 Métis and Cree warriors. The Northwest Field Force was dispatched under the command of Major General Frederick Middleton.

It comprised roughly 6,500 British regulars and Canadian militia and 1,500 irregulars and police. After a series of engagements, Riel was captured on 15 May and hanged for treason on 16 November 1885.[29] The unsuccessful North-West Rebellion effectively ended Indian attempts to violently resist settler expansion and governmental policy.

COPYRIGHT ERNEST BROWN, EDMONTON.

INTERIOR OF FORT PITT. JUST BEFORE THE REBELLION OF 1885
1. FIRE SKY THUNDER, 2. SKY BIRD(Big Bear's Son), 3.MATOOSE, 4. NAPASIS, 5. BIG BEAR,6. ANGUS MC.KAY(H.B.CO.), 7. DUFRAIN(H.B.Co.Cook), 8.L.Goulet, 9. STANLEY SIMPSON(H.B.Co.)10. ALEX MC.DONALD, 11.ROWLEY,12.CORP. SLETCH — 13. EDMUND,14. HENRY DUFRAIN.   —(Killed at Cut Knife)

ILLUS. 2. Big Bear (centre-left) at Fort Pitt, Saskatchewan, April 1885, shortly before the outbreak of the North-West Rebellion. This photograph was taken only thirty years prior to the outbreak of the First World War. *Library and Archives Canada, C-008183.*

The last armed Indian resistance in Canada before the First World War occurred in 1897 under Saskatchewan Cree Almighty Voice. After being arrested in October 1895 for illegally slaughtering a cow, he shot and killed a NWMP officer. He, his brother-in-law, and his cousin then evaded police forces for nineteen months. The affair ended in May 1897 in a confrontation that resulted in the deaths of all three Indians as well as three Mounties.[30]

By 1914, Euro-Canadian control over land, resources, and government was firmly established, with Indians marginalized to allocated parcels of Crown-owned land. Indian children were forcefully removed to missions and schools to acquire a European education. Indian cultural attributes were outlawed, and most aspects of life were controlled by Indian Affairs directly, or via local Indian agents. The Indian population of Canada was at the lowest point, having been reduced through warfare, disease, and socio-economic hardship. To the Canadian government and Euro-Canadian populations, this was evidence that their Indians were doomed to extinction under the logic of Social Darwinism. Policy was therefore intended to ease this demise while providing assimilationist avenues to incorporate the civilized remnants into Canadian society. As an Ojibwa chief from Ontario aptly contended, "You came as a wind blown across the Great Lake. The wind wafted you to our shores. We rcd [received] you—we planted you—we nursed you. We protected you till you became a mighty tree that spread thro our Hunting Land. With its branches you now lash us."[31]

Chapter Two

The Image of the Indian

In 1904 J.M. Barrie's play *Peter Pan, or The Boy Who Wouldn't Grow Up* debuted in London to great acclaim; it was followed by the novel *Peter and Wendy* in 1911. In modern times, Barrie's depiction (and that of the 1953 and 2002 Walt Disney movies) of the fictional Piccaninny Indians has come under criticism for its stereotypical prejudices. This condemnation, however, is historically unwarranted. His representation of "the Piccaninny tribe, and not to be confused with the softer-hearted Delawares or the Hurons," is symbolic of the image of the Indian that existed in contemporary British and Canadian societies.[1] It also epitomizes the racial construct of the noble savage in the years immediately approaching the First World War. The character Tiger Lily also embodies the "Indian Princess" ideal, which evolved from the legendary early seventeenth century chronicle of the Powhatan Indian Pocahontas: "Tiger Lily, proudly erect, a princess in her own right. She is the most beautiful of dusky Dianas and the belle of the Piccaninnies."[2]

In his description of Piccaninny warriors, Barrie conformed to the pervasive belief that Indians possessed innate martial prowess, within the paradigm of the noble savage: "Down the war-path … come the redskins.… They carry tomahawks and knives, and their naked bodies gleam with paint and oil. Strung around them are scalps.… Observe how they pass over fallen twigs without making the slightest noise.… The redskins disappear as they have come like shadows." He continues his account of the warriors, led by "the terrible Great Big Little Panther," and their "unwritten laws of savage warfare": "Through the long black night the savage scouts wriggle snake-like, among the grass without stirring a blade.… Not a sound is to be heard, save for when they give vent to a wonderful imitation of the lonely call of the coyote. The cry is answered by other braves, and some of them do it even better than the coyotes, who are not very good at it at all. So the chill hours wear on, and the long suspense is horribly trying to the paleface who has to live through it."[3] After Peter saves Tiger Lily from the pirates, the Lost Boys and their traditional enemy the Piccaninny become friends and allies:

> They called Peter the Great White Father, prostrating themselves before him…. "The great white father," he would say to them in a very lordly manner, as they grovelled at his feet, "is glad to see the Piccaninny warriors protecting his wigwam from the pirates." "Me Tiger Lily," that lovely creature would reply; "Peter Pan save me, me his velly nice friend. Me no let pirates hurt him." She was far too pretty to cringe this way, but Peter thought it his due, and he would answer condescendingly, "It is good. Peter Pan has spoken." Always when he said, "Peter Pan has spoken," it meant that they must now shut up.[4]

In the end, Captain Hook's pirates defeat and subjugate the Piccaninnies, and as for the warriors, "No more would they torture at the stake. For them the happy hunting-grounds now."[5] In a description reminiscent of American Indian massacres, such as Sand Creek (1864), Marias (1870), and Wounded Knee (1890), Barrie concludes that, "It is no part of ours to describe what was a massacre rather than a fight…. To what extent Hook is to blame for his tactics on this occasion is for the historian to decide."[6]

The paternalistic policies regulating indigenous peoples of the British Empire were dependent upon contemporary racial and class theories, persistent in European dialogue and culture, that were imported to settler societies: "Colonial settlers, the offspring of European imperialism, refused to integrate with the indigenous population. Moreover, they kept Europe as their myth of origin and as a signifier of superiority even when formal political ties and/or dependency with European colonial powers had been abandoned. This sense of identification with the 'mother country' has not, however, mitigated the unevenness and fragility of settler identities, which were often forged in defence against metropolitan contempt."[7] In the absence of large noble and gentry populations, the original, primarily lower class, British settlers of the "White Dominions" instinctively filled the vacuum. While the colonies afforded new opportunities, and the ability to transcend the regimented tiers of European society, the hierarchies did not vanish. Settlers found indigenous peoples, Asian labourers, and "inferior" immigrants to fill the lower rungs of class and racial hierarchies. Racial estimations were manifest in martial race theories, which directly affected the utility of Indians within Canadian military formations, including those of the First World War.

The categorization of indigenous peoples in the British Empire stemmed from an Anglo-Saxon perception of superiority; therefore, it seemed natural to spread civilization, and its religious and political appendages, to the vast expanses of the globe. Frontier warfare, and the increasingly vitriolic relationship between indigenes and colonials, magnified European and settler beliefs that the indigene was devoid of any appreciation of the benefits of European civilization. However, as one Mi'kmaq Indian aptly contended: "If France, as thou sayest, is a little terrestrial paradise, art thou sensible to leave it?... To come to a strange and barbarous country which thou considerest the poorest and least fortunate of the world.... Since we are wholly convinced of the contrary, we scarcely take the trouble to go to France ... seeing, in our own experience, that those who are natives thereof leave it every year in order to enrich themselves on our shores."[8]

Mutual suspicion and profiling of the "other" were the inevitable consequences of contact between incompatible cultures. The Mi'kmaq were appalled by the food, stench, and facial hair (a sign of stupidity) of Cartier and his crew, who "drank blood and ate wood" (wine and stale biscuits). Based on oral traditions, other indigenes of the Americas believed the pale-skinned visitors were deities. The Aztec thought that Hernando Cortes was the god Quetzalcoatl, and Hawaiians viewed Captain James Cook as the manifestation of Lono.

Alternatively, Indian practices such as polygamy, human sacrifice, and shamanism, their communal land philosophies, and their lack of any perceived political structures, when misunderstood by Europeans, gave credence to the belief that they were "uncivilized heathens." The more violent and cannibalistic rituals were perceived as intrinsic blood lust. C.J. Jaenen comments that this was obtuse of Europeans, "who believed in transubstantiation and literally eating their Lord in their communion service." J.R. Miller elaborates, "Surely people of countries who guillotined, hanged, drew, and quartered those guilty of hundreds of offences, and who put heads on pikes as a warning to others, should have been able to understand the symbolic, cheerleading, and deterrent purposes of such native North American practices."[9]

By the time Charles Darwin published his *On the Origin of Species* in 1859, patriarchal administration and custodial practices regarding Indians permeated British-Canadian policies, and the concept of "the savage" was engrained in settler perceptions. Social Darwinism and racial theories simply buttressed previously held beliefs and gave them a spacious framework in which to be employed, modernized, and justified. The indigenous populations of Canada, devastated by war and disease, were moribund. To the resident Euro-Canadian populations, this was proof of Herbert Spencer's notion of "survival of the fittest" (see Table 1).[10]

Indians were, according to the widely accepted belief, destined to extinction in the inevitable natural struggle against modernity and more advanced races. The residual populations would be assimilated or absorbed through miscegenation (a term coined in England in 1863).[11] In 1910 journalist and poet Ernest McGaffey referred to the "doomed races" of Canada: "For it is so that the wilderness falls before the axe, that the old order passes as the new regime comes in; that you cannot stay the current development by a dogged refusal to go with the tide; and that the iron pen of history has written time and time again, the survival of the fittest is the law of nations."[12]

Year	Euro-Canadian Population	Indian/Eskimo Population
Contact (1500)	N/A	300,000-350,000
1841	1,540,109	N/A
1851	2,436,297	158,960 (1856)
1861	3,229,633	N/A
1867	3,463,000	N/A
1871	3,689,257	102,358
1881	4,324,810	108,547
1891	4,833,239	107,638
1901	5,371,315	109,698
1911	7,206,643	103,661 Indians, 4,600 Eskimos
1914	7,879,000	103,774 Indians, 3,447 Eskimos
1916	8,001,000	105,561 Indians, 3,298 Eskimos
1918	8,148,000	105,998 Indians, 3,296 Eskimos

TABLE 1. Canadian and Indian/Eskimo Populations
Note: Statistics prior to confederation in 1867 indicate the combined totals of all colonies of British North America. Sources: Government of Canada, *Statistics Canada* at www.statcan.gc.ca; Colonial Office, *Colonial Office Lists 1901–1918* (London: Waterlow and Sons, 1914–1919); Canada Census and Statistics Office, *The Canada Yearbook: Years 1891–1918* (Ottawa: Census and Statistics Office); Department of Indian Affairs, *Annual Report of the Department of Indian Affairs: Years 1864–1919* (Ottawa: King's Printer).

During the nineteenth century, academic theorists supported what became a relatively accepted belief, that races varied in potential and in the progression of evolution. Darwin believed that civilized races had attained heights of progress through natural selection and racial struggle: "Looking to the world at no very distant date, what an endless number of the lower races will have been eliminated by the higher civilized races throughout the world."[13] Theorists generally agreed that the process of "animality [sic] through savagery and barbarism to civilization was an uneven one, with many races confined to the earlier phases of evolution."[14] This stagnation was seen in the condition of Indians, specifically in the perceived characteristics of lower intellect, laziness, licentious behaviour, an imitative childlike demeanour, and a penchant for violent and erratic outbursts.

Racial discourse was part of a pan-European deliberation about the differences among human populations and nations that accompanied the extension of European empires. The word *race* was used to describe variations of biology, nation, and culture. Most theories promoted the concept of an evolutionary stratum of racial tiers. The bottom was occupied by Aboriginal Australians, followed closely by Africans. North American Indians occupied the next tier, then Asians and Middle Eastern peoples, followed by Polynesians, including Maori. Eastern Europeans came next, followed by Mediterranean peoples. Western Europeans, who had formulated most of these theories, were the obvious apex of evolution, with Anglo-Saxons as the very summit, in British opinion. This was the established categorization in most imperial European nations and in the British dominions, including Canada.[15]

In a glaring contradiction of colonialism, however, Indian women were the object of sexual attention. Kay Schaffer explains that the "sexual exploitation of [indigenous] women was endemic to British imperialism—the romance between dusky, dark-haired maidens and pioneering heroes was at the core of the colonial adventure tale.... So long as European women were absent, indigenous women could be used to satisfy what were perceived to be natural needs." The sensationalized and quite fictional account of the Powhatan Indian Pocahontas, who became a celebrity in London before her death in 1617, illustrates this observation.[16] The romanticized legend of her saving John Smith in 1607, their subsequent love affair and her conversion to Christianity, her choice to live with English settlers rather than her own people, her marriage to John Rolfe, and her triumphant entry into British society evolved gradually to illustrate the potential of Indians to be assimilated and saved from barbarity. From the first engraving of her likeness in 1616, paintings and engravings depicted her as increasingly more European in appearance. The myth of her life was exploitable propaganda for settlers, religious orders, and politicians to justify their actions and policies.[17]

While Indian women were the object of lust and rape, miscegenation in Canada was not widely socially accepted. The Métis, however, were evidence of its occurrence. Two early historians of the Métis wrote, only half-jokingly, that "the Métis nation was created nine months after the landing of the first European."[18] The Canadian government incorporated the frequent marriage of white men to Indian women into its assimilationist strategy. As mentioned, the 1869 *Indian Act* removed "status" from any Indian female who married a non-Indian—a penalty also imposed on the children. This law was not rescinded until 1985. Such a policy was designed to reduce the number of status Indians within the larger Canadian populace.

In reality, susceptibility to disease and alcohol, direct or circuitous involvement in colonial wars, and socio-economic disparity had drastically reduced Indian populations by the turn of the twentieth century. To Canadians this was evidence of the fatal impact theory. Canada instituted paternalistic policies controlling most aspects of Indian life, with the aim of assimilating the surviving Indian population. Duncan Campbell Scott, deputy superintendent general of Indian Affairs from 1913 to 1932, viewed the future of Indians as part of an irreversible trend of Social Darwinism and believed "final results may be attained, maybe in four centuries ... by the merging of the Indian race with the whites [through] treaties, teachers, missionaries and traders—with whatever benefits or injuries they bring in their train."[19] As J.R. Miller contends, "To Scott it was obvious that, if First Nations would not voluntarily do what Indian Affairs knew to be best for them, then compulsion would have to be applied."[20]

According to Ronald Haycock, in his study of the perception and popular media coverage of Indians at the dawn of the twentieth century, there were three basic conceptions, singularly or in combination, about Indians. The first was that the Indian was doomed to extinction because, like the Beothuk of Newfoundland, he was unable to survive the competitive evolutionary struggle. The responsibility of the white population and the government was to "make the death struggle of the primitive as soft as possible." The second conception was that of the noble savage. Indians had distinguished records of military allegiance to the

British, which influenced their corresponding duality as both the noble and the savage. Canadians could not ignore the historical benefits of this alliance or the exemplary examples of Joseph Brant, Tecumseh, and Crowfoot. The dichotomy of the Indian as a savage brute or a noble warrior provided an exploitable and convenient framework whereby the Canadian population and government could justify the inconsistency of military and Indian policies while maintaining a phlegmatic posture. The "noble" Indian was extolled by government officials and citizens alike, but only when it suited their interests. The "good Indian" and the "bad Indian" were often used on an individual basis. The concept of this duality was reinforced by common media and literature, including J.M. Barrie's *Peter Pan* and "Wild West" shows. The Indian was either depicted as a treacherous, blood-lusting savage or as a righteous, astute warrior. James Fenimore Cooper's characters in *The Last of the Mohicans* (1826) illustrate this ubiquitous dichotomy: Chingachgook, the Mohican, represents the noble, while Magua, a Huron adopted by the Mohawk, represents the savage.[21]

The third conception was that the Indian had been unwillingly, or unknowingly, corrupted by the degenerate portion of the white population and that the honourable white segment was obligated by virtue to assimilate the Indian "to hitherto unprecedented levels of civilization and salvation, fashioned on the white model." As such, reserves were intended to be temporary holding locations until a time when the remaining Indian population was fully assimilated and integrated into white society.[22] In 1910 journalist Elizabeth Walmsley summarized the position of the Indian in Canada: "The 'brave' no longer lives in a wigwam or 'tepee' as his forefathers did, more or less exposed to the inclemencies [sic] of all weather and consequently hardened to them, but in a 'shack' much like an immigrant settler's. But he cannot accustom himself to the white man's mode of life.... For the nature of the Indian is still Indian, and until he can be taught how to adapt himself to the higher standards of comfort which contact with civilization has brought him, the result must inevitably be extinction."[23] In the years approaching the First World War, the legal and social position of the Canadian Indian did not render him a suitable candidate, in British-Canadian opinion, to defend the empire, despite past allegiance to the Crown.

Nevertheless, racial perceptions, in combination with the settler-state experience, formed the basis for the martial profiling of indigenous peoples within the British Empire. The concept of martial races—the belief that certain identifiable peoples or societies had an innate and exceptional capacity for war—was a construct engineered in India and exported across the British and other European empires. Martial race theories were derived from a pragmatic approach to internal state security, as a consequence of the 1857 Indian Mutiny and the subsequent shifting *sepoy* ratios in the Indian Army of the British Raj to favour men from the Punjab, Nepal (Gurkhas), and the Northwest Frontier (Afghanistan).[24]

In Canada, the Iroquois Confederacy, specifically the Mohawk, represented the pinnacle of martial accomplishment among Indians. The Iroquois had been the dominant military Indian coalition in northeastern North America prior to contact, a position they maintained until the close of the War of 1812. The confederacy also established a long-standing alliance with the British Crown and rendered invaluable service during the colonial wars in North America. In western Canada, the Blackfoot Confederacy (Blackfoot, Blood, Piegan, and later the allied Sarcee) was also recognized for its military prowess as a result of its long-standing animosities with the Crow, Sioux, and Cree and its penchant for attacking white settlers.

At the turn of the century, the Plains Indian warrior, with headdress and horse, was the romanticized ideal of the noble savage in the minds of most Canadians. The West had been recently "civilized," the North-West Rebellion still resonated, and Canadians wanted, and invented to some extent, an equivalent to the mighty Sioux, led by Sitting Bull and Crazy Horse, of the Battle of the Little Bighorn (1876). At the onset of the North-West Rebellion, Canadian politicians and media made frequent reference to a "Canadian Little Bighorn" and to "Custer's Last Stand." In a sense, it was really the last stand of Indian autonomy.[25]

The idea that Indians possessed innate martial talents was a common belief during the nineteenth and early twentieth centuries. A recent commentator remarked that Indians were natural-born soldiers who "possessed the skills and discipline of modern commandos and special forces ... who were capable of adapting to whatever situation they encountered."[26] Given this belief, then, prudence warned against arming and training Indians in a military capacity, for fear of insurrection.

Likewise, Cynthia Enloe argues in *Ethnic Soldiers: State Security in a Divided Society* (1980), that the martial proclivities of minorities were judged by their "political reliability," which included population ratios and proof of allegiance during colonial warfare. After a weighted assessment by governmental and military authorities, specific groups were assigned military

ILLUS. 3. With Headdress and Horse: Blood Indians in Full Regalia, 1907. *Library and Archives Canada, C-018881.*

occupations, or formed into minority units, consistent with the goal of maintaining state security.[27] American Indian historian Tom Holm argues, through a paradigm he labels the "Gurkha Model," that "It was only after Indian assimilation policies had been put in place, the Native population had dwindled to less than one percent of that of the United States as a whole, and Native soldiers and Marines had proven themselves in combat in World War I, that Indians were judged a politically 'safe' minority group."[28]

The inclusion of Indians in the CEF during the First World War was predicated upon contemporary racial theories and martial race perceptions, including those based on previous involvement in colonial warfare. The calculated decision to admit Indians into the CEF was made after carefully weighing military needs, specifically for manpower after 1915, against the need to maintain the status quo of Indian-white relations. This approach and its consequent practices, although magnified during the prolonged and more sacrificial Great War, were not a departure from, but rather a continuation of, past policy during colonial warfare. This pragmatism was also apparent in the deployment of Canadian expeditionary units preceding the First World War, most notably those raised for service during the Second Anglo-Boer War.

Chapter Three

Modern Warfare and the Noble Savage

In 1811, shortly before the outbreak of the War of 1812, William Henry Harrison, the governor of the Indiana Territory, paid tribute to the Shawnee leader Tecumseh and his tribal confederacy in a report to his superiors in Washington:

> The implicit obedience and respect which the followers of Tecumseh pay him, is really astonishing, and more than any other circumstance bespeaks him one of those uncommon geniuses which spring up occasionally to produce revolutions, and overturn the established order of things. If it were not for the vicinity of the United States, he would, perhaps, be the founder of an empire that would rival in glory Mexico or Peru [Maya, Aztec and Inca civilizations]. No difficulties deter him … and wherever he goes he makes an impression favorable to his purposes. He is now upon the last round to put a finishing stroke on his work.[1]

After the siege of Fort Detroit in August 1812, Major General Sir Isaac Brock remarked that although his Indian allies were "going and coming," Tecumseh's influence "has kept them faithful—he has shewn [sic] himself to be a determined character and a great friend of our Government." At their first meeting, a month prior, Brock, who thought Canada was a backwater and distrusted Indian motives, exclaimed that "a more sagacious or gallant Warrior does not I believe exist." By all indications, he was thoroughly impressed with Tecumseh as a warrior and as a statesman. Tecumseh, a commanding orator in English and several Indian languages who stood almost six feet with a muscular frame, sized up the six-foot-two Brock and allegedly exclaimed, "Ho-o-o-e: This is a man."[2] These men have been immortalized in history and are regarded as founding fathers of Canada, although, ironically, neither man was Canadian. Their relationship, however, represents the alliance between the Crown and Indians to safeguard common interests, and also bears witness to the fact that Canada was born of Indian and Euro-Canadian cooperation and blood.

Canada had a long history of British-Indian alliance throughout the settler-state experience. Indian nations, most conspicuously the Iroquois Confederacy, had been worthy British allies. Indians were given honorary British ranks, exemplified by Mohawk captain Joseph Brant, and awarded British citations and medals.[3] Following the 1817 Rush-Bagot Treaty and the American Monroe Doctrine of 1823, which nullified future American and external European threats, Indians lost their importance as military allies. However, while Indians lost their military importance as a collective, individual Indians continued to support British military campaigns after the War of 1812 when mustered by imperial/Canadian authorities. Warriors from the Six Nations reserve assisted Canadian militia units in ending the Fenian raids of the 1860s. Eighty-six Indians, predominantly Mohawk, were recruited as voyageurs and paddled General Lord Garnet Wolseley's 1884–85 relief force up the Nile to the besieged city of Khartoum.[4] Wolseley had previously employed 140 Indian scouts on his expedition to restore order during the 1870 Red River Rebellion. Wolseley identified the need for Indian-specific skills during both operations and recruited accordingly.[5]

Furthermore, Indian faithfulness to the British Crown was exemplified by the refusal of many Indian nations, including the Blackfoot Confederacy, to join Métis or Cree forces during the North-West Rebellion, while small numbers of Cree, Blackfoot, and Ojibwa scouts were used by Major General Frederick Middleton's Northwest Field Force. The long-standing military alliance between the Crown and Indians, although diminished, was not extinct by 1914. For the vaunted Six Nations Iroquois Confederacy, the Silver Covenant Chain was certainly tarnished, but it was by no means broken. Given this pattern of allegiance to the British Crown, Indian enthusiasm towards the First World War was not historically unfounded.

The Second Anglo-Boer War, however, serves as the most emblematic example of Indian-exclusionist military policy in Canada prior to the First World War. French-Canadian prime minister Sir Wilfrid Laurier initially hesitated to send forces in aid of a British imperial campaign. In July 1899 the colonial secretary, Joseph Chamberlain, asked if the Canadian *Militia Act* could be interpreted so as to justify the use of Canadian soldiers outside of Canada. Laurier replied that the "Militia Act was concerned only with the defence of Canada and that the theatre of war had little to do with it."[6] The purpose of the Canadian militia was to support the civil authorities in times of strikes, riots, and rebellion, and its size clearly reflected this role. The permanent force numbered 1,000 men, whose daily pay was half that of an unskilled labourer, while the part-time militia consisted of 35,000 poorly trained civilians of limited military value.[7]

Most historians agree that Laurier was bullied into his final decision by English-speaking ministers, the Colonial Office, governor general Lord Minto, and the British commander of the Canadian militia, General Edward Hutton. They used the press, which printed sensationalized stories of Boer atrocities, and back-room hustling to gain public support and to trap Laurier into granting some form of participation, even if it meant disregarding the terms of the *Militia Act* and Parliament's right to be consulted.[8] Behind the scenes in Ottawa, an agent of the Imperial South African Association, financed by Cecil Rhodes, founder of DeBeer Diamonds, lobbied to get a clear commitment from Canada by greasing the palms of some influential ministers.[9]

On 13 October 1899, without summoning Parliament, a special Order in Council was drawn up stating that Canada would raise, outfit, and send a volunteer force of 1,000 men, to be paid for by Britain. Laurier's explanation for participation was given in a stirring speech to the embarking troops: "The cause for which you men of Canada are going to fight is the cause of justice, the cause of humanity, of civil rights and religious liberty. This is not a war of conquest.... The object is not to crush out the Dutch population, but to establish in that land ... British sovereign law, to assure all men of that country an equal share of liberty."[10] This short-term and limited commitment excluded any possibility of Indian service in its precedent-setting expeditionary adventure, despite the fact that Indians were active in domestic Canadian military units.

Indians had been present in non-permanent active militia units (reserve units—the permanent active militia represented Canada's small regular force) since the militia's official creation in 1868. The *Militia Act* did not bar them from service, and enlistment remained at the discretion of the commanding officer. Indian boys also received rudimentary military training through the residential school system, although this practice was by no means uniform throughout Canada. As early as 1896, William Hamilton Merritt, an honorary chief of the Six Nations reserve, requested the formation of a regular unit composed of, and reinforced by, Indian boys from Canada's residential schools. In a letter to the governor general, John Hamilton-Gordon the Earl of Aberdeen, he outlined his intention to "form a permanent Imperial Corps recruited from our Indians." He continued:

> I would consider it very kind if you could ascertain from the Principals of the Industrial Schools how they would view the project of a certain picked proportion of their boys being drafted into a regiment on completing their education at the school, and how many it is likely could be supplied each year to recruit such a regiment if established. It has been held that the natural inborn instincts of the Indian lad suits him admirably for the profession of soldiering.... I suppose you would consider that there would be no difficulty in recruiting a regiment from the Indians of Canada who could speak English, and who are qualified to make excellent soldiers, and who have proved themselves to be true and Loyal Subjects of the British Crown.

Although in 1898 Merritt even lobbied the War Office, the proposal was dismissed for two reasons. The first argument against it concerned the financial expenditure of educating the boys only to deploy them on operations. Exporting educated, assimilated, and "worthwhile young Indians" would inherently deplete their numbers within Canada, diminishing the impact they could have on their communities. Secondly, it was deduced that the scheme would "appear as a draft," without Indian approval, and could violate treaty agreements.[11] Nevertheless, certain residential schools did institute cadet training, predominantly in Ontario, Manitoba, and Alberta.[12] There were also attempts to form complete Indian militia units in the decades prior to the First World War. Although the United States had formed all-Indian units as early as the Civil War (1861–65), and continued to do so through to General John Pershing's "Punitive Expedition" to capture the Mexican revolutionary Pancho Villa in 1916, Canada had no similar background.[13] The earliest attempts at forming an all-Indian militia unit in Canada coincided with the Second Anglo-Boer War.

In September 1866, the 37th Haldimand Battalion of Rifles was formed at Dunnville, Ontario, neighbouring the Six Nations reserve. It was composed of six companies, of which four (Dunnville, Caledonia, Oneida, and Walpole) were predominantly Indian, save for a majority of white officers.[14] In addition, large numbers of Six Nations (and Ojibwa and Potawatomi) men were active in the 26th Middlesex Light Infantry (in London). Given the high percentage of Indians in these militia units, in February 1896 Six Nations chief Josiah Hill petitioned the Department of Indian Affairs, through his regional agent Captain D.E. Cameron, to form a regiment on the reserve: "The Six Nations Indians feel on account of their loyalty to the Crown for over one hundred years, and having fought side by side with Soldiers of the Crown in the War of Independence and the War of 1812-1814 that a Regiment bearing the name of the Royal Six Nations whose rank and file shall be composed of Indians with the head quarters at the Council House on the Grand River Reserve be established, over 1000 men can be raised if necessary...to be commanded by Capt. Cameron our popular Indian Agent."[15] Chief Hill's request was not endorsed by all council chiefs. Chief Isaac Hill protested to Indian Affairs that the council was unable to reach a consensus, and "they [did] not want to reject the ancient way of consulting on that affair," which was through resolution by consensus, under the traditional Longhouse Great Law of Peace.[16] Nevertheless, Cameron proceeded to forward the request to Hayter Reed at Indian Affairs, complete with drawings of a proposed regimental uniform (kilt with Indian headdress), colours, and a *guidon* with battle honours, including the American Revolution and the War of 1812.[17] Uncharacteristically, Reed enthusiastically approached the deputy minister of Militia, Colonel Charles E. Panet: "I may say that this Department heartily endorses the proposed movement and is prepared, should the idea be favourably entertained by your Department, to encourage and assist the Indians in carrying out the proposal to a successful issue." Although the idea was submitted to the governor general, John Hamilton-Gordon, in March, it was rejected on the grounds of funding and interdepartmental "complications."[18]

With the outbreak of hostilities in the Transvaal and Canada's formal commitment of an expeditionary force on 13 October 1899, Chief Josiah Hill sent a letter directly to Queen Victoria on behalf of the sovereign entity of the Iroquois Confederacy: "I humbly beg herewith to transmit to Your Most Gracious Majesty a decision of the Chiefs of the Six Nations Council ... offering Your Majesty a contingent of Chiefs and Warriors, officered by Indians or those in connection with them to serve Your Majesty in the Transvaal, in conformity with the customs and usages of their forefathers and in accordance with existing Treaties with the British Crown." A second appeal was sent by the Six Nations in December.[19]

In November a request by the Ojibwa, Potawatomi, and Odawa of the Saugeen reserve (Southampton, Ontario) to send warriors was submitted through their local agent, W.H. Scott: "The Indians of the Saugeen Reserve are anxious to go to

ILLUS. 4. Iroquois Chiefs from the Six Nations Reserve reading Wampum Belts, 1871. Left to Right: Joseph Snow (Onondaga); George Henry Martin Johnson (Father of Pauline Johnson, Mohawk); John Buck (Onondaga); John Smoke Johnson (Father of George Henry Martin Johnson, Mohawk); Isaac Hill (Onondaga); John Seneca Johnson (Seneca). *Library and Archives Canada, C-085137.*

the Transvaal in case another contingent be sent. They want to go as scouts in a company.... They are anxious to show their loyalty."[20] Similar requests were sent by the Chippewa (Ojibwa) of Nawash/Cape Croker and Sarnia, Ontario. In January 1900, the Duck Lake Cree of Saskatchewan "asked to fight to assist the British to fight the Boers."[21]

With offers of Indian warriors flooding in from across Canada, both the Colonial Office and the government of Canada finally dismissed the requests. The colonial secretary, Joseph Chamberlain, replied directly to Chief Hill on behalf of the Queen in February 1900: "I have received Her Majesty's comment to desire you to convey to the Chiefs of the Six Nations our extension of Her sincere thanks for the loyalty and sympathetic assurances contained in the resolution and of Her regret at being unable to avail Herself of their patriotic offer." In April, Indian Affairs followed the British exclusionist example and served notice to all agents that "no Treaty Indians can enlist for service."[22] There were reports and rumours circulating of Indians, mostly in western

Canada in the wake of the North-West Rebellion, "wishing to join the Boer force in the Transvaal" out of sympathy for the Boers' repression at the hands of the British. There was also a fear that the provision of military training and the organization of Indian regiments could be utilized against Canada itself.[23] The most palpable example of the British-Canadian policy barring Indians from service was that of John Brant Sero, a Mohawk from the Six Nations reserve: "I have just returned from South Africa, disappointed in many respects, but I do not wish these lines to be understood as a grievance. I went to that country from Canada hoping that I might enlist in one of the mounted rifles; however, not being a man of European desent [sic], I was refused to do active service in Her Majesty's cause as did my forefathers in Canada.... I was too genuine a Canadian."[24]

Although the government banned the enlistment of Indians for service in South Africa, a limited number did manage to evade this protocol. Since enlistment was on an individual basis and no account of "race" was registered on any military records, the precise number of Indians who served is not known. However, a select number of Indian men were among the 7,368 Canadians to see service during the Boer War, including Private Walter White of the Anderdon Huron reserve near Windsor, Ontario. White was killed on 18 February 1900 during the Battle of Paardeberg.[25] Private George McLean of the Okanagan nation of British Columbia served with the 2nd Canadian Mounted Rifles (CMR) in South Africa. McLean enlisted again during the First World War and was awarded the Distinguished Conduct Medal (DCM) during the Battle of Vimy Ridge (9–12 April 1917) for killing nineteen Germans and capturing fourteen more while wounded.[26] Joseph Hanaven of the Six Nations reserve served with the 6th CMR. He was denied the allocation of a land grant for returning soldiers because he did not apply by the deadline. However, non-Indian soldiers who applied after the closing date of 31 December 1913 were "grandfathered" and given parcels of land as outlined in the *Service Act*.[27]

Canadian Indians also actively contributed to the Canadian Patriotic Fund. For example, in lieu of sending warriors, the Saugeen reserve donated thirty-six dollars, while their sister Ojibwa communities of Cape Croker and Sarnia donated thirty-five dollars each.[28] The relatively small scale of the South African War, and of the corresponding force supplied by Canada, did not necessitate the inclusion of Indians. The exclusionist policies of the government of Canada with respect to its Indian population, and the patriotic response of Indians, during the Boer War would be mirrored at the onset of hostilities in 1914.

The Boer War, however, exposed the deficiencies in British doctrine and the inadequacies of the Canadian military. After British forces withdrew from Canada in 1871, military expenditure and reform were left in relative abeyance. The 1904 *Militia Act*, which was current at the outbreak of the First World War, authorized a significant expansion of the Canadian permanent and militia forces.[29] In 1909 the Canadian Defence League was formed; it called for universal military training and mandatory cadet instruction for schoolboys. Such a drastic program was neither economically feasible nor sanctioned by the government, but by 1911 six provinces, including Quebec, offered cadet training. By 1913, 40,000 Canadian boys were active in this program, including many of the 4,655 Indian boys aged sixteen to twenty years old within the residential school system.[30] During that same year, the permanent force peaked at 3,100 and the militia at 43,000, both still well under the authorized strengths of 5,000 and 60,000, respectively.[31]

The 1904 *Militia Act* also identified those Canadians eligible for military service. Section X stated, "All the male inhabitants of Canada of the age of eighteen years and upwards, and under sixty, not exempt or disqualified by law and being British subjects, shall be liable to service in the militia; provided that the Governor-General may require all the male inhabitants of Canada capable of bearing arms."[32] Those "exempt under law" were listed, and they included conscientious objectors, such as Doukhobors, and "unexpendable" professionals. The act, however, made no specific mention of Indians, which raises some interesting questions.

Given that Indians were "British subjects," was it simply implied that Indians were included, most notably because they were active in the militia? Within the twelve military districts of Canada, commanding officers of militia units had the freedom to recruit directly from the local population. Commanders of units centred in regions with high Indian populations—such as the 37th Haldimand Battalion of Rifles, headquartered beside the Six Nations reserve, and the 26th Middlesex Regiment in London, which had the Oneida settlement and the Chippewa and Munsee-Delaware reserves in close proximity—enlisted Indian volunteers who were fit for service. Given that race was not recorded on attestation papers for either the Boer War or the First World War, was it assumed that only Euro-Canadians would be recruited, as evidenced by the Boer War? Or were Indians consciously omitted from the act based on treaties, which excluded most, but not all, Indians from service? After all, Merritt's 1896 and 1898 proposals to form an Indian regiment were dismissed for fear of violating treaty rights. Furthermore, during the Boer War the government specifically stated that "no Treaty Indians can enlist for service." Was this, perhaps, a conscious omission to avoid confirming official policy, so that Indians could be denied service when suitable to authorities or, when required, utilized at the discretion of the government in the future? Indians had a long history of allegiance and military service alongside British and Canadian soldiers. Although their use and value had diminished after the War of 1812, in times of need they were still called upon to provide their valuable skills in assisting Canadian or imperial ventures.

Indeed, the failure to mention Indians is puzzling, and the only clear answer is that no official policy existed concerning Indian service in the militia, home defence forces, and expeditionary formations, or under conscription legislation. The absence of an official policy was manifest immediately at the outbreak of the First World War and led to confusion within the Ministry of Militia and the Department of Indian Affairs and among recruiters, Indian volunteers, band councils, and Indian agents.

Chapter Four

The Privileges of Civilized Warfare, 1914

Duncan Campbell Scott, through his influential position as deputy super-intendent general of Indian Affairs from 1913 to 1932, was the driving force behind the propagation of paternalistic and assimilationist policies. As he declared, "I want to get rid of the Indian problem.... Our objective is to continue until there is not a single Indian in Canada that has not been absorbed into the body politic and there is no Indian question, and no Indian Department."[1] He was also the most influential government official regulating Indians and the war effort, and he dominated all aspects of their military service. Following official sanction to enlist Indians in December 1915, Scott, in keeping with contemporary political and social conventions, viewed military service as a convenient windfall to his program of assimilation:

> These men who have been broadened by contact with the outside world and its affairs, who have mingled with the men of other races, and who have witnessed the many wonders and advantages of civilization, will not be content to return to their old Indian mode of life ... thus the war will have hastened that day, the millennium of those en-gaged [sic] in Indian work, when all the quaint old customs, the weird and picaresque ceremonies, the sun dance and the potlatch and even the musical and poetic native languages shall be as obsolete as the buffalo and the tomahawk, and the last tepee of the Northern wilds give place to a model farmhouse. In other words, the Indian shall become one with his neighbour in his speech, life and habits, thus conforming to that world-wide tendency towards universal standardization which would appear to be the essential underlying purport of all modern social evolution.[2]

With the initiation of hostilities, Scott, in a view shared by the majority of British and Canadian politicians and senior commanders, believed that the "war would be over by Christmas." Within this general atmosphere he initially promulgated an unofficial exclusionist policy regarding Indian enlistment.

The war, however, was not short-lived, and both Canadian and Indian contributions, overseas and on the home front in support of Britain, increased dramatically over the course of four and a half years of horrific warfare.

ILLUS. 5. Duncan Campbell Scott, c. 1933. *Library and Archives Canada, C-003187.*

Following Britain's declaration of war on 4 August 1914, support of men and materials was immediately offered by the government of Canada. This commitment was affirmed in the Canadian House of Commons by Prime Minister Sir Robert Borden: "As to our duty, all are agreed; we stand shoulder to shoulder with Britain and the other British dominions in this quarrel ... not for love of battle, not for lust of conquest, not for greed of possessions, but for the cause of honour."[3] Until the 1931 Statute of Westminster, Britain retained control of Canadian foreign policy, including the ability to declare war independently. Therefore, unlike the Second World War, former Canadian prime minister Sir Wilfrid Laurier's 1910 maxim, "When Britain is at war, Canada is at war. There is no distinction," was the legal arrangement for Canada in August 1914.[4]

Canada had the autonomy, however, to decide the scope of men and materials offered to the imperial war effort. It formally committed a contingent of 25,000 men (1st Canadian Division) on 31 July. Heightened trade and export potential accompanied war, and Canada sought to secure enhanced portfolios and new contracts for munitions, materials, and agrarian products to boost an economy in the midst of recession.[5] George H. Perley, Canadian high commissioner to Britain, expressed to Borden at the onset of hostilities that "this war sure to alter situation and relationship various parts Empire. What Canada does at this time immensely appreciated and will not be forgotten."[6] The pledging of an expeditionary force was one avenue to gain favour in the contest for British and other Allied war contracts. On 7 September Borden requested that Perley "confidentially sound [Colonial Secretary] Harcourt [as to] our expeditionary force being increased to say forty thousand men [but] no more should come than we can manage to pay for." In the same telegram, he instructed Perley to ascertain in confidence, "how many Australia and New Zealand propose to send."[7] Manpower was the foremost criterion for securing accolades and financial recompense via war contracts.

Recruiting stations in Canada, possessing few, and outdated, contingency plans for mass mobilization, were overwhelmed with volunteers during the first months of the war, and attesting officers had the ability to be highly selective. This outpouring of support, although driven by a jingoistic furore, was also the result of high unemployment rates throughout Canada in the midst of a global economic downturn. Nevertheless, positions within initial Canadian formations were quickly filled by men of European, primarily British, stock. In 1914 the population of Canada was 7.88 million (excluding 103,774 Indians and 3,447 Eskimos). Of the total population, 54 percent were of British ancestry, with 10.89 percent born in Britain itself. Of the 36,267 soldiers of the first CEF contingent, 9,635 (27 percent) were English-speaking born Canadians, 1,245 (3.4 percent) French-speaking born Canadians, and 23,211 (64 percent) British by birth.[8]

Although the majority of Indian leaders and peoples offered their immediate support to the war effort, their active participation remained dependent on the existing 1904 *Militia Act* or, in the absence of any clear policy, on the whims of the federal government. Throughout 1914 the general policy towards Indian service followed contemporary racial assumptions and past policy and practice, and it remained one of exclusion or limited involvement. Throughout

1914 and early 1915, in the absence of vast deployments to European theatres, white manpower was sufficient to meet the demands of Canadian commitments, still in relative infancy, in the context of a war that was anticipated to be short-lived. In November 1914 the Canadian commitment was raised from 25,000 to 50,000 men, and by the end of 1914, 59,144 soldiers had been enlisted for service overseas. The 2nd Canadian Division, however, did not arrive in France until September 1915. No Canadian or other dominion units were active on the Western Front until the independently raised Princess Patricia's Canadian Light Infantry (PPCLI) Battalion entered trenches near Ypres on 6 January 1915, followed by the 1st Canadian Division in March.[9]

The precedent for the employment of indigenous men as combatants, however, was set by both Britain and France during the opening battles of the war, as the dominions hastened to form expeditionary forces. France quickly put into effect its plans to mobilize indigenous colonial soldiers for a European war, and then dispatched them to the Western Front. Four battalions of Moroccans, dubbed *les Bataillons des Chasseurs Indigènes*, were incorporated into the Sixth French Army on 20 August 1914, and on 1 October two battalions of colonial Algerians arrived in France.[10] In October a Senegalese brigade (*Tirailleurs Senegalais*) suffered a casualty rate of nearly 75 percent while successfully holding its portion of the line on the Yser River.[11] While the dominions were scrambling to train expeditionary forces, Britain, in need of manpower, deployed a British (East) Indian contingent, Indian Expeditionary Force A, consisting of the 3rd (Lahore) Division, the 7th (Meerut) Division, and the 4th (Secunderbad) Cavalry Brigade, which arrived at Marseilles on 26 September 1914. By the close of 1914, over 2,000 *sepoys* had been killed on the Western Front.[12]

Under the *British North America Act* and the *Indian Act*, Canadian Indians did not have the rights and responsibilities of citizenship; therefore, the government of Canada did not expect, or need, them to take up arms in a foreign war. Indians remained wards of the Crown. The British War Office initially agreed with this policy, stating that "such an appeal to all the scattered remnants of tribes throughout the immense domain, and in varying degrees of civilization, would be practically impossible."[13] On 8 August 1914, four days after the British declaration of war, the minister of militia, Sir Sam Hughes, received a query from Colonel W.E. Hodgins, Number 1 Military District commander, asking, "Is it intended that Indians who are anxious to enlist for service Overseas are to be taken on the Contingent?" The Number 1

District of southwestern Ontario contained numerous Indian communities in and around London, Sarnia, Windsor, and Owen Sound that comprised an estimated total of 3,577 Indians (3.5 percent of the total Indian population). Hughes replied on the same day: "While British troops would be proud to be associated with their fellow subjects [Indians], yet Germans might refuse to extend to them the privileges of civilized warfare, therefore it is considered ... that they had better remain in Canada to share in the protection of the Dominion."[14] The last sentence, however, is nebulous, as it is unclear whether Hughes was insinuating that they should be utilized in the home defence force to help protect the actual dominion, or whether he was implying that they should simply remain in Canada, safely barred from any form of military service. Given future policies and events, the latter appears more likely.

Many historians have incorrectly applied Hughes's statement to represent an official policy of exclusion, while others inaccurately argue that this passage was not widely disseminated. First, although the Ministry of Militia tried to dissuade Indian enlistment in 1914 and 1915, no official policy of exclusion was ever promulgated. Second, this passage was identically reproduced, and extensively circulated, in correspondence concerning Indian service, from its first usage in August 1914 until December 1915, when official authority was finally given to enlist Indians.[15] Hodgins, who received the initial reply from Hughes, became the adjutant general of militia shortly thereafter. When replying to enquiries concerning his ministry's Indian enlistment policy, Hodgins simply quoted the passage relayed to him earlier by his superior. Eventually, this passage was frequently used by officials in the Ministry of Militia and the Departments of Indian Affairs and Justice. It became the unofficial policy surrounding Indian service until December 1915. P. Whitney Lackenbauer surmises that while "others hold this policy up as an example of simple racism, it was careful to proclaim that British soldiers would welcome serving alongside Indians"—a residual extension of the colonial alliance fostered between Indian nations and the British Crown.[16]

There was also apprehension that including Indians in an expeditionary force could violate treaties, as evidenced by the position of the government during the Boer War. During the negotiations of Treaties 1 through 6 (1871–86)—which covered roughly the southern half of the provinces of Manitoba, Saskatchewan, Alberta, and western Ontario—Indian chiefs specifically asked about military service. In October 1873, during the discussions of Treaty 3, governmental representative Alexander Morris was asked by an Ojibwa chief from Fort Frances, Ontario, "If you should get into trouble with the nations, I do not wish to walk out and expose my young men to aid you in any of your wars." To this Morris replied: "The English never call Indians out of their country to fight their battles." [17] Morris echoed this sentiment to Cree chiefs at Fort Carlton and Fort Pitt, Saskatchewan, in August 1876 during consultations over Treaty 6A: "I assured them, you will never be asked to fight against your will; and I trust the time will never come of war between the Queen and the great country near us.... My words, where they are accepted are written down, and they last; as I have said to others, as long as the sun shines and river runs."[18] (This theme will be discussed in greater detail in Chapter 6, most notably concerning Indians and conscription.)

Treaties were signed collectively, not by Canada, but in the name of Queen Victoria; thus, Indian nations saw treaties as an alliance with the Crown through Canada, not with Canada itself. Indians often related more to the British Crown than to Canada, because treaties signed on behalf of Queen Victoria signified sovereignty in partnership with Britain. Many Indians referred to the queen as "the Great White Mother" and in 1914 acknowledged that the "Queen's grandson needed help."[19] This belief was guided not only by treaties but also by past military partnerships and by the 1763 Royal Proclamation, which stated that Indian Affairs and any political activities between Indian nations and the state remained the responsibility of the Crown; thus, the proclamation was a historic recognition of the Indian nations' sovereign status.

In August 1914 Chief F.W. Jacobs of the Sarnia, Ontario, Chippewa (Ojibwa) reserve, and president of the Grand Council of the Chippewa Nation of Western Ontario, wrote to Duncan Campbell Scott that his people were willing to offer "help towards the Mother Country in its present struggle in Europe. The Indian Race as a rule are [sic] loyal to England; this loyalty was created by the noblest Queen that ever lived, Queen Victoria." The Chippewa of Sarnia, Kettle, and Stoney Point also unanimously pledged $1,000 from their band funds for "aiding the Mother Country in this present war with Germany."[20] Similarly, the Ojibwa of the Sucker Creek reserve (Manitoulin Island, Ontario) offered $500 on 26 August 1914, to defray "the enormous expenses in which our Great King is engaged at present. In the wars of 1812 our forefathers fought faithfully under the British Flag. In 1870 four members of this Band went on the war expedition with Sir Garnet Wolseley to Red River." On 1 September, their sister Ojibwa at

Shequiandah, Ontario, also pledged $500 "to show our loyalty and sympathy to our Great Father the King of Great Britain in his conflict with other nations in Europe." One day later, Indian Affairs received $100 from the Christian Island Ojibwa (Penetanguishene/Midland, Ontario), "as our help in good will and respect of the British Flag in which we belong."[21]

Such conveyances of support were not limited to Ontario. On 11 September, the Cape Mudge band at Kwawkewlth, British Columbia, gave $100 "for purposes of the war in which Great Britain is now engaged." Offers of men and money were also sent by the Blood and Blackfoot of Alberta and by the Duck Lake Cree of Saskatchewan during "these trying times of the World Wide War in which the British Empire and her Allies are now engaged in defence of Liberty and the Honour of the Empire." By 24 March 1915 Indian Affairs had received offers of money from Indians across the country totalling $16,968.95. [22]

The most striking example of this affiliation with the Crown—and the inherent belief in Indian sovereignty—came from the Six Nations of the Grand River, the largest Indian community in Canada, which boasted a population of 4,716 in 1914 (or 4.6 percent of the total Canadian Indian population). When war was declared, the band council offered warriors and $1,500 directly to Britain. The chiefs told Scott that the Six Nations "do not belong to Canada and wish to make their contributions direct [through] their brother Chief Ka'rah'kon'tye the Duke of Connaught Governor-General of Canada … as a token of the alliance existing between the Six Nations and the British Crown."[23] This position of sovereignty was maintained by the council, and independently by the majority of chiefs, throughout the war in regards to patriotic donations, recruitment, and the actual service of Six Nations men, leading Scott to declare that this stance was "to such a degree as to constitute a serious hindrance to their advancement and efficiency."[24] In other words, the refusal of the Six Nations to assimilate, to relinquish traditional government, or to recognize the authority of Canada and the *Indian Act* was viewed by Scott as a form of unofficial treason and was a thorn in the side of his department. This would result in serious consequences for the Six Nations in 1924, when the RCMP, at the request of Indian Affairs, forcefully deposed of the traditional council, arrested the chiefs, confiscated wampum belts, and installed an *Indian Act* council in its place. Nevertheless, outside of political spheres, the Six Nations community supported the war effort through enlistment, donations, and women's patriotic work. The community remained, as usual, a loyal ally to the king.

The vast majority of Canadian Indians and band councils greeted war with enthusiasm and offered immediate support in men and money. With no existing pan-Indian political organization, individual reserves and councils relayed their support through their Indian agents, to Scott, or to the king. It was not only the traditionally warlike Indian nations, such as the Blackfoot and Iroquois Confederacies, which offered warriors; so too did nations with little martial prowess, such as those of British Columbia. Scott, although ignorant of the martial histories of certain Indian nations, recognized that the Indians of British Columbia were "not so warlike in disposition as those of the central and eastern parts of the Dominion."[25] As an alternative, on 1 September 1914 Thomas Deasy, agent at Massett, British Columbia, offered the services of his Haida wards for local home defence, to relieve white soldiers for overseas duty. His offer was duly dismissed.[26]

Throughout 1914 Indian men rushed to recruiting depots for reasons other than loyalty to the British Crown. Although the warrior ethic had stagnated as a result of residential schooling, religious education, and isolation on reserves, it had not been completely repressed. While many joined for money, adventure, and employment, as did their white comrades, scores of others enlisted to revive the warrior tradition and gain social status within their communities.[27] War in Europe seemed a feasible means to circumvent governmental policies and the *Indian Act*, and it offered freedom and escape from docile reserve life. According to Mike Mountain Horse, "From the outset of this colossal struggle the Red Man demonstrated his loyalty to the British Crown in a very convincing manner.... My uncle, Chief Bull Shield, had been a great warrior of the plains. But the war proved the fighting spirit of my tribe was not quelched [sic] through reservation life. When duty called, we were there and when we were called forth to fight for the cause of civilization, our people showed all the bravery of our warriors of old."[28]

In 1914, although the 1904 *Militia Act* made no specific reference to Indians, the government unofficially discouraged their enlistment, despite the fact that many were active in militia units. Scott bluntly stated on 12 August 1914 that "no unit composed solely of Indians will go to the front with the Canadian Contingent," but neither he nor his department (nor the Ministry of Militia) made any official statements concerning individual enlistment.[29]

Policy was not uniform, and correspondence from the Ministry of Militia and the Department of Indian Affairs was inconsistent, reflecting the nature of the Canadian government; cross-departmental planning and correspondence was, in general, negligible during this time period. For example, while Hughes's phrasing of 8 August 1914 was circulating, as was other correspondence discouraging enlistment, other communications advised the opposite. J.D. McLean, assistant deputy and secretary for Indian Affairs, wrote on 13 October 1914 that the individual Indian "should be allowed to enlist if he so desires. A number of Indians throughout Canada have already enlisted."[30] In December 1914 Duncan Campbell Scott instructed his agents, "If the young men of the Indian band in their particular district desire to enlist for active service during the present war ... take them to the local recruiting office and offer their services."[31]

In summary, unofficial policies of exclusion and inclusion were operating conjointly until December 1915, although exclusion remained the dominant premise. This dichotomy led to great confusion within departments and among Indians and their agents as to the regulations pertaining to Indian service. Correspondence from agents, chiefs, and individual Indians asking for clarification of policy flooded into both the Department of Indian Affairs and the Ministry of Militia throughout 1914 and 1915. Most, but not all, replies were consistent with an exclusionist policy. Astonishingly, in 1917 a commentator writing for the *New York Times* recognized this ambiguity and remarked that Indians "would have been there [the Western Front] nearly three years ago had not an order from the Canadian Militia Department, for some reason never quite explained, forbidden recruiting among the Indians when the war commenced.... In several other instances recruiting officers winked at the regulations and enlisted individual Indians [who] offered their service to the British Crown."[32]

Many Indians applied for overseas service. Most were immediately turned away. Many others were released after their Indian status was discovered. However, under the frantic "call to arms" of the minister of militia, Sir Sam Hughes, units recruited directly from their regions, without interference from the Ministry of Militia or the DIA. Local recruiting officers, therefore, had absolute discretion over whom they enrolled, provided recruits met the medical standards.[33] This policy was reiterated by the chief of the general staff, Lieutenant General Willoughby G. Gwatkin, in a 13 November 1914 memorandum concerning "coloured enlistment," which included not only Indians, but also blacks and Asians.[34]

The success or failure to attest Indian volunteers, therefore, depended on two factors. The first was the need for battalion commanders to fill their unit quotas. Given the overwhelming response to recruitment, officers had little trouble meeting demands, and, as the statistics show, they filled initial positions with men predominantly of British origins. The second and more likely factor depended on the recruiters' racial perceptions of Indians within the dichotomy of the noble savage. While many would have viewed Indians with disdain and rejected volunteers, others assumed Indians possessed martial talents and enrolled them accordingly.[35] Although race was not recorded on enlistment documents, some recruiting officers listed "Indian" under the section entitled "Description of [Name] on Enlistment—Complexion" on the attestation form. For example, Albert Mountain Horse was listed as Indian on his enrolment documents and thirty-two (or 11 percent) of the 292 men who volunteered from the Six Nations reserve were recorded as such.[36]

Many Indians circumvented the unofficial exclusionist policy, with or without the collusion of their commanding officers. By 28 August 1914, for example, eight Indians from the Six Nations and two from the Mississauga of the Credit were reported by the Brantford area Indian agent to have enlisted. The 1st Canadian Division, which disembarked in England on 14 October 1914, therefore did contain a small number of Indian soldiers, as did the independent PPCLI Battalion, in which there were at least two Indians.[37] According to R.F. Haig of the Fort Garry Horse, some British civilians were disappointed to witness that the newly arrived colonial soldiers from Canada were not all red-skinned, decorated and dressed in feathers and pelts, and wearing traditional headdress.[38]

Many of these first Indian soldiers were snipers and scouts, including the famed Ojibwa sniper Corporal Francis Pegahmagabow of the 1st Battalion— the muse for Joseph Boyden's acclaimed, and effectively mainstream, novel *Three Day Road* (2005).[39] Enlisting on 14 August 1914, the twenty-three-year-old Pegahmagabow bluntly stated, "I went to war voluntarily just as quick as the white man." William Ireland, editor of the Parry Sound *North Star*, wrote of Pegahmagabow's enlistment at length: "His grandfather was a warrior and chief and fought for the British in the War of 1812, so the boy comes from a long line of fighting ancestors who fought in the Indian wars. We are all hoping Francis will distinguish himself as his forefathers did and will return home covered with glory and medals. His example might well be followed." Pegahmagabow did not disappoint. He returned home to his Parry Island reserve in 1919, having won the Military Medal three times (one of only thirty-eight Canadians to accomplish this feat) while tallying an unofficial 378 kills and 300 more captured.[40]

ILLUS. 6. Non-commissioned Officers of the 1st Battalion. The individual at the extreme left of the group is Corporal Francis Pegahmagabow. *Library and Archives Canada, PA-00383.*

Shortly after the declaration of war in August, there were numerous unsuccessful attempts to create all-Indian units throughout Canada, despite the fact that there was no historical precedent for such units. The first effort was made in October 1914 by Glen Campbell, chief inspector of Indian agencies for western and northern Canada, and militia veteran of the 1885 North-West Rebellion. Campbell proposed the formation of a corps of scouts or irregular cavalry made up entirely of Indians, something similar to the mounted infantry unit in which he had confronted Métis/Cree forces during Louis Riel's second uprising.[41] Concurrently, in Alberta the Reverend John McDougall, a Methodist missionary to the Alberta Indians, petitioned Indian Affairs: "Indians at one time fought in battles amongst themselves, and some of them are the best scouts in the world.... I would suggest the taking of a certain number of Indians from each tribe and from each reserve, and making up a regiment of about 500."[42]

On 1 November 1914 Colonel William Hamilton Merritt, honorary chief of the Six Nations Iroquois, tried, as he had done during the Boer War, to arrange with the Ministry of Militia the formation of two Six Nations companies, which he personally offered to fund. He did not, however, consult the Six Nations council. On 26 November the council rejected the offer to mobilize a distinct regiment, asserting that they would only respond to a request from King George V. By allowing the Canadian government control of a Six Nations regiment, the council would tacitly acknowledge the government's jurisdiction, something they were not prepared to do. While the council supported the war effort, they decided to force the government to recognize the Six Nations Confederacy as a sovereign ally of Britain, equal to the Dominion of Canada. According to Scott Trevithick, "By making their acceptance conditional upon recognition of their independent political status the Chiefs hoped to force the government to make a concession. When the government did not, it provided a further affront to Six Nations nationalism." The Militia Council in Ottawa had also decided that the offer was simply "too inconvenient," and it bluntly stated that "under no circumstances [would the government allow] the Canadian-Indians to furnish a contingent for war service in Europe."[43]

All attempts to create all-Indian units or sub-units were rejected conjointly by the DIA and the Ministry of Militia throughout the early months of the war. Scores of requests, however, continued to be sent by band councils, Indian agents, and private citizens to both regarding the enlistment of individual Indians or the formation of Indian units. There remained confusion among Indian communities, their agents, and district military commanders as to the regulations concerning Indian enlistment. This ambiguity was only rectified by the Ministry of Militia in December 1915, after the 1st Division had been drained of manpower in the 1915 battles at Ypres, Givenchy, and Festubert. As the CEF expanded and suffered greater losses, the need for manpower increased, and governmental policy slowly shifted in favour of recruiting Indians to meet these mounting demands. It was the British requests for Indian soldiers in October 1915, however, that finally prompted the shift in policy.

Throughout 1914 the war was generally met with a jingoistic outpouring in the British segments of Canada, and support for the imperial government was given in the form of men, material, and money. The outward support for the war given by most Indian leaders did not in all cases reflect the opinions of those whom they purportedly represented. Many Indians did not endorse the recruitment of their men for a European war. This was no different from the divisions within the Euro-Canadian populations and should be viewed as such. Most French-Canadians, and some Irish-Canadians, did not back the war effort either.

For many Indian leaders seeking full and equal sovereignty, support offered directly to the Crown was viewed as a means to lobby the imperial government to pressure Canada to alter oppressive laws. The actions of the Six Nations council surrounding the creation of a distinct Six Nations battalion offers the most emblematic example of this belief. Many other leaders also cited treaties and offered support in the name of Queen Victoria while seeking acknowledgement of sovereignty from both Canada and the Crown.

Aware of these Indian grievances and demands, in 1914 the Canadian government actively resisted, blocking Indian attempts for inclusion in the war effort when possible. With manpower sufficient at this point in the war to meet demands and commitments, Indian participation was not needed and, therefore, not generally accepted. Inclusion remained in keeping with past practice and contemporary racial constructs. A select number of Indians circumvented the non-official and confusing policy of exclusion to enlist in the CEF; however, most were denied enlistment privileges. According to James Walker, at the onset of war the participation of Indians was guided "by a set of presumptions about their abilities which dictated the role they were to play [or not play] and which limited the rewards they were to derive."[44] As the war progressed, and Canadian forces expanded and accrued the horrific casualty rates of modern trench warfare on the Western Front, Canadian policies regarding Indian service were substantially altered to provide for greater inclusion. Racial concerns were progressively discarded to meet the pragmatic requirements for manpower.

Chapter Five

In the Interest of the Indians, 1915–16

By the close of 1914, the 125,000 "old contemptibles" of the BEF had suffered 90,000 casualties. Although the dominions mobilized expeditionary forces and conducted training both at home and abroad, no dominion forces participated in major campaigns during 1914. During 1915 and 1916, however, those forces expanded and became key components of the fighting strength of the BEF on the Western Front and at Gallipoli. High casualty rates accompanied this participation, and the swelling expeditionary forces required increasing reinforcements to sustain their national formations. The increasing overall strength of Allied armies was accompanied by the immediate need for service and support auxiliaries, such as labour battalions, forestry corps, and pioneer battalions. Britain increasingly looked to her dominions as a source of men and materials. Amplified dominion participation, however, was accompanied by greater demands for inclusion in strategic and operational counsel by dominion prime ministers, most notably by Borden, to satisfy nascent domestic national consciousness.

Within this general atmosphere, in October 1915 the British War Office issued the most important imperial documents of the war pertaining to indigenes of all dominions. Official inclusion of Indians in the CEF and the clarification of policy in December 1915 were directly linked to the requests of the imperial government. While Canadian scholars have noted the drastic shift in policy towards greater Indian inclusion after October 1915, not one has referenced these documents, nor made any connection to the demands of the senior British government. On 8 October 1915 all governors general and administrators of British dominions and colonies received a confidential memorandum from the Canadian-born colonial secretary, Andrew Bonar Law:[1] "The [War] Cabinet have asked for a report as to the possibilities of raising native troops in large numbers in our Colonies + Protectorates for Imperial service. What is wanted is an estimate of the numbers that could be raised; the length of time needed for training; an opinion as to their fighting value; and any pertinent remarks on such points as climatic restrictions on their employment, the influence of religion...[and] the difficulty of officering." A second request was sent on 18 October.[2] War exigencies now required the military inclusion of indigenous men. The colonial secretary also specifically addressed Canadian Indians by comparing them to other dominion indigenes: "There were striking differences.... The Red Indian was more romantic and picturesque."[3] In the British interpretation, the loyal service of Indians during the colonial period still resonated and was again requested in aid of the empire.

The 1st Canadian Division arrived in France on 16 February 1915. On 3 March battalions entered the lines at Fleurbaix and took part sparingly in the Battle of Neuve Chapelle (10–13 March 1915). The 1st Division suffered 320 casualties in March, in what was labelled a "familiarization period." During its tour in the Ypres Salient, between 15 April and 3 May, the division suffered 6,104 casualties out of roughly 16,500 engaged (37 percent)— the majority between 22 and 25 April. During these four days, although the number of Indians present in the division was small, eight became casualties, including five killed.[4] During subsequent actions at Festubert (22–24 May) and Givenchy (15 June), the division suffered an additional 3,000 casualties. Furthermore, while the division was not involved in any large-scale battles until actions at St. Eloi Craters in March 1916, "wastage" accounted for roughly 650 casualties per month from September 1915 to March 1916.[5]

Compounding the need for manpower in the face of these casualties was the drastic expansion of the CEF in 1915. The 2nd Division, authorized on 9 October 1914, joined the 1st Division in France in September 1915, facilitating the creation of the Canadian Corps. On 30 October Borden increased the authorized strength of the CEF to 250,000, despite sober counsel from Gwatkin that "there is a limit to our production.... You cannot put every available man into the firing line at once. Casualties must be replaced. It takes 3,000 to place 1,000 infantrymen in the field and to maintain them there in numbers and efficiency for a year."[6] Nevertheless, a 3rd Division was formed from surplus reserves in France on 24 December 1915. On 31 December Borden doubled the authorized strength of the CEF to 500,000, an increase that was accompanied by this threat to the British government:

It can hardly be expected that we shall put 400,000 to 500,000 men in the field and willingly accept the position of having no more voice and receiving no more consideration than if we were toy automata. Any person cherishing such an expectation harbours unfortunate and even dangerous delusion. Is this war being waged by the United Kingdom alone or is it a war waged by the whole Empire?... Procrastination, indecision, inertia, doubt, hesitation and many other undesirable qualities have made themselves entirely too conspicuous in this war.... Another very able Cabinet Minster spoke of the shortage of guns, rifles, munitions, etc., but declared that the chief shortage was of brains.[7]

Since the beginning of October, Borden had been relentless in demanding greater involvement in the direction of the war. According to Borden, nationalist considerations could not be ignored if recruitment was to be sustained, as the "Governments of Overseas Dominions have large responsibilities to their people for conduct of war and we deem ourselves entitled to fuller information and to consultation respecting general policy in war operations."[8]

In late 1916 Borden craftily enhanced Canada's position within the political spheres of London. In November, he forced the resignation of the minister of militia, Sam Hughes, explaining, "his conduct and speech were so eccentric as to justify the conclusion that his mind was unbalanced."[9] Borden thought it "essential to curtail the activities of Hughes and to place in the hands of a responsible Minister in London, the disposition of all such matters affecting the welfare of the Canadian Army ... and thus relieve the Government of the unfortunate results of Hughes' visits abroad."[10] To circumvent the legalities of British control over Canadian foreign affairs, Borden used the 1914 *War Measures Act*, internal to Canada, to achieve his desires.[11] On 28 October 1916 the Ministry of Overseas Military Forces of Canada was established in London to ensure that Canada was kept informed of developments and to express concerns "in all matters connected with the government, command and disposition of the overseas forces of Canada"; it "shall be responsible for the administration of the affairs of the military forces of Canada in the United Kingdom and on the Continent of Europe."[12] No other dominion initiated any matching organization, although in June 1917 South African General Jan C. Smuts became a permanent member of David Lloyd George's imperial war cabinet, which saw sporadic attendance by dominion prime ministers.[13]

In reality, Borden's commitment of 500,000 men, in light of casualty rates, would require the immediate enlistment of 250,000, and an additional 25,000 men per month (300,000 annually) if its strength was to be sustained. Senator James Mason reported to his colleagues that these figures "will not be obtained under the present system of enlistment."[14] As of January 1916, the total strength of the CEF stood at only 218,260, and on 20 January the 4th Division was authorized by Borden. The total enlistment for 1915 was 158,859—an average monthly enlistment of 13,238.[15] To meet Borden's imperious and idealistic promises, Canada needed to significantly bolster recruitment.

ILLUS. 7. The 1,000 Yard Stare: Canadians Returning from the Somme Front, November 1916. *Library and Archives Canada, PA-000832.*

To meet the demand for manpower in November 1915, the government authorized prominent individuals and communities to recruit and raise battalions for overseas service outside of official military circles, with the consent of the Ministry of Militia, which did not forego financial responsibility. Throughout 1915 confusion prevailed as to the legality of enlisting Indians, and scores of requests were submitted to the Ministry of Militia and the DIA. For example, in October 1915 Cape Croker Chippewa Indian agent A.J.

Duncan questioned Indian Affairs as to why three men from his reserve were denied enlistment at four different stations while other Indians had been accepted.[16] In November Scott simply replied to offers and complaints, "[I] would not put any obstacle in your way [but] The Militia Department, however, does not seem to be very willing to enlist Indians for overseas service." Hughes's August 1914 passage concerning Indians, Germans, and civilized warfare was still being circulated throughout 1915 within both departments and to individual agents and chiefs. Major General Eugene Fiset, surgeon general and deputy minister of militia, wrote to Scott on 22 October 1915, "With respect to Indians enlisting I would point out that several cases of this nature have been reported and respecting these offers I would point out that it has been decided that while British troops would be proud to be associated with their Indian fellow subjects, the Germans might refuse to extend to them the privileges of civilized warfare."[17] Nevertheless, Scott was advocating in his personal replies to queries that Indians should "enlist in the usual way."[18]

ILLUS. 8. Cree Recruits from File Hills, Saskatchewan, October 1915. Left to Right: David Bird; Joe McKay; Leonard McKay; Leonard Creely; Jack Walker; Harry Stonefield. *Glenbow Museum Archives, NA-3454-41.*

On the Six Nations reserve, Merritt continued to press for the formation of Indian companies and acquired the assistance of Six Nations–born Mohawk Frederick O. Loft, a militia veteran of seven years and an accountant at the Toronto-based Provincial Lunatic Asylum. Loft addressed the council and warriors "who were present in large numbers" on 24 March 1915. The council, "after touching on the various relations existing between the Chiefs of the Six Nations and the British Crown," offered their decision. According to the council minutes, "The chiefs did not deem it proper that they should ask the government to allow them to form companies when they already have the 37th Battalion on the reserve and are standing ready to respond when called to do so by the [British] Department of War."[19]

Nevertheless, in November F.R. Lalor, MP for Dunnville, Ontario, and Lieutenant Colonel Edwy Sutherland Baxter, 37th Haldimand Rifles commanding officer, appealed to Sam Hughes to raise a battalion in the Dunnville-Caledonia-Six Nations area. Although it was to include Indians, it was not initially intended to be solely an Indian unit. Baxter was known to the Six Nations and was "one of the most popular men in the opinion of the Indians," according to a December 1915 article from the local *Brantford Expositor*. While the Ministry of Militia approved the battalion, no mention was made concerning Indians, as recruitment remained within the discretion of local commanders, in this case Baxter. He believed that he could muster 200 to 250 Indians from the Six Nations reserve, given that many of these men were already active in his militia unit.[20]

The request of Lalor and Baxter, in addition to unrelenting appeals from Deasy in British Columbia, William Charles McKay in Saskatchewan, Glen Campbell in Manitoba, and Lieutenant Colonel B. Robson, commanding officer of the 135th Middlesex Battalion (London), to recruit large numbers of Indians, influenced the decision of the Ministry of Militia to officially endorse Indian service in early December 1915. McKay had been requesting authority to raise Indian companies throughout 1914 and 1915, and he was supported in this by his MP, S.J. Donaldson: "I must say that I would be very much in favour of you allowing Mr. McKay to carry out his proposition.... If you had 300 or more of these Indians at the Front they would make good snipers as they are crack marksmen and they are as tough as any class of people I have ever met in this country."[21] In late 1915 Donaldson took a commission as lieutenant colonel and raised and commanded the 188th Battalion at Kamsack,

Saskatchewan, which contained Indians from the Fort Pelly Agency.[22] Campbell, who had sought permission to form an Indian unit in 1914, was loaned by the DIA from his position as "Chief Inspector of Agencies, Reserves and Inspectorates in Manitoba, Saskatchewan, Alberta and the Northwest Territories" to the Ministry of Militia to raise a battalion. On 9 July 1915, at fifty-two years of age with virtually no military experience, he was tasked with assisting in raising the 79th Battalion in Brandon, Manitoba. (It should be noted that he was not the commanding officer.) On 24 November Campbell was transferred from the 79th Battalion, mandated to raise the 107th Battalion in Winnipeg, and appointed its commander as a lieutenant colonel.[23]

Following the 8 and 18 October 1915 requests from the War Office for indigenous soldiers, a third, albeit not as direct, call was written by the colonial secretary, Andrew Bonar Law, on behalf of the king on 25 October: "More men and yet more are wanted to keep my armies in the field.... I ask you men of all classes to come forward voluntarily."[24] A November 1917 report from the Ministry of Militia replied to the question of "whether there was any General Order of the Department by which Indians were not allowed to enlist. No Such General Order was issued. Towards the latter part of 1915, the number of Indians who volunteered to enlist was continuously increasing, and representations were made from the Crown ... that they should be allowed to do so, and the following circular letter was issued on December 10, 1915. This regulation has never been altered since that time."[25] The aforementioned circular from the Ministry of Militia "to OC Divisions and Districts, Inspector-General of Eastern Canada and Inspector-General of Western Canada" stated: "I have the honour, by direction, to state that owing to the large number of applications for enlistment of Indians, authority is hereby granted to enlist Indians in the various Units for Overseas Service, provided, of course, that the enlistment Regulations as to medical fitness and otherwise are fully observed." This instruction was then filtered down to all Indian agents and battalion commanders.

Prior to this directive, authority had been granted to individual battalions to enlist Indians. On 2 December 1915 Robson (135th Battalion) had been granted verbal approval from Hughes to recruit Indians. Lalor, Baxter, and Deasy were verbally informed the following day. On 4 December Hughes cabled Donaldson and McKay, "that you may get them [Indians] down and enlist them and recruit all the good Indians you can get provided they pass the examination." On 9 December Fiset wrote to Indian Affairs stating that authority had been given to recruit Indians nationwide, specifically on account of the extension given earlier to Baxter and the 114th Battalion.[26] For the first time in the war, two months after the first British request, Canadian authorities relented and officially allowed Indians into the CEF. While Indians were given admittance, other minorities, such as blacks and Asians, were still unofficially barred from military service for the time being. This differentiation afforded to Indians illustrates the common belief in their enhanced martial proclivities and their continued reputation as fierce warriors.

Although policy towards individual enlistment had been officially clarified, the issue of homogenous Indian units still remained vague. Throughout January 1916 requests to form all-Indian units came from Indian agents, battalion commanders, and civilians in Ontario, Manitoba, Saskatchewan, and British Columbia. On 3 January 1916 Hodgins wrote McKay, stating that although permission had been granted to recruit Indians, "It is not considered advisable that Indian should go as separate Companies or Units." On 6 January Gwatkin issued a memorandum within the Ministry of Militia:

> If 500,000 men are to be raised, we must take all we can get; but it is useless to enlist Indians, and train them, unless we intend to employ them at the front. And how are they to be employed at the front? As a battalion, or by companies, or as individuals? If as a battalion, or by companies, we must come to some understanding with the [British] War Office; and the best plan would be, I think, after consultation with the War Office, to earmark one or more companies as Indian companies, and keep them up to strength by drafts specially prepared. How Indians would stand trench warfare I do not know; nor do I know whether, coming from different tribes, they would fight among themselves. What does the Minister intend? At one time he decided that there were not to be Indian battalions, but that individual Indians were to be allowed to enlist into any battalion they pleased. Since then he is reported to have told the Press that Indian and Japanese and negro battalions would all be raised; so we are not quite sure where we are standing.[27]

An important and previously overlooked component of this communication was that Fiset recognized the chain of command and sought to secure the approval of the British War Office before implementing any official Canadian policy concerning homogenous Indian units or sub-units.

The response to the change in Indian enlistment policy was overwhelming. A clear example of the drastically increased acceptance of Indian volunteers was the enlistment of American Oneida brothers Albert and Enos Kick of Green Bay, Wisconsin, who were attested as "Indian" on 28 January and 3 February 1916, respectively, into the 135th Middlesex Battalion[28]: "My brother [Albert] and I enlisted almost at the same time, first month of 1916, because we have families and didn't want to see Germans kill the little ones. We tried to go over in 1914, but we couldn't on account of us being Indians, so we couldn't very well pass as a white man, so we waited until our chance came, so both of us went to the same Battalion and the same Company and everything the same.... But I miss my brother Albert, he is over there yet."[29] (Albert was killed at Cambrai on 1 October 1918.) The 135th Battalion embarked for England in August 1916 containing seventy-seven Indians, including the American Kick brothers. On 13 April 1916 Indian Affairs received a letter from Jennie Kick, wife of Enos, temporarily living on the Muncey Ontario reserve:

> I cannot support my 4 Poor little Indian children.... I am not healthy I am sickly most of my life and cannot be with out my husband. We need him in the worst way. We have no place to go to. But when my husband is here we allways have a place to go too, he left us at his fathers and his mothers, and they turned us out on the road and every since that we are all over the reserve. We do not Belong here. Our home is near Green Bay Wisconsin place called Oneida Wis., Brown County. So I Beg and Beg you to have my husband Enos W. Kick Released ... anybody can tell you the way we are fixed should you want to know more about it.... I am begging every night and day for God sakes sent my husband to us. We are poor every since my husband is away. We want help so send my husband to me.

Indian Affairs simply replied that it could not force his release and that discretion remained with Enos himself. Enos survived the war and returned to his family in December 1918.[30]

It is not known how many American Indians served in the CEF prior to the U.S. declaration of war on 6 April 1917. In total, 35,612 Americans served in Canadian units during the war.[31] The Indian population of the

United States in 1917 was roughly 330,000 (three times larger than that of Canada). The exact total figures for American Indian service, as for Canadian Indian service, are not known. An accurate estimate, based on the 1920 annual report of the commissioner of Indian Affairs, Cato Sells, and secondary sources, reveals that between 10,000 and 12,000 American Indians served in the American Expeditionary Force (AEF)—6,509 are known to have been drafted and another 5,000 to 6,000 are thought to have voluntarily enlisted. As a point of comparison, 3.9 percent of the total Indian population of Canada voluntarily served, whereas the 3.3 percent of the U.S. Indian population that served includes those who volunteered *and* were drafted. Like his Canadian counterpart Duncan Campbell Scott, Sells viewed the military service of Indians as an avenue of assimilation. By November 1918, 17,000 (including the 6,509 who were drafted) had been registered for the draft. Sells stated in his 1918 report that "many Indians from our northern reservations enrolled in Canadian military organizations before the declaration of war by the United States." According to Thomas A. Britten, "press reports indicated that hundreds of Native Americans from the United States enlisted in the Canadian army between 1915 and 1917."[32]

In 1919 Joseph K. Dixon interviewed and surveyed 2,846 American Indian veterans. Of the 2,315 who listed a specific national formation, seven reported that they had served in the CEF. An extrapolation of this percentage, based on the total service of 12,000, would place the overall number of American Indians in the CEF at thirty-six. Given that Dixon used American enlistment papers to locate his subjects, his sample group would have excluded most Indians with CEF service. While the number is certainly higher than the projected totals of Dixon's surveys, it is doubtful that it exceeded 300.[33] In August 1919 an inquiry was made by the U.S. administration as to how many American Indians served in the CEF. The reply from the Ministry of Militia simply stated that "no differentiation between Indians and other Canadians was attempted in the Canadian Forces."[34]

On 6 December 1915 Baxter received written authorization specifically to recruit Indians for his 114th Battalion.[35] However, the chiefs and community of the Six Nations were split in support of active recruitment for the 114th Battalion. On 18 December 1915 Baxter complained to Major George H. Williams, Number Two District recruiting officer, that two "desposed [dehorned, in Iroquoian phrasing] Chiefs … are doing all in their power to prevent the enlistment of Indians with the 114th O.S. Battalion."[36] Baxter's initial recruitment drive was a failure, yielding only thirty-five Six Nations men by the end of 1915. He complained bitterly to Scott and Logie that other battalions had been poaching Indians from his area, and he requested their transfers, and those of all other Indians in Ontario battalions, to the 114th. He confided to Scott that he could not raise his battalion to strength without a significant number of Indians (as his "township was composed principally of German immigrants") and asked for permission to recruit outside of his geographical area "from any reserve or reserves in Canada."[37] On 19 January 1916 Scott wrote to Logie asking "whether there are any general orders attaching Indians recruited to the 114th Battalion. I am anxious to do anything that is possible to promote recruiting from the different Indian bands in Ontario." Scott also asked if transfers of those Indians already recruited were mandatory. Several battalions had already transferred their Indians to the 114th, but following complaints by other battalion commanders, who were also trying to fill battalion quotas, Logie instructed Baxter that transfers were not mandatory and discretion remained with the Indians themselves. Many battalion commanders stated bluntly that they wanted to keep their "good Indians."[38]

On 25 January Scott wrote Baxter insinuating that Charles A. Cooke, an Ojibwa-Mohawk clerk at the DIA, could be dispatched to assist in "enlisting persons of his own race." Cooke, the "only male Indian employed at the Service in Ottawa," was officially attached on 31 January. Cooke arrived at the Six Nations reserve on 5 February, after having consulted with members of the Ministry of Militia and Indian Affairs as well as local Indian agent Joseph McGibbon. By 8 February he had enlisted ninety-six men. On 16 February he was bestowed with the honorary rank of lieutenant to enhance his professional appearance. Cooke toured Ontario and Quebec reserves throughout 1916 recruiting for the 114th Battalion.[39]

Although he initially formed the 114th Battalion, Baxter's tenure of command lasted just over two months. He died of disease on 15 February 1916 and was replaced by Lieutenant Colonel Andrew T. Thompson, who was born in Cayuga in 1870, near the Six Nations reserve.[40] Descended from an affluent, aristocratic family, Thompson had previously served in the Canadian militia as private to colour sergeant with the Queen's Own Rifles of Canada. He then joined the 37th Haldimand Rifles as a captain in 1892 and proceeded to serve as the regiment's commanding officer for eight years. He went on to command the

5th Infantry Brigade for four years and served as commander for the Canadian Coronation Contingent at the crowning of King Edward VII in January 1902.[41] Thompson, a lawyer and editor by trade (he was editor of the *Canadian Military Gazette* for many years), also served as member of Parliament for the constituency of Haldimand and Monck from November 1900 to November 1904 in Prime Minister Wilfrid Laurier's Liberal government.[42] Given his prior service with the 37th Haldimand Rifles and his political experience, Thompson was a logical choice to command the 114th Battalion, with its Indian composition. Thompson's grandfather had fought alongside Six Nations warriors at the Battle of Queenston Heights with Major General Sir Isaac Brock, and Thompson's two sons, Andrew and Walter, were serving lieutenants, having joined the 114th on 8 December 1915. Thompson himself was an honorary chief of the Six Nations; his Iroquoian name was *Ahsaregoah,* meaning "the sword."[43]

On 1 March 1916 Thompson was given special permission to enlist Indians, both within and outside the battalion's military district, but not exclusively above other local battalions.[44] This arrangement was supported by Brigadier General W.A. Logie, commander of Number Two District, Toronto, and also by Duncan Campbell Scott: "I thought I should write you [Logie] and state how much I am interested in the welfare of the 114th Battalion; I hope to see a solid half of the battalion composed of Indians, and I trust that District No. 2 may be able to produce them. It is in the interest of the Indians, I think, that we should have at least two full Indian companies. Personally and officially I have been doing everything possible to bring this about."[45] In April Thompson recognized Scott's support by making him a honorary member of his battalion's mess, while stressing in the same letter that the 114th still required "MORE MEN."[46]

During active recruiting and in the media, the 114th was advertising itself as "the Indian Unit," and at least a dozen battalions transferred their Indian recruits to the 114th. However, not all Indians wanted to serve in the 114th Battalion, as they preferred "not to fight alongside Mohawks." During the colonial wars, Iroquois warriors (specifically the Mohawk) had earned a reputation as fierce combatants by conquering or assimilating other nations, some to the point of near extinction, as in the case of the Huron and the Mahican Confederacies.[47] This reluctance to transfer to, or join, the 114th lends credence to Gwatkin's concerns on 6 January 1916 as to "whether, coming from different tribes, they would fight among themselves." Furthermore, Cooke met resistance to recruitment from certain Six Nations chiefs and on many northern Ontario Ojibwa reserves, some going so far as to conceal their young men during his visits. Angered by the Six Nations Council's refusal to endorse recruitment, Cooke bitterly concluded to Scott that "the much boasted loyalty of the nation to the British throne from the stand-point of the chiefs is more of a myth than a fact." Similarly, the Parry Island Band, home to Corporal Pegahmagabow, opposed Cooke's efforts, claiming that the government and Crown failed to uphold its promises of presents and pensions after the War of 1812. As usual, Scott tried to mollify these uncooperative Indian communities: "I consider that any Indian who joins it [114th] will be well treated and that his association with the battalion would be a credit to him in the future.... There are already a good many Ojibbeways [sic] in the battalion and anyone ... would feel quite at home there.... It is in the interest of the Indians, I think, that we should have at least two full companies of Indians."[48]

The reluctance of certain Indian communities to welcome Cooke, or any other aspect of recruitment, is evidence of the strategies initiated by Indians to promote their agendas and to confront the paternalistic edicts of the *Indian Act* and the control of the DIA; they were not spectators of the ongoing process of colonization and the convergence of cultures. J.R. Miller and P. Whitney Lackenbauer recognize that Aboriginal peoples "were active agents who adopted strategies of 'resistance, evasion and defiance to counter attempts to control their lives and eradicate their traditions,' and that Indian Affairs bureaucrats recognized the weakness of their position and were reluctant to provoke confrontation."[49] Indians did not represent a monolithic, homogenous entity; rather, they were a diverse collective of nations with distinct cultures, histories, and experiences. This point is exemplified by the differing responses of various Indian communities in Ontario and Quebec toward Cooke's drive to enlist Indian men. Some viewed him as an Indian who could promote their welfare and grievances within the DIA, while others criticized him as an assimilated appendage to the oppressive Canadian administration. Both estimations, however, are indicative of a choice to either promote or protect community-specific interests.

Cooke's recruitment drive was not as successful as expected, much to his own disappointment and that of Scott and Thompson. Nevertheless, he successfully recruited Mohawks from Kahnawake and Kanesatake (Oka) in Quebec, and from Akwesasne/St. Regis (Quebec/Ontario/New York State), as well as a number of Cree and Ojibwa from northern Ontario and Manitoba. On 29 May, twenty Mohawks from Tyendinaga (Bay of Quinte Mohawks near

Belleville) who were already training with other battalions willingly transferred to the 114th after Cooke explained the voluntary transfer policy and dispelled the rumour that Indians "are not to be recognized as Indians overseas … and that Indians were being sent to the front under the guise of Italians."[50]

In July 1916 a report of the Number Two Military District revealed that the 114th had 348 Indians (including five officers), while another 211 were included in fifteen other units.[51] Given the lower than expected recruitment rates and the non-mandatory transfer policy, an all-Indian battalion was untenable. In all, 353 Indians (287 from the Six Nations reserve) served in the 114th Battalion, in which two of the four companies, including most of the officers, were Indian. Of the Six Nations men, 52 percent had previous militia experience, the majority of which were with the 37th Haldimand Battalion. A thirty-five-man regimental band, all from the Six Nations, was also formed. The band toured the British Isles for recruiting and patriotic purposes and included traditional garments and war dances in their performances.[52]

Although only two companies were composed of Indians, special concessions were asked for by Thompson in a letter to the Ministry of Militia on 25 March 1916:

> This battalion is recruiting largely from the Six Nation Indians. Already more than two hundred of them have enlisted, and I confidently expect three hundred and fifty to four hundred more. The ancestors of these men fought for Great Britain in every battle on the Niagara frontier in the War of 1812, and were with General Brock in large numbers when he fell at Queenston Heights. To this day they venerate his memory, and the name for which I ask, "Brock's Rangers" would greatly add to our prestige with them, and gratify them exceedingly. The "white" half of the battalion comes from Haldimand County, one of the Niagara Peninsula group, and many of these men too had ancestors with Brock in 1812.

Permission was granted to use the name "Brock's Rangers" two days later.[53] The regimental crest featured two crossed tomahawks below the motto "For King and Country." The crest also bore the name "Brock's Rangers" and a crown, all superimposed on a maple leaf. The Six Nations Women's Patriotic League embroidered a 114th Battalion flag, which they adorned with Iroquoian symbols. Thompson proceeded to gain approval from the Ministry of

Militia for his battalion to carry this flag alongside the king's colours and their regular regimental colours.[54] The battalion was mobilized to proceed overseas on 29 September 1916. The last inspection before sailing was conducted on 17 October 1916 at Camp Borden, by Major General F.L. Lessard, who concluded: "This is a good Battalion in which there are 300 Indians ... 15 men trained in Scouting ... of Good Class and Physique."[55]

The only other CEF unit to mirror the Indian composition of the 114th was the 107th Battalion, raised in Winnipeg, Manitoba, in December 1915, shortly after governmental permission was granted to enlist Indians. Lieutenant Colonel Glen Campbell, who had attempted to construct a similar unit in 1914, was responsible for the configuration and recruitment of the battalion and became its first commanding officer. If Canadians created legendary folk heroes like those of the United States, Campbell would be equivalent to the celebrated American frontiersman, soldier, and politician David "Davy" Crockett. He is deserving of a lengthy interlude, as his life epitomizes the Canadian frontier experience.

ILLUS. 9. Lieutenant Colonel Glenlyon Archibald Campbell, 1917. *Courtesy of Glenlyon Campbell.*

Glenlyon Archibald Campbell was born on 23 October 1863 at the Hudson's Bay Company (HBC) post, Fort Pelly, Saskatchewan. Glen's father, Robert Campbell, an immigrant from Glen Lyon, Scotland, was a fur trader for the HBC for interrupted periods between 1830 and 1871.[56] Through his trading expeditions, he helped map the final portions of northern Canada, giving name to many geographical features in the Yukon Territory. In fact, in 1840 he became the first known non-Indian or Eskimo to cross into the Yukon River watershed from the east. The present-day 602-kilometre-long Robert Campbell Highway (Highway 4) in the Yukon roughly conforms to his 1840s route.[57]

Robert Campbell's vocation had an early impact on his son Glen's life. In 1870 Glen and his two siblings accompanied their mother to Scotland, where shortly thereafter she died of typhoid.[58] The children were taken in by an aunt in Perthshire and spent their time between Scotland and Manitoba. Glen attended Glasgow Academy and Merchiston Castle School in Edinburgh. At nineteen years of age he found himself in the Montana Territory, at his father's request, to work on a cattle ranch and learn stock-raising. In 1884 Glen returned to Manitoba to live with his father on the family ranch near Riding Mountain in the Russell District of Manitoba.[59]

Unlike Andrew Thompson, Campbell's only military service prior to taking command of the 107th Battalion had come during the 1885 North-West Rebellion. In early April 1885 Major Charles Arkoll Boulton was given permission from the Canadian government to recruit an irregular mounted infantry unit from the population of the Russell-Birtle district in Manitoba. The unit, known variously as "Boulton's Mounted Infantry," "Boulton's Horse," and more commonly as "Boulton's Scouts," consisted of 5 officers and 123 men, including Glen Campbell. The unit joined General Frederick Middleton's column as the advance guard en route to Fish Creek and the Métis capital of Batoche. On 13 May, following the Battle of Batoche, Major Boulton promoted Campbell: "I now appointed Captain Campbell, a son of an old Hudson's Bay officer.... He was installed amid cheers of the men."[60]

In actuality, the Campbell/Riel connection dated back to the Red River Rebellion (1869–70). In fear of Métis pillaging and reprisal, Glen's father, by then a chief factor in the HBC, sent his year's quota of furs to London, England, via Sioux country, which was engulfed in the American-Sioux War (1862–90). Glen, his mother, and his siblings accompanied the military escort from Manitoba and disembarked in London. This action led to Robert's dismissal from the HBC the following year.[61]

After his brief period of military service, Glen Campbell returned to ranching, hunting, and trapping. Between 1897 and 1898, during the Klondike Gold Rush, he unsuccessfully attempted the arduous overland route from Edmonton to Dawson City. Then, like his counterpart Thompson, Campbell too became a politician. After being defeated in the race for the seat of Dauphin in the Legislative Assembly of Manitoba in 1892 and 1896, he won the reconstituted constituency of Gilbert Plains[62] in 1903 and again in 1907 as a Conservative. In 1908, aided by his brother-in-law, MP Clifford Sifton, he was elected to the House of Commons for the federal riding of Dauphin.[63] From all accounts, the six-foot-four Campbell made an impression on his fellow members of Parliament with his "towering figure, bronzed swarthy face, large brown eyes, capped off with a cowboy hat."[64] Although he spoke infrequently, on 17 March 1911 Campbell was involved in a bellicose dialogue with an Alberta MP, a confrontation labelled "one of the tensest situations and exciting scenes ever witnessed in Canadian Parliament" by the *New York Times*.[65] On another occasion, after listening to a speech by an eastern member who used eloquent yet confounding language, Campbell made his rebuttal in a combination of Cree and Latin.[66]

Campbell, although a Conservative, was defeated in the 1911 election, which saw Robert Borden replace Wilfrid Laurier as prime minister. However, he was appointed chief inspector of agencies, reserves, and inspectorates of Manitoba, Saskatchewan, Alberta, and the Northwest Territories within the DIA by the new Conservative administration. Campbell had strong ties with the Indian communities of Manitoba through ranching and trapping. He had also married Harriet Burns, daughter of Saulteaux (Ojibwa) chief Keeseekoowenin, in 1886. Campbell remained in this position with Indian Affairs, centred in Winnipeg, until July 1915.[67]

As mentioned, in October 1914 Campbell unsuccessfully petitioned Ottawa to raise an irregular unit of Indian scouts similar to that in which he had served under Major Boulton during the 1885 rebellion. On 9 July 1915 he was loaned to the Ministry of Militia by the DIA, given the rank of major, and tasked with assisting in raising the 79th Battalion in Brandon, Manitoba. On 24 November Campbell was transferred from the 79th, mandated to raise the 107th Battalion in Winnipeg, and appointed its commander as a lieutenant colonel.[68]

On 3 February 1916 Campbell sought permission from Scott to recruit Indians from the Elkhorn and Brandon industrial schools in Manitoba. Campbell argued that "were those lads with me, they would be under closer and more kindly supervision than in any other Battalion in the west ... even if they were not quite eighteen years of age." Scott endorsed the proposal with trepidation, concerned that parents and band councils might complain if the DIA used its influence to persuade under-age Indian pupils to enlist, but added, in paradoxical logic, that those who did so would be "breaking their treaty obligations, as they promised to be loyal citizens and it is anything but loyal to prevent recruiting." Scott went on to state that "there should be some good material at Elkhorn," as the students received drilling instruction within their curriculum.[69] At this time in Manitoba, 795 Indian boys were attending various "Indian Schools and Institutions." In Canada, for the fiscal year of 1915–16, 12,799 Indians were enrolled in one of 350 residential and day schools.[70] Scott also encouraged Campbell to visit western reserves for recruiting prospects.[71] In order to monopolize Indian recruitment in the West, on the same day he wrote to Scott, Campbell fraudulently reported to the officer commanding his Number Ten Military District (Manitoba, Saskatchewan, Territory of Keewatin, and District of Thunder Bay). His superior relayed his message to the Militia Council: "I was informed by Lt-Colonel Campbell ... who is very familiar with matters of this nature, that, in his opinion, it would not be possible to raise a Battalion at the present time from the available Indians in the country; in fact, he states that nearly all the useful and available men have already enlisted in Overseas Battalions, individually."[72]

The recruiting drive by Campbell himself, however, was a success. Unlike the 114th Battalion, which was linked to the one-half Indian militia unit of the 37th Haldimand Rifles, the 107th did not have the benefit of such a relationship. Complete with a pipe and drum band and the regimental march "The Campbells are Coming," Lieutenant Colonel Campbell enticed 1,741 volunteers, both Indian and non-Indian, to join his battalion. He rejected over 700 of these men and achieved full strength within three months of the battalion's conception—45 officers and 861 other ranks. Over 500 of these soldiers were Indian, although Campbell initially only intended "to form a platoon of Natives in my Battalion." Unlike in the 114th, however, only two officers of the 107th were Indian, lending credence to the comments of Inspector General Lessard that the Indian "NCOs and men are very good, of good physique and above average intelligence, though very few hold certificates [diplomas]."[73] For the most part, a non-battlefield commission in the CEF still required an education, which eluded most western Indians. In 1914, according to Indian Affairs, only 31 percent of Indians in Manitoba spoke English, 22 percent in Saskatchewan, and 15 percent in Alberta, compared with 67 percent in Ontario, home to the 114th Battalion.[74]

Many of the Indian soldiers of the 107th did not speak English, or spoke very little, and they came from a variety of nations, predominantly the Blackfoot Confederacy, Cree, and Ojibwa, with lesser numbers of Iroquois, Sioux, Delaware, and Mi'kmaq. To remedy this, Campbell often instructed training and conducted administrative and disciplinary matters in Indian languages, as he was fluent in Cree and Ojibwa. English language instruction was also given to Indian soldiers in the battalion.[75] Similarly, Lieutenant Colonel James K. Cornwall, commanding officer of the 8th Battalion, Canadian Railway Troops, which contained more than fifty Indians, had lived among the Indians of Alberta and Manitoba, hunting and trapping before becoming the Peace River MPP in the Alberta Legislature. He was fluent in Cree, Chipewyan, and Dogrib. Not only did he interpret, he also taught his Indian soldiers to speak rudimentary English.[76]

The 107th had a cap badge that embodied its Indian configuration. It depicted a crown bearing the battalion number, reinforced with a backdrop of a stalking wolf. The 107th became known unofficially as the "Timber Wolf Battalion." The origin of the cap badge and nickname was explained by Steven A. Bell: "My Grandfather was a rancher in the Canadian West during the Great War. Four of the Native Canadians who worked for him joined the 107th. Only one returned. He gave my family a 107th cap badge. He claimed the Timber Wolf was selected because it was a common totem to many of the Native soldiers. He used the name 'Timber Wolf Battalion' to refer to the unit. No other explanation regarding the origin of the cap badge was discovered in the records at the National Archives."[77] Another theory, according to Glenlyon Campbell (the great-grandson of Lieutenant Colonel Campbell) was that Campbell's wife, Harriet, "was full-blooded Ojibwa, daughter of Chief Keeseekoowenin, and her family was Wolf Clan. I assume that is why the 107th had the timber wolf on their patch."[78]

The thirty-two officers and 965 other ranks of the 107th, including Glen's son Lieutenant Jack Campbell, arrived in Liverpool on 25 October 1916, followed by the thirty officers and 679 other ranks of the 114th on 11 November. Like many Canadian battalions raised after 1915, the 114th was broken up soon after its arrival in England; its members were used to reinforce other units. Some Indian members, primarily officers, were transferred to the 107th at Campbell's insistence, but the majority were sent to bolster the 35th (Toronto) and 36th (Hamilton) Battalions. The 114th's regimental Six Nations band toured until the end of 1917, when its members were sent to active formations.[79]

A number of other battalions raised after December 1915 also had a high percentage of Indians, although none rivalled the 107th and the 114th:

> ➤ 135th Middlesex (seventy-seven Ojibwa, Oneida, and Munsee-Delaware from London, Ontario, and surrounds)

> ➤ 149th Lambton (sixty-seven Ojibwa, Odawa, and Potawatomi from Walpole Island, Sarnia, Kettle, and Stoney Point reserves, Ontario)

> ➤ 160th Bruce (sixty-five Ojibwa, Odawa, and Potawatomi from the Saugeen, Cape Croker, and Manitoulin Island reserves near Owen Sound, Ontario, and surrounds)

> ➤ 52nd "Bull Moose" New Ontario (sixty-five northern Ontario Ojibwa and Cree)

> ➤ 188th Saskatchewan (Nahane from the Pelly Agency)

> ➤ 203rd Winnipeg Rifles (forty-two Ojibwa and Cree).

All were dispatched overseas in 1916, although most were broken up as reinforcements. Nevertheless, the increasing number of Indians training within the CEF in the United Kingdom did not go unnoticed by British authorities.[80]

In April 1916 the Canadian high commissioner in London, Sir George Perley, asked Duncan Campbell Scott for weekly updates on Indian Affairs and Indian war participation at the request of the Colonial and War Offices. Scott's first cable to London, on 20 April, began by addressing the alliance between Indians and the Crown: "A striking example of loyalty has been shown by the Indians of Canada, who have never failed when Britain Arms and British loyalty called them to action. Shortly after the participation of Great Britain in the war, the Indian Department began to receive letters from the various bands of Indians throughout the Dominion, stating that they desired to assist the Mother Country in any way in their power.... They have contributed over

$20,000.00 and ... A great many Indians have enlisted, but as our records are very incomplete, the exact number could not be given." Upon hearing of the donations and service, Scott was instructed by the king's private secretary to draft a letter of thanks on the king's behalf:

> I am deeply touched by your loyal generosity. Reading the speeches made by former Governors to the Indian sachems [Iroquoian for chiefs] and their replies, I find that there is constant reference to the silver chain which bound together their mutual interests, and each new meeting and renewal of friendship made the chain brighter and stronger. I find in your late action evidence that you wish the chain to be preserved, and, for my part, I accept your gifts and acknowledge that the chain has been brightened and strengthened by them. When peace is again restored, you may all feel that you have done your part and have had your share in the great events which have taken place. [81]

It is interesting to note that Scott referenced the alliance between the British and the Iroquois Confederacy, represented by the Silver Covenant Chain, or Two Row Wampum Belt, to signify the allegiance of Canadian Indians as an entire entity. As mentioned, it was originally agreed to by the Confederacy and the Dutch in 1613 and was extended to the British, via the covenant chain, in 1677 (or arguably in 1664) and to the United States in 1794. The two parallel beaded purple rows (never touching) signify the mutual coexistence of two sovereign entities—the Iroquois and a European partner—in North America.

Like the king, Canadians were also beginning to take notice of Indian contributions to the war effort, and they extolled Indians' martial abilities, almost to the point of bragging about "their Indians." Throughout late 1915 and 1916, newspapers and magazines from across the country were proudly reporting on Indian participation. In communities where large numbers of Indians volunteered in locally raised battalions, home newspapers lauded their patriotism. On 14 November 1915 the Port Arthur *Evening Chronicle* ran an article, "Over 20 Indians Will Fight in the Ranks of the 52nd: Eight Bands of Red Men are Represented by Local Recruits." The piece proudly declared, "These boys are all crack shots and should be valuable as snipers and scouts." In relation, the Port Arthur *Daily News-Chronicle* published an article entitled "Indians are Proving their Loyalty to the British Empire: Have Enlisted in Large Numbers All Through Canada and Make Fine Soldiers—High Class Marksmen" on 2 November 1916. The article argued that Indian enlistment "will doubt-less lead to better recognition of them by the white people.... Civilization is having its effect in moulding the lives of these citizens [sic] of the Dominion and at the present many of them are fighting a battle for that civilization. When it is over Canadians must not forget this." The *Saskatchewan Journal* (a weekly magazine) of 7–14 November 1915, in an article entitled "Red Indians of Canada want to take Warpath for the Empire," praised Indians' patriotic fund contributions, their loyalty to the Crown, and the fact that "several regiments of warriors of unexcelled prowess can be recruited if it is considered necessary." A 1918 *Brandon Sun* entry, "Indians Prove Great Fighters, Officers Aver: Late Col. Campbell Says His Redmen Would Put Many a White Man to Shame," proclaimed that the "more than 500 Indians of the 107th, can see danger quickly and know just what to do, for they use their natural instincts." The *Brantford Expositor*, which had been frequently publishing articles on the recruitment and progress of the 114th Battalion, exclaimed "'Brock's Rangers' an Appropriate Title for Six Nations' Indians" on 10 April 1916.[82] In addition, newspapers often published excerpts of letters from Indian soldiers engaged on the Western Front.

Scrolling through contemporary newspapers, not to mention reading the examples above, it is obvious that the literary depiction and cultural perception of the noble savage was as prevalent as it had been prior to the war. Most articles comment on Indians being used as "sharpshooters" and scouts and celebrate the innate martial prowess of the Indian brave.[83] As the *New York Times* stated in August 1917, "Tales of wonderful Indian snipers who were a law unto themselves and amply earned their exemption from disciplinary rule prescribed for their pale-skin comrades by bringing scores of Germans to the earth found their way into print early in the war."[84]

In November 1916, roughly one year after the official sanction, the distribution of known Indian enlistments was released by the DIA (see Table 2) and was widely published in newspapers across the country.[85] The same report stated that Indians had donated $24,679.30 to various war funds (of which $10,250.00 was refused, because Indian Affairs asserted that "the bands in question were unable to afford the outlay"). It also mentioned that seventy-eight officials in assorted positions within the DIA had enlisted.

ILLUS. 10. Cree Recruits from Saskatchewan's File Hills Community pose with Elders, Family Members and Indian Agent, W. M. Graham before departing for War. *Library and Archives Canada, PA-66815.*

Province	Enlistments	Male Indian Population Ages 16 to 65 (1915)	Percent
Ontario	862	6,185	13.9
Quebec	101	2,535	4.0
Manitoba	89	2,567	3.5
Saskatchewan	57	1,968	2.9
Prince Edward Island	24	78	30.8
British Columbia	17	6,665	0.26
Nova Scotia	14	558	2.5
New Brunswick	12	428	2.8
Alberta	9	1,529	0.59
Yukon Territory	2	428	0.47
Northwest Territories	N/A	1,121	N/A
TOTAL	1,187	24,062	4.9

TABLE 2. Known Indian Enlistments, November 1916

The numbers reflect three factors. First, initial recruitment efforts were directed at Indians in eastern Canada, who were less isolated, deemed more assimilated, and spoke more English. In fact, the total number of Indians able to speak English or French in 1914 was 46,748, or 45 percent of the total Indian population of 103,774. Of this total, however, only 17,805 (17 percent) could write either language. Of these literate Indians, roughly 70 percent lived east of Manitoba. Second, by extension, higher enlistment rates occurred east of Manitoba, within the more traditionally warrior-based nations with a history of military allegiance, such as the Iroquois.[86] Last, as Mike Mountain Horse explained, many men (most notably in the West, where more recent treaties had been signed) believed that "Certain treaties with the Great White Father stipulated that they would lay down their weapons of war and fight no more."[87]

Recruitment in the West had been largely ignored throughout 1915 and early 1916. In February 1916 Scott questioned Fiset as to whether "it is the wish of your Department to make any effort to enlist Indians in British Columbia as is at present being done in the Province of Ontario and also in some of the western provinces." In his reply, Fiset related that the officer commanding Number Eleven Military District (British Columbia and the Yukon) had stated that his Indian wards "would not be suitable as soldiers."[88] Nevertheless, Scott spent the month of June 1916 in British Columbia promoting Indian enlistment while conducting other obligations of his office.[89]

The failure to promote recruiting in western Canada was also noticed by private citizens in close contact with Indians and by military officials. Both believed that western Canada could provide a large number of Indian soldiers who had previously been overlooked "for [Borden's commitment of] a Canadian Expeditionary Force of 500,000 men." In March 1916 Stuart Henderson of Ashcroft, British Columbia, wrote directly to Sam Hughes, dramatically extolling the innate soldierly qualities of western Indians and promoting the formation of an all-Indian battalion with detailed figures of male Indian populations of the four western provinces and the two territories:

> It thus can be safely estimated there is a possible recruiting field approximating 12,000 able-bodied men.... These 12,000 men are of a fine type and will equal the white in all that goes to make up a soldier in the ranks, in strength, endurance, keenness, alertness, tirelessness, and ambition. They are excellent shots, scouts and fine travellers, live

in the open air with or without tents. They have scrapped with nature all their lives and are surely fitted for this greatest scrap of all times, and have not had the training, education and civilizing influence to neutralize their natural aptitude for struggle of a physical nature.... If there is anything ... that would tend to make a race of natural soldiers, these men certainly must possess the predisposition and have the raw material of first class fighting men ... killing does not minimize but excites the primal instinct in them.... But the strongest argument in favour of the Indian as a soldier is his facility in using a gun ... every Indian is a marvellous shot.

Henderson closed his letter by stating that the civilizing influence of army discipline, education, and cleanliness would be a benefit to both Indian populations and Canada as a whole, which contradicted his earlier stressing of the virtues he was adamant would make Indians natural soldiers. In contrast to this assimilationist viewpoint, he argued that Indians should form distinct battalions, as "too many remarks might be made by his fellow [white] soldiers" if they were in mixed units.[90]

Similarly, in November 1916 Lieutenant Maxwell Graham (253rd Battalion) submitted an extensive report to his commanding officer, Lieutenant Colonel P.G.C. Campbell, and Indian Affairs. It was based on comprehensive research and statistics of Indian men ages sixteen to sixty in all provinces (a total of 23,408): "In the opinion of the undersigned [Graham] a great opportunity was missed shortly after the war started, at that time until the fall of 1915 [when enlistment was authorized], the Indians of the Dominion at large, who depended on trapping and employment in lumber camps etc., were many of them in danger of starvation. Tactful recruiting agents through the promise alone of three full meals a day, could have secured many able bodied Indians." Graham also stressed that the West had been wholly ignored and that recruitment in remote areas would yield large numbers of Indian recruits if "select Indians now overseas be brought back for recruiting purposes ... that photographs be shown the Indians of this Dominion, of their compatriots in uniform." In accordance, in late 1916 Scott authorized a second major shift in policy. To enhance Indian recruitment in western Canada and on the more isolated reserves in eastern Canada, a military recruiter, often an Indian repatriated from the front, was paired with a member of Indian Affairs. Charles

Cooke again offered his service to recruit outside of Ontario, believing, like Scott and Graham, that the remainder of the Indian populations "have been completely overlooked."[91]

Some offers to recruit in remote areas in late 1916 were perhaps overzealous, or unproductive, since many men were hunting or trapping far outside any communities or reserves. In August 1916 C.M. McCarthy, police magistrate for Elk Lake District, Ontario (Kirkland Lake area), wrote to the DIA claiming that he "could get six or seven hundred good Indians from the north this winter and next spring." In October he wrote to Scott stating, "I did not succeed in everything I was after in connection with getting up an Indian Battalion ... things were not coming my way." He did, however, recruit "40 Indians from Moose Factory and Ruperts House ... for the 228th O.S. Battalion." In December 1916 this battalion was remustered as the 6th Battalion, Canadian Railway Troops.[92] Nevertheless, government policy had shifted from unofficially preventing Indians from enlisting in 1914, to official inclusion and sanctioning individual recruitment efforts in late 1915 and into 1916, to becoming directly involved in promoting the recruitment effort by late 1916.

The October 1915 British requests influenced Canadian policies affecting other minorities, which then saw changes during 1916. In 1914 the total black population of Canada was roughly 20,000, with the majority of that population living in Nova Scotia and southern Ontario—a residual effect of the Loyalist movement and the "underground railway." Throughout 1914 and 1915 official policy forbade the enlistment of black Canadians, although, like Indians, a small number successfully enlisted at the discretion of recruiting officers either free of colour prejudice or needing to fill battalion strengths. The 106th Battalion Nova Scotia Rifles is known to have enlisted at least sixteen blacks during late 1915.[93] Most battalion commanders, however, shared the concerns of Lieutenant Colonel George Fowler, commanding officer of the 104th Battalion, who turned away over twenty black volunteers: "I have been fortunate to have secured a very fine class of recruits, and I did not think it was fair to these men that they should have to mingle with negroes."[94] In April 1916 Gwatkin circulated a blunt memorandum to all military district commanders: "The civilized negro is vain and imitative ... in the trenches he is not likely to make a good fighter; and the average white man will not associate with him on terms of equality.... It would be humiliating to the coloured men themselves to serve in a battalion where they are not wanted. In France, in the firing line, there would be no place for a black battalion, CEF. It would be eyed askance; it would crowd out a white battalion; it would be difficult to reinforce." He concluded that nothing prevented individual battalions from enlisting blacks at their own discretion, and that a segregated labour battalion could be raised to meet their desire to serve in some capacity.

On 19 April 1916 Borden agreed to the formation of such a battalion and authorization that the imperial government would "be glad to accept such a battalion of Canadian Negroes" was given by the War Office on 11 May.[95] The War Office had previously asked Canada to mobilize labour battalions in February 1916, and at roughly the same time it was courting South Africa for expeditionary Native labour units. The segregated South African Native Labour Contingent (SANLC), 21,000 strong, eventually served in France from November 1916 until September 1918.

On 5 July 1916 the No. 2 Construction Battalion, led by white officers,[96] was officially announced and was given authority to recruit blacks from across the country. Objections from military commanders over disease and the troublesome nature of such a unit in winter quarters (although they were Canadians) were immediately voiced. Moreover, recruitment had not been as high as expected, despite the fact that in February 1917 authorization was given to accept blacks from the United States and the Caribbean (171 men from these areas eventually served in the battalion).[97] The battalion even recruited five Indians from Windsor, Ontario. During training these Indians, contrary to the stereotype of the "drunken Indian," were appalled with the drinking and gambling in the unit and demanded a transfer. When the response was slow, Tuscarora chief Thunderwater, great sachem of the Great Council of Tribes (centred at Akwesasne/St. Regis) appealed to the Ministry of Militia, claiming "a natural dislike of association with negroes on the part of Indians." They were eventually transferred to the 256th Railway Construction Battalion, which had a large Indian component. Thunderwater demanded of Gwatkin that he "arrange that Indians and negroes are kept from the same Battalions."[98] Lieutenant Colonel Thompson, commanding officer of the 114th Battalion, rejected the offer of black volunteers, claiming that "The introduction of a coloured platoon into our Battalion would undoubtedly cause serious friction and discontent."[99]

ILLUS. II. Soldiers of the No. 2 Construction Battalion, 1917. *Canadian War Museum, George Metcalf Archival Collection, 19930012-397.*

On 28 March 1917 the 624 men of the black battalion left Halifax for Liverpool well short of the authorized 1,038-man strength. This prompted Major Bristol, the secretary to the minister of Overseas Military Forces, to remark that "these Niggers do well in a Forestry Corps and other Labour units [but] the prospects of maintaining a battalion are not very bright."[100] Given its size, it was reconstituted as the No. 2 Construction Company in May 1917 and attached to the Canadian Forestry Corps in the Jura Mountains, France. To sidestep policies of confinement and segregation similar to those imposed on the South African Native Labour Contingent, the Canadian Ministry of Overseas Military Forces deliberately despatched the company to this location, which was in the French area of operations, free from such racial policies. When General Headquarters issued instructions to conform to imperial standards, the Canadian forestry commander, Colonel J.B. White, refused: "The men of this Unit are engaged in exactly the same work as the white labour with whom they are employed ... no change will be made."[101] The No. 2 Construction Company remained equal to other Canadian forestry units until its return to Canada on 4 December 1918. In all, over 1,000 Canadian blacks served in various battalions during the war (5 percent of the total black population), the majority in No. 2. This representation is equivalent to that of Euro-Canadians and Indians.[102]

Asian Canadians were also barred from enlistment until the summer of 1916, when the Ministry of Militia officially authorized their recruitment. Of the known 222 Japanese who saw service, almost all were enrolled in infantry battalions, primarily the 10th, 50th, and 52nd battalions. It is known that fifty-four were killed and ninety-two were wounded, while thirteen won the Military Medal—all overrepresentations, and a testament to their bravery, given the relatively low number of Japanese who saw service.[103]

While enlistment privileges were extended to certain minorities during late 1915 and 1916, those from enemy countries were treated with harsh restrictions. The 80,000 "unnaturalized enemy aliens" from Germany and Austria-Hungary within Canada were not only refused the right to serve and to vote, but 8,579 were also imprisoned in twenty-six "special camps" under the *War Measures Act*.[104] Another 80,000 citizens, mostly Ukrainians, were required to carry identity papers and had to periodically report to local police forces. Even at this juncture in the war, the need for recruits did not wholly supersede or countermand mercurial and often unwarranted racial tensions, which were heightened by war hysteria.

The variances in policies toward different minorities is interesting, especially the creation of a homogenous black unit, which begs explanation. French-Canadians (save for those in the 22nd Battalion), Indians, and Asians were scattered across CEF units. In a glaring contradiction, blacks, unlike Indians and Asians, were enfranchised. However, they were at least in political opinion not welcome in ordinary CEF battalions. In racial terms, according to the accepted hierarchy of races, Indians and Asians were viewed as more civilized, and therefore more easily assimilated into the military fold. Likewise, Indian martial prowess could not be dismissed. It is well to remember that, unlike other minorities, the vast majority of blacks served as non-combatant labourers. In this military application, Euro-Canadians were more enthusiastic about Indians than blacks and were more willing to associate with Indians.

There were, however, other reasons why an all-Indian infantry battalion never materialized during the First World War. The first was the availability of reinforcements without conscription. Given the high casualty rates and the relatively low Indian male population of military age (18–40)—roughly

11,500—it was considered unlikely that enough replacements could be mustered to support a battalion once it engaged in combat. By way of comparison, had the homogenous New Zealand Maori Battalion been designated an infantry rather than a pioneer unit, it is doubtful that it would have been able to maintain its strength, given the lack of volunteers after 1916 and the failure to enforce conscription on Maori.

Second, as Gwatkin remarked, there was concern within the DIA and the Ministry of Militia regarding a potential Indian unit formed piecemeal from various Indian nations, "whether coming from different tribes, they would fight among themselves." Certain Indians' reluctance to transfer or join the 114th supports his argument. In addition, many Indians did not speak English; therefore, exercising proper command and control would have been difficult given the scope of Indian languages that would make up any all-Indian unit. Scott recognized this problem during the initial Indian recruiting campaign of early 1916: "The usual routine of drill must be undergone by every soldier to fit himself to take his place in the ranks; and lack of knowledge of English is a very great disadvantage in receiving instruction. Under the circumstances I am of the opinion that it would be well to confine the efforts in recruiting to reserves ... where most of the Indians have been in closer touch with white people and have a knowledge of the English language."[105] Many government officials and senior military personnel also regarded the CEF as a tool of assimilation in keeping with contemporary Indian Affairs policy. It must be remembered that the Ministry of Militia (and Arthur Currie) did not endorse the concept of homogenous French-Canadian battalions either, thus alienating a great number of French-Canadian men who would otherwise have enlisted. Had an all-Indian unit been formed, the French would have objected, or demanded the same conditions, thereby adding to an already volatile ethnic situation. As Jonathan Vance states in his widely acclaimed *Death So Noble: Memory, Meaning, and the First World War* (1997): "English Canadians confidently expected ... the war's legacy would provide the impetus for both groups to become, not Native Canadians or French-Canadians, but Canadians pure and simple."[106] In other words, the war would serve as the ultimate impulsion for final reconciliation and assimilation into English Canadian society.

Third, the well-documented susceptibility of Indians to tuberculosis troubled the senior staff of the Canadian Red Cross and military authorities: "When they went into lower altitudes, and became subjected to poisonous gasses, this tendency would also immediately break out into tuberculosis and instead of the Indians being an assistance in numbers they would be a burden on the medical and Red Cross service."[107] Finally, W.M. Graham, inspector general of Indian Agencies for southern Saskatchewan, argued that Indians,

> would do much better if they mingled with whites, allowing them to pick up their work much more quickly and would be more contented among whites, especially as nearly all the enlisted Indians are educated and could easily fall in line with their white brothers. Then again, if they went into the front as a unit, and if by chance they went into action and suffered tremendous casualties, there would always be a feeling among their friends at home that their sons had been placed in a more dangerous position than the whites. Of course this would not have been the case, but one must remember that the old Indian is quite primitive and does not understand things as we do.[108]

In retrospect, Graham's insight, albeit containing elements of assimiliationist policy and prejudice, was quite remarkable. Many colonial and dominion units were perceived by their home governments (which exercised little discretion over their soldiers, especially prior to 1918) as being used as "cannon fodder" by the BEF commander in chief, Field Marshal Douglas Haig, and his senior staff. In his controversial book *The Donkeys* (1961), Alan Clark popularized the notion that British and Commonwealth soldiers were "lions led by donkeys."[109]

The 114th and 107th Battalions were the closest any units came to being Indian. The 114th was broken up in November 1916 to reinforce other units, including the 107th. Shortly after arriving in England, on 1 February 1917, the 107th, containing over 500 Indians, was officially converted into a pioneer battalion. Pioneers were primarily infantry soldiers trained to perform basic combat engineering assignments in the front lines. However, they were not support troops like those of entrenching battalions, railway companies, or tunnelling companies, nor were they educated and skilled engineers like those of the engineering field companies. Pioneers were armed, trained in infantry tactics, and employed in combat roles when not performing minor engineering tasks. There is no evidence to suggest that the decision regarding the 107th was influenced by the Maori unit of the same designation. By this time, all newly formed Canadian battalions were being broken up for use as reinforcements. There was, however, a need for auxiliary units in the Canadian Corps.

Lieutenant Colonel Campbell pleaded with authorities to have his battalion re-mustered as a pioneer battalion, citing his Indian soldiers' "ability to adapt themselves without complaint to awkward circumstances and bad weather, which rendered their efficiency as a pioneer battalion far above the average."[110]

After augmented training in England, Campbell and his pioneers disembarked at Boulogne, France, on 25 February 1917. By 1 March they had joined the Canadian Corps in the Vimy region, as part of General Horne's British First Army. The 107th was the last complete unit from western Canada to join the Canadian Corps.[111] The unit participated in the preparations for and the battle of Vimy Ridge, performing such functions as burying wire and cable to ensure stable communications, raising casualty clearing stations, helping to build light railway, digging trenches, and erecting defensive obstacles and barbed wire. On 9 April, the opening day of Vimy and the British Arras offensive, three companies were "under orders to assist in burying cable and improving communication forward through NO MAN'S LAND." During Canadian Corps actions at Vimy, the unit suffered ten casualties, including three deaths.[112]

Having incurred another twenty-five casualties during the month of July, the battalion's first true combat initiation coincided with newly promoted Canadian Corps commander Lieutenant General Sir Arthur Currie's first operation at Hill 70 (15–25 August 1917). Until this assault, despite having held a portion of trench line from late June to mid-July, the 107th had been used exclusively for pioneering purposes. During the attack on Hill 70, the 107th was in direct support of the 3rd Infantry Brigade, 1st Division. The first Canadian troops went over the top at 0425 hours on 15 August.[113] The 107th followed the lead waves with a view to digging communication trenches across the 300 to 500 yards of no man's land linking the original Canadian front lines to newly captured positions. A secondary task, if required, was to act as primary reinforcements to the attacking infantry units and defend against inevitable German counter-attacks. Under fire from enemy artillery, including gas shells, members of the 107th Battalion's three forward companies carried out their prescribed responsibilities throughout 15 and 16 August, suffering twenty-one killed and 140 wounded (including nine gassed) out of 600 men engaged.[114]

On the night of 17 August, the battalion was ordered to rotate back to the rear rest areas. One company containing many Indian scouts, augmented by other members of the battalion, volunteered to "search and bring in wounded" from the battlefield, an offer Lieutenant Colonel Campbell immediately authorized. Thirty dead were recovered and buried, while another twenty-five wounded were brought to dressing stations. Unfortunately, German artillery laid down a gas-shell barrage during the process, poisoning eighty-four members of the detail and wounding four others. Two Indian members of the 107th, privates O. Baron and A.W. Anderson, were awarded the Military Medal for bravery during this action.[115] In addition, Campbell received a letter from Lieutenant Colonel D.M. Osmond of the 10th Battalion on 28 August thanking the 107th for "the splendid assistance you gave us on the night of 17–18th, 1917 … car[ing] for a number of our wounded." A second letter of appreciation was sent to Campbell from Osmond's direct superior, Brigadier General Frederick O.W. Loomis, commander of the 2nd Brigade. The rescue mission was even known to Currie, who wrote Campbell on 31 August: "I want to tell you that I have heard, with a great deal of pride and satisfaction, the reports of the gallantry and devotion to duty displayed by … your Battalion during the recent operations.… My sincere congratulations."[116]

On 28 May 1918, shortly after Campbell's death from kidney failure on 20 October 1917 (three days shy of his fifty-fourth birthday), the 107th was disbanded after over one year of service and its members scattered across the 1st Canadian Engineer Brigade.[117] Campbell is buried at the Etaples Military Cemetery, France, alongside 1,144 other Canadian and 9,628 Allied dead.

At the close of 1916, Gwatkin summarized the position of the Indian within the CEF, including all-Indian units, while referring directly to the correlation between their admittance and the need for manpower: "We have already attempted to raise a complete battalion—the 114th (Lieut-colonel A.T. Thompson). Mr. C.A. Cooke assisted. The attempt was not entirely successful. The battalion never reached full strength, and soon after its arrival in England it was broken up. Whether the Red Indian will make good *in trench warfare* is doubtful. But we need everyman we can get.… Let us by all means go on enlisting individual Indians."[118] The need for manpower, in conjunction with conscription in 1917, generated further changes in policy towards Indians during the final two years of the war, including their specific recruitment for non-combat forestry, railway, construction, and rear-echelon battalions.

Canadian recruitment policies at the outbreak of war and into 1915 could not sustain national formations in the face of mounting casualties, a decline in voluntary enlistment, and an expanding expeditionary force. Pragmatism required policies be altered to allow for the inclusion of Indians, and eventually for their conscription. On 5 January 1916 Britain introduced the first of a series of *Military Service Acts*, which initiated conscription (New Zealand quickly followed suit). Canada introduced conscription with the controversial Military Service Bill on 11 June 1917, to the indignation of most French-Canadians. Confusion and capricious policy concerning the position of Indians was immediate and pronounced.

From the outbreak of war, Indian policy was anything but concrete. In 1914, based on the 1904 *Militia Act*, no official policy existed, and uncertainty and contradiction plagued government decisions pertaining to Indian participation. In 1915 official policy was extended to allow for the enlistment of Indians. By 1917, however, with the increased tempo of the war and the corresponding need for manpower after the Allied catastrophes at Verdun and the Somme, the Canadian government was faced with greater uncertainty concerning the conscription of Indians. Indicative of the indecision surrounding Indian participation from 1914 to 1915 were the policies of conscription and registration. The record of the decision-making process concerning Indians and conscription is convoluted, to say the least, but it is evidence of the fact that neither the Ministry of Militia nor the DIA thought such a situation would ever arise.

Chapter Six

All the King's Men, 1917–18

Historian John Keegan dubbed 1916 "the year of battles."[1] During this year, the intensity and scale of the war dramatically increased. Both the Allies and the Germans launched fruitless large-scale offensives against fortified entrenched defensive positions. Stalemate and attrition permeated operations on the Western Front, and the horrific nature of the war was fully realized. During the Battle of Verdun (February to December 1916), the French sustained 380,000 casualties, while the Germans suffered 330,000, for a total of roughly 710,000 (of which 306,000 were killed). Shockingly, the Battle of the Somme (July to November 1916) produced even more devastating results. On 1 July, the opening day of the battle, British imperial forces suffered almost 60,000 casualties, including 20,000 dead. The Newfoundland Regiment (battalion) was virtually annihilated at Beaumont-Hamel. Of the 801 men who went over the top, 733 became casualties in less than thirty minutes. Campaign casualties for the Allies were 625,000, counting 147,000 killed. The British Empire suffered 420,000 casualties, including 24,000 Canadians, while the French contributed another 205,000. Estimates for German losses hover between 470,000 and 550,000. In total, in less than five months approximately 1.5 million men were killed, wounded, or missing in a battle space covering no more than nineteen kilometres of trench-line and an Allied axis-of-advance reaching ten kilometres.[2] The carnage of the war was reaching epic proportions. Paul Baumer, the narrator and main character of Erich Maria Remarque's classic *All Quiet on the Western Front* (1928), provides a human face for these statistics:

> We see men living with their skulls blown open; we see soldiers run with their two feet cut off, they stagger on their splintered stumps into the next shell-hole; a lance-corporal crawls a mile and a half on his hands dragging his smashed knee after him; another goes to the dressing station and over his clasped hands bulge his intestines; we see men without mouths, without jaws, without faces; we find one man who has held the artery of his arm in his teeth for two hours in

order not to bleed to death. The sun goes down, night comes, the shells whine, life is at an end. Still the little piece of convulsed earth in which we lie is held. We have yielded no more than a few hundred yards of it as a prize to the enemy. But on every yard there lies a dead man.[3]

ILLUS. 12. "Once more unto the breach, dear friends": Canadian Soldiers at the Somme, October 1916. *Library and Archives Canada, PA-207187.*

The year of battles took a ghastly toll on the field forces of all nations. By 1917 the need for manpower to sustain Allied formations became increasingly important as events unfolded on both the Western and Eastern Fronts. By the close of 1917, the Allies faced numerous, and immediate, strategic and operational problems. Unrestricted German submarine warfare wreaked havoc on trans-Atlantic supply lines. Reinforcements were dwindling, manpower in Allied forces was shrinking, and there were increasing numbers of deserters in the French army. Although the United States entered the war on 6 April 1917 and had the potential to tip the scales in favour of the Allies, it would be months before a significant and competent field force was ready for deployment. Britain, the dominions, and France continued to shoulder the weight of the war. In addition, after the disaster at Caporetto in October and November

1917, the Italians struggled to maintain a sizable, professional army.[4] More-over, there was no Allied or German breakthrough on the Western Front—stalemate and attrition continued.

To compound the Allies' problems, they witnessed the capitulation of their Russian ally and the collapse of the Eastern Front in November 1917. From mid-1917 on, the Germans began to relocate men and material to the Western Front in preparation for a massive offensive. By the time the Treaty of Brest-Litovsk was signed on 3 March 1918, forty-four German divisions had already been relocated. Between November 1917 and 21 March 1918, when the five-stage *Kaiserschlacht* offensive began, the Central Powers had increased their fighting strength on the Western Front by 30 percent. By comparison, Allied strength fell by 25 percent over the same period, the result of the devastating losses sustained during the Passchendaele offensive and the dearth of imme-diate replacements.[5] Canada, like its allies, was in need of reinforcements to sustain the Canadian Corps and sought avenues to mobilize the military and industrial strength of the nation.

In September 1916, the National Service Board was created to take a cen-sus of Canada's population. The registration of all men and women over the age of sixteen occurred in the winter of 1916–17, with the stated objective being to "gather information in the cause of increased production from an agricul-tural point of view; to ascertain where labour for essential industries may be found; and to prepare a system of rationing food should it become necessary." A special section was added confirming that Indian registration was mandatory and warning that "the result of failure to register will be so serious that very much hardship and suffering may occur on your Reserve."[6] Correspondingly, in February 1917 Duncan Campbell Scott issued all Indian agents with a standard "Return of Indian Enlistments" form on which agents were instructed to update original enlistment registers and to provide monthly recruitment returns. This was the first official attempt to determine the number of Indians in uniform.[7]

Confusion among Indians was immediate. The chiefs of Wanikewin, Ontario, south of Sudbury on the French River, wrote to Indian Affairs on 9 January 1917 desiring "to know if we have to sign up on those cards issued by the Government ... let us know if the Indian is exempt unless he wishes to sign." The reply simply stated, "Indians as well as white people are expected to sign these cards."[8] Many viewed the registration as a means to conscription; others viewed it as conscription itself. Chief Meeshe Keepinais, from the Swan

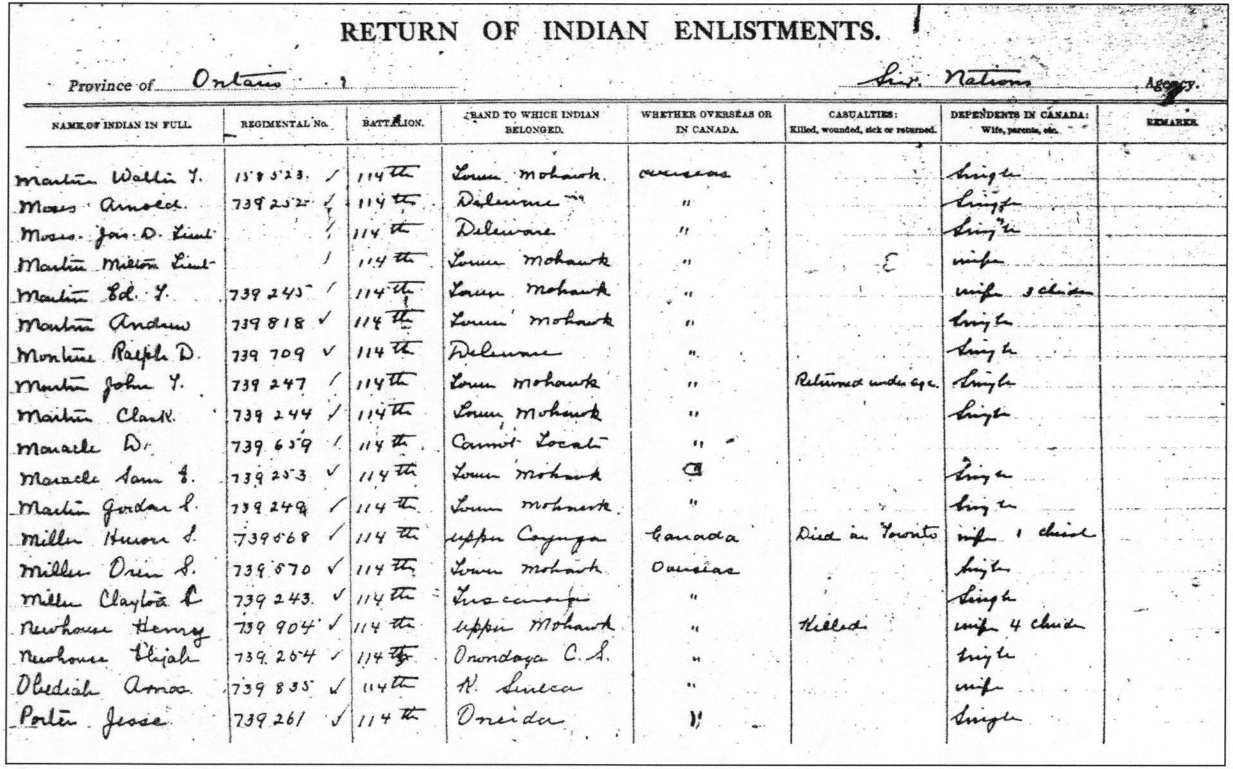

RETURN OF INDIAN ENLISTMENTS.

Province of Ontario Six Nations Agency.

NAME OF INDIAN IN FULL.	REGIMENTAL No.	BATTALION.	BAND TO WHICH INDIAN BELONGED.	WHETHER OVERSEAS OR IN CANADA.	CASUALTIES: Killed, wounded, sick or returned.	DEPENDENTS IN CANADA: Wife, parents, etc.	REMARKS.
Martin Wallie Y.	158523	114th	Lower Mohawk	overseas		Single	
Moses Arnold	739252	114th	Delaware	"		Single	
Moses Jas. D. Lieut.		114th	Delaware	"		Single	
Martin Milton Lieut.		114th	Lower Mohawk	"		wife	
Martin Ed. Y.	739245	114th	Lower Mohawk	"		wife 3 children	
Martin Andrew	739818	114th	Lower Mohawk	"		Single	
Montour Ralph D.	739709	114th	Delaware	"		Single	
Martin John Y.	739247	114th	Lower Mohawk	"	Returned under age.	Single	
Martin Clark	739244	114th	Lower Mohawk	"		Single	
Maracle D.	739659	114th	Cannot Locate	"			
Maracle Sam S.	739253	114th	Lower Mohawk	[illegible]		Single	
Martin Gordon S.	739249	114th	Lower Mohawk	"		Single	
Miller Huron S.	739568	114th	Upper Cayuga	Canada	Died in Toronto	wife 1 child	
Miller Oren S.	739570	114th	Lower Mohawk	Overseas		Single	
Miller Clayton C.	739243	114th	Tuscarora	"		Single	
Newhouse Henry	739904	114th	Upper Mohawk	"	Killed	wife 4 children	
Newhouse Elijah	739204	114th	Onondaga C.S.	"		Single	
Obediah Amos	739835	114th	N. Seneca	"		wife	
Porter Jesse	739261	114th	Oneida	"		Single	

ILLUS. 13. Return of Indian Enlistments Form. *Library and Archives Canada, RG10 Vol. 6768, File 452-20.*

Lake Manitoba reserve, wrote to Scott asking if "the Government is going to take the young men all over this country and send them away to the war, we want to know at once if that includes the young Indians of these reserves, according to our treaty agreement with the Government we were not to be compelled to go to war for the Government and we object to having our young men taken away to the war." The Port Simpson, Nisga'a, and Kitkatla Bands in British Columbia sent a petition to Borden, Laurier, and Scott, adamant that conscription did not apply to them.[9]

John Gadieux from Fort William, Ontario, wrote a blunt letter to his agent in January 1917 and attached his blank national service card: "*Go to hell.* Me to sign my name on that card, sign out your own name an leave me alone and if you think that everyone is a fool like yourself you need not think that I am one. Mr Agent you have been at me all summer enough that you might just as well make up your mind not to try an crack tis nut."[10] Many men, such as Bloods Peter Black Rabbit, George Long Time Squirrel, and John Pace, refused to sign their cards, while others in remote locations were simply ignorant of the registration.[11] Indian Affairs released a statement to its agents in February 1917 that "the Indians are under obligation.... Understand that these cards do not mean enlistment in the overseas battalions, but a census of the industrial strength of the Dominion." It is unclear if any legal action was taken against Indians who refused to register. Gadieux's letter was passed to the National Service Board, since Indian Affairs was not responsible for the enforcement of regulations.[12]

The worry that the registration was the basis of conscription was not unfounded; the Canadian Corps was suffering sustained casualties. From April 1916 to April 1917 the Canadians suffered 75,065 casualties; a further 43,837 were accrued during the remainder of 1917.[13] In January 1917 the total strength of the CEF was 303,149, far below Borden's 1916 pledge of half a million men. Monthly volunteer rates had plummeted from 28,185 in January 1916 to roughly 5,000 a month for August to December 1916. Total recruitment for the year 1917 was an unpromising 63,611, compared to 176,919 for 1916.[14]

In May 1917, when casualty rates were more than twice that of recruitment, Borden announced his intention to introduce military conscription, because "the battle for Canadian liberty and autonomy is being fought today on the plains of France and Belgium."[15] It was a fateful decision that further divided English- and French-Canadians. On 11 June 1917 Borden introduced the Military Service Bill with the objective of securing more men to promote

Canadian interests and autonomy while legally demanding Québecois partici-pation. On 23 September 1918 Toronto's *Evening Telegram* declared that con-scription would not have been required "if the racialists of Quebec had joined the colours in proportion to their numbers as the Indians of Ontario joined the colours in proportion to their numbers."[16]

Immediately, Scott was flooded with correspondence from both chiefs and agents asking what the regulations were pertaining to Indians. For example, on 27 June 1917 Chief F.W. Jacobs of Sarnia, representing the Grand Council of the Chippewa Nation of western Ontario, wrote a simple one-sentence let-ter: "Are the Indians included in the proposed Conscription?" Scott replied that the bill was not yet law; however, he did presume that, if made law, it would apply to all British subjects in Canada, including Indians. This answer was relayed to other chiefs and agents inquiring about the position of Indi-ans and mandatory service. Many chiefs and band councils reminded Scott of treaties that prevented Indians from being compelled to go to war in service of Canada, or, more specifically, outside of Canada.[17]

. On 29 August the *Military Service Act* (*MSA*) legally sanctioned conscrip-tion. The act applied to all male British subjects in Canada, including Indians, Asians, and blacks, between the ages of twenty and forty. Men were placed in six classes based on age, marital status, and dependant status. Those specifi-cally mentioned for exemption were conscientious objectors, the clergy, and certain professionals. There was no mention of Canada's arctic Eskimos—a logical realization of the impossibility of enforcing the act, given their remote-ness and relatively miniscule population of roughly 3,400—which, unlike that of Indians, was still in decline. In addition, Eskimos were not recognized under the *Indian Act*. The registration deadline for those men included was 10 November, in order to apply for individual exemptions. Of the 142,588 Canadian men registered under the *MSA*, only 24,132 joined active Canadian battalions. Nevertheless, driven by the necessities of the war, Canada's policy towards Indian military service had shifted to the opposite of its 1914 position. Ottawa was now demanding, under law, Indian participation.

Petitions flowed to Ottawa and to the king from Indian (and Japanese) councils demanding that, because they did not have rights of citizenship, they should not be forced to perform the duties of a fully enfranchised Canadian. According to the British Columbia Port Simpson and Kitkatla bands:

We ... object to the Militia Act and a ruling which has been made under it conscripting our men, on the grounds that at no time have our Indians had any say in the making of the laws of Canada. We have always been treated by the Government as minors and wards of the Government...We also have a land case which has been before the Government of Canada for a very considerable time, and we consider the Government's attitude towards us in respect to our land troubles and in refusing to extend to us the position of citizens of Canada are unreasonable, and until we receive just treatment at the hands of the Canadian Government and are recognized as citizens and given a say in the making of laws of Canada we consider that we should not be subject to conscription.

Many Indian communities reminded the government of its obligations under the numbered treaties, and of the promises of negotiator Alexander Morris, which excluded Indians from conscription. For example, Chief John Prince of the St. Peter's Band, Manitoba, wrote to Scott in November 1917:

When I gave my country to the Great Mother Queen in the year 1871, I was told that time ... that our Great Mother Queen should never fight us in her war because I was told that time she wants to look upon us as a child ... she would never enter your Indians in her war because She is strong enough and her soldiers are strong enough.... We are going to tell you what we have done to help our King George of England.... We up hold a collection of treaty money the sum of $51.65 ... helping our King on his war.... Lots of our boys went off from their own accord to the war there is some are killed and wounded and some are out there still fighting for the King and Country also there is some are coming back unable to do the work for themselves.[18]

Widely circulated newspapers also ran articles stating these same cases on behalf of the Indian population. Within these objections lie the articulations of the war aims of Canadian Indians: if they were to share in the burdens of the war, they must receive in return an extension of equality and citizenship. The Mohawks at Tyendinaga, Ontario, told Scott specifically that "they don't have to go out of Canada to fight as they are minors and have no vote in the country."[19]

The Six Nations Council wrote to the king in October explaining their refusal to comply with Canadian conscription. They reiterated their belief that the Iroquois Confederacy represented a sovereign ally of both Canada and the Crown, and that they were not citizens but "Indian Allies of the Crown." The letter was carefully worded so as not to suggest they were subject to British conscription either. Similarly, Chief Peter Angus of the Lake of Two Mountains (Kanesatake/Oka) Mohawks, Quebec, wrote the king on 13 November:

> I am in need of a favour from you, I want to know if you gave any orders to your servant here in Canada to inlist us poor Indians here as we were always told by our fore fathers that we were not to battle any more since the last that our fore fathers fought for British. I have called on the Department [Indian Affairs] to see to this matter for us for he knows very well that we have no right to fight any more according to the laws that was made in 1862 but the Department said he could not do anything in my favour ... well we know very well that you have placed him there for to protaked us.... So now I want to ask you our Earthly father to write to the Department to look in this matter for us and not to disturb your children who are but a few of us ... hoping that you will understand all what I want, my writing is plain but its your child's best.

Both letters were referred back to the governor general, Prime Minister Borden, the Ministry of Militia, and the DIA by Colonial Secretary Walter Hume Long.[20]

In addition to the protest correspondence directed at Ottawa and London, many Indians refused to register, while many remote Indians did not know of the regulation. As with the earlier National Service Board registration, some entire reserves refused to comply out of defiance, a few going so far as to conceal their young men. On the Sarcee reserve in Alberta, the agent, disgusted with the regulations of his government, registered all eligible men only to exempt them, citing a fictitious outbreak of tuberculosis in the paperwork submitted to his superiors in Ottawa. On numerous smaller reserves throughout Canada all eligible men had already willingly volunteered.[21]

On 1 October 1917 Scott incorrectly informed the Ministry of Militia and the deputy minister of justice, E.L. Newcombe, that the policy of his department "is that the Act should apply to Indians. There are no existing treaties which promise immunity from military service."[22] Scott had already rejected an appeal from Ontario Indians covered under the Robinson Treaty (1850) for exemption based on treaty rights. Treaty agreements, however, had prohibited Indians from enlisting during the Boer War and were used, in part, until December 1915 to exclude Indians from the CEF. Nevertheless, the Ministry of Militia endorsed Scott's decision: "Indians are British subjects and come under the terms of the Military Service Act, just as any other British subjects."[23] All male Indians of military age were expected to register by 10 November 1917. Astute representatives of Indian Affairs questioned the feasibility and practicality of this undertaking.

The Indian agent at Kenora, Ontario, R.S. McKenzie, wrote to Scott asking how any registration "could be done at the present time is hard to say and it would cost a vast amount to have this done, even if we attempted to do so, as the Indians are all scattered over the country, and out to their Hunting grounds at this season of the year." Many other agents in remote areas shared this concern and wrote to Scott in disbelief at the responsibility implied in the arduous task of completing the registration. Scott replied that "while Indians are subject to the Military Service Act, the officers of this Department are not responsible for the enforcement of the Act," thereby relieving agents of direct involvement in the conscription process.

Scott, therefore, had carefully and furtively removed his department and his staff from direct association with the *MSA*. This did not go unnoticed by the Military Service Branch of the Department of Justice. Scott wrote to Newcombe on 5 November informing him that he had instructed his agents to transmit this message to any *MSA* official who was inquiring about its application to Indians: that the "Military Service Act applied to Indians, and that the Military Service Council had been requested to write the Registrar accordingly." His agents were to have no involvement in completing any aspect of the registration. He did, however, instruct them to inform band councils, chiefs, and individual Indians that the act did apply to them and that "they must register and file claims for exemption before the 10th instant."[24]

Given the confusion surrounding Indians and the *MSA*, and the reluctance of Indian Affairs to aid in registration, on 12 November the Department of Justice issued a notice to "Hunters, Lumbermen and Others [read *Indians*]." It was a reminder that the deadline had passed and that those who had failed to register were liable to five years imprisonment. Those who were unaware of the registration and in default were to write the Military Service Council

MILITARY SERVICE ACT, 1917.

TO

HUNTERS, LUMBERMEN AND OTHERS.

Have you reported for service or claimed exemption under the Military Service Act, 1917?

On the 13th October, 1917, a Proclamation issued requiring all British subjects who were bachelors and widowers without children, whose age on that date was between twenty and thirty-four years, nine months and thirteen days to report for service or claim exemption by the 10th November, 1917.

Men who failed without reasonable excuse to comply with the Proclamation are guilty of an offence and liable to five years imprisonment.

Any man who did not hear of this Proclamation and is consequently in default, should write at once to the address given below, explaining the circumstances, and if the application is well founded, the Minister of Justice will consider the propriety of extending the time for the individual in question, as he has power to do.

Write to:-

DEPARTMENT OF JUSTICE,

MILITARY SERVICE BRANCH,

OTTAWA; ONTARIO.

sued by Military Service Council.
OTTAWA, 12th November, 1917.

ILLUS.14. *Military Service Act* Notice, November 1917. *Library and Archives Canada, RG10 Vol. 6768, File 452-20.*

explaining their circumstance in order to avoid penalty.[25] This appeal and process was a last unrealistic attempt to enforce the *MSA* on Indians. The reality was that many Indians were in fact uninformed of the act or were still in the bush engaged in traditional activities. Furthermore, many remote Indians, who would have failed to comprehend the *MSA*, as they did not read or write English, were ignorantly ordered to write to the Service Council. There were, however, individual cases of charges laid against Indians for failing to register. Clefus DeCoine of Lake Wabasca, Alberta, 250 miles north of Edmonton, was charged with breach of the *MSA*. At the trial, DeCoine needed a Cree interpreter, and it was obvious to all that he had no concept of the act. The charges were quickly dismissed.[26]

The Department of Justice relented two days after issuing the notice. On 15 November, to avoid problems associated with taking legal action against those who failed to register, the deadline for Indians was extended to 1 February 1918. By this time Borden had become directly involved in the issue and was requesting information from Newcombe and the Department of Justice pertaining to the legal rights of Indians. In turn, Newcombe was pleading with Scott for "special consideration and such instructions ... as will ensure the most convenient and economical handling of the cases of Indians."[27] In addition, Scott's staff outlined for him relevant passages of treaties exempting Indians from military service, "which showed him the folly of stonewalling conscription." Scott fruitlessly argued that Indian exemption under treaty or constitutional rights was folly, as not all status Indians entered into, or were covered by, treaty; rather, they should be exempted because they did not enjoy the franchise or citizenship.[28]

Before the closing date of 1 February arrived, however, Ottawa passed legislation exempting Indians (and Japanese) from the terms of the *MSA*, which to Scott was "a compromise, and a half-way face-saving measure." Contrary to Scott's earlier assertion that no treaties exempted Indians from mandatory service, on 17 January 1918 an Order in Council (PC111) stated:

> Whereas petitions and memorials have been received from and on behalf of Indians pointing out that in view of their not having any vote, they should, although natural born British subjects, not be compelled to perform militia service, and that in the negotiations of certain treaties, expressions were used indicating that Indians should not be so compelled, an instance of this recently brought forward being the expression of the Lieutenant Governor in negotiating the North West Angle Treaty as it appears in the despatch of the 14th of October, 1873, quoted in Morris, Treaties of Canada with Indians, pp. 50 and 69;...

> 14a. Any British subject who, under the laws in force from time to time is disqualified from voting at a Dominion election, otherwise

than under Section 67 of the Dominion Election Act R.S.C. 1906, or Section 6 of the War Times Elections Act 7-8 George V, Chapter 39, shall be entitled to exemption from combat military or naval service, unless he has in fact voted at a Dominion election although at the time disqualified from doing so.

18a. Any Indian agent may make application for the exemption of any Indian attached to the Reserve over which such agent has jurisdiction and it shall not be necessary for the Registrar to assign to a local tribunal any application made or transmitted by an Indian agent on behalf of an Indian, but the Registrar shall forthwith issue to such Indian and transmit to the Indian agent for delivery to him a certificate of exemption from combatant military service. In the event of any man thus exempted from combatant military service being hereafter called upon to perform any military duty he may then put forward any claim for exemption even from non-combatant service which he may then have.[29]

An important, often overlooked inference of PC111 is that it applied to all Indians. It must be remembered that not all Indians were covered or represented by treaty, most notably in British Columbia and the territories. Nevertheless, to avoid complications and administrative hassles, the Ministry of Militia circulated a memorandum stating that "*no distinction* made based on Treaty or non-Treaty Indians."[30]

The order also contained provisions whereby any Indian who had enlisted, or been drafted since the *MSA* was passed, could apply for guaranteed discharge. A stipulation was that these men could make a submission for discharge on their own behalf only through their agent, not through a relative, band council, or chief. Another clause of PC111 declared that although all Indians were exempt from military service, all Canadian men and women over the age of sixteen, including Indians, were still compelled to register under the *MSA* by 22 June 1918.[31] An unpublicized glitch within PC111, which could have caused great embarrassment to the government of Canada, was that both regulations 14a and 18a stated that "Indians were exempt from combat duties." This suggested that Indians could volunteer and serve in home defence units, at reasonable pay rates, without ever leaving Canada. It also meant that those overseas could request transfer back to Canada and serve out the remainder of the war in the home defence force.

For French-Canadians, who strongly opposed conscription, if this special treatment afforded to Indians had been known, it would have been met with fierce opposition. Rioting had already plagued Montreal during the two days following the passing of conscription, and on the Easter weekend of 1918 Quebec City was engulfed in anti-conscription violence that led to the death of four civilians. Auspiciously, for Scott and the government of Canada, few Indian soldiers discovered these loopholes. There was, however, one exception.

On 31 August 1918 Harry Stonechild, a Peepeekisis who was still serving after being wounded and gassed in France, wrote the following letter to his Saskatchewan superintendent, W.A. Graham, who proceeded to forward it to Scott: "I beg your assistance to kindly inform me as to whether these instructions apply to me that were issued by Ottawa at the last Federal Elections. Concerning to Indians who have been drafted into the ranks. May be released from the Army if application is made by themselves or relations. As the Indians do not enjoy their Franchise they have the privilege of now leaving the army if desiring to do so."[32] Although Stonechild volunteered in August 1915 and was not drafted, he wanted clarification of his rights as an Indian soldier under current law. Scott told Graham that each case should be judged on its own merit, but stated that it would be a dangerous precedent to recommend returns to those already in uniform; it might cause undue resentment among other segments of the population, specifically French-Canadians: "It has been thought that a recommendation for the return of one Indian might cause dissatisfaction in the event of a large number of applicants being made.... I may add that there is no truth that enlisted Indians are to be allowed to return to civil life on account of not having the privilege of franchise."[33]

Stonechild and PC111 (14a) referred to amendments made to the *Voters Act* by a fretful Borden before the bitter general federal election of 17 December 1917. To ensure victory for conscription, Borden introduced two laws to slant the voting in favour of his newly formed Union government (which included selected opposition members in Cabinet). The first, the *Wartime Elections Act* (20 September 1917), disenfranchised conscientious objectors and Canadian citizens who were born in Central Power countries and immigrated after 1902. The law also gave female relatives of servicemen the vote. Thus, the 1917 election was the first federal election in which some women were allowed to vote, although not Indian women: "Accordingly it follows that Indian women cannot vote." Second, the *Military Voters Act* (27 November 1917) provided a special provision for the enfranchisement, for the upcoming election only, of all soldiers, including Indians. In addition, a special clause for Indian veterans (of the Great War only) stipulated that a governmental representative would be dispatched to reserves in order for them to vote.[34] The *Indian Act* specified that enfranchisement meant the loss of "Indian status"; however, the *Military Voters Act* superseded these articles.[35]

In reality, Indian servicemen had already obtained the right to vote before these alterations, albeit without their knowledge. On 4 May 1916, in parliamentary debate, the minister of justice, Charles Doherty, quoted a passage from the active *MSA*: "Canadian soldiers on Active Military Service during the present war [have the right] to exercise their electoral franchise ... [it] makes no exception of Indians."[36]

In October 1918 Major H.P. Cooke, the deputy registrar of the Military Service Council, wrote to Indian Affairs questioning the exemption of Indians under 14a, given its wording and the fact that Indian soldiers had voted in the 1917 election: "You will see that an Indian who was disqualified from voting as these men were, and in fact did vote although disqualified, as these men did, is not entitled to exemption from combatant service." J.D. McLean, assistant deputy and secretary of Indian Affairs, responded that voting was not a factor in determining the status of an Indian, and they were exempt from combatant service under treaties, the *Indian Act,* and PC111, whether they had voted in 1917 or not. Responding to similar questions, Scott simply replied that he "was not wishing to interpret the Military Service Act." This, again, is a clear example of contradicting policy and illustrates the fact that neither the Ministry of Militia nor Indian Affairs ever considered an occasion where this dilemma would arise. The question of Indians serving overseas, and thereby gaining the right to vote, was never considered and was, subsequently, duly dismissed to avoid friction. In relation, the issue of exemption for enfranchised Indians who had gained the vote by relinquishing status and rights to reserve lands under various acts was never approached, nor did it ever arise as a problem.[37]

On 23 February 1918 the government authorized a second national registration of men and women over sixteen years of age. It was to be carried out on 22 June 1918, the same day as the deadline for Indians to register and apply for exemption from the *MSA*, which augmented existing confusion among Indians, councils, and agents. Again, Scott was flooded with correspondence, as is evident in his letter to the chairman of the Canada Registration Board, Senator G.D. Robertson: "I have had enquiry on behalf of the Six Nations Indians as to whether they will be required to register.... This is the second enquiry and I anticipate many more." The registration council had learned from the previous attempt of 1916–17 and the enforcement of the *MSA*, evidenced by Robertson's reply: "Indians located on Reserves and under the supervision of your Department ... are to be registered, but no attempt will be made to register those in roving tribes, who are not directly under the supervision of the Department of Indian Affairs." Indian Affairs dispatched a circular to all agents to try to assuage the inevitable resistance and backlash to the registration. It praised the "splendid response" of Indian contributions to the war and stated that registration in relation to the Indian "is [to] show that he is willing to place himself on the side of the King and to prove that he is a law-abiding resident of Canada." [38]

As with the previous registration, many Indians refused to fill out the cards. Some believed it was a ploy to reverse their exemption from conscription. Others simply vanished into the bush. The Montagnais (Innu) at Pointe Bleue, Quebec, refused to register. They believed that registration meant war service for the men, and that for women it was a scheme to send them to British Columbia as surrogates to breed children to replace Indian war dead. The Six Nations Council again wrote to the king and refused to support the registration, stating that "they are not British subjects, and that they are a separate nation governed by ancient treaties with the Crown." The Council informed Scott that they would hold their own registration and turn over to the government only that information they decided would be required. To set an example, on 12 July the government fined Mohawk Wesley Martin $100 with the option of one month incarceration after he vehemently refused to register. [39]

In July 1918 Mohawk chiefs Joseph Gabriel, Louis River, and Mitchell Martin of the Lake of Two Mountains (Kanesatake/Oka) again petitioned the king that registration was a violation of the historic agreements made between the Iroquois Confederacy and the Crown. They began their letter with reference to the 1763 Royal Proclamation: "As the laws was strictly forbidden taking advantage of our simplicity, or molested or disturbed and Indian In his Hunting ground." In a separate letter to Scott, the chiefs urged him to clarify the intention of the registration through a representative at Kanesatake, who would outline to the Indians that it "has nothing to do with Military service, It force no one to Military Duty." Charles Cooke relayed to Scott after his recruitment campaign at Oka in February 1917 that the chiefs "will not do anything for the Government in connection with the war, in fact one, Mitchell Martin, stated that he wants the Germans to win the war so that the Government, together with the Seminary, could be removed from the country."[40] This should be viewed, however, as more disdain for the *Indian Act* and the Seminary (which had been a source of friction since 1717) than pro-German sentiment.

Shortly before the registration deadline of 22 June, the government passed another piece of legislation, on 4 April, to "utilize to the best advantage the human energy of Canada for purposes essential to the prosecution of the present war." This was known as *War Regulations against Idleness*. Although exempt from the *MSA*, Indians were included in its provisions, which mandated, "Every male person [aged 16–60] residing in the Dominion of Canada shall be regularly engaged in some useful occupation.... Any person violating the provisions hereof shall be guilty of an offence and shall be liable on summary conviction before a Magistrate." Scott instructed his agents to relay these regulations to their Indian wards, although Indian Affairs never intended to enforce this mandate.[41]

In 1919, Duncan Campbell Scott summarized the position of the Indian and the *MSA*:

When the Military Service Act was put into force in 1917, it was decided to exclude Indians from its operation, and an Order-in-Council to that effect was passed on January 17th, 1918. This action was taken in view of the fact that the Indians, although natural-born British subjects, were wards of the Government, and, as such, minors in the eyes of the law, and that, as they had not the right to exercise the franchise or other privileges of citizenship, they should not be expected to assume responsibilities equal to those of enfranchised persons. It was also taken into consideration that certain old treaties between the Indians and the Crown stipulated that they should not be called upon for military service. It may, therefore, be emphasized that the Indian participation in the war was wholly voluntary and not in any degree whatsoever subject to the influence of compulsory measures.[42]

In a sense, Indian allegiance to the Crown through treaties ultimately excluded them from conscription.

Scott also alluded to an underlying reason for the second registration of 1918. He claimed it was a safeguard, and necessary "in order that certificates of exemption might be issued to them for their protection in the event of their being confused with eligible whites and also to prevent whites and half-breeds [and Métis] from passing themselves as Indians, a trick that was frequently resorted to by deserters after the passing of the Order-in-Council [PC111] exempting the former." Band registers were used to investigate these claims, and most white claims to Indian status were quickly dismissed.

However, two notable whites who claimed Indian heritage voluntarily enlisted in the CEF as Indians. British-born Archibald Belaney, or Grey Owl, joined the 13th Battalion (Black Watch) in 1915 claiming he was Apache and Scottish and adopted by the Ojibwa. He served as a sniper, was wounded twice, and was honourably discharged in November 1917. Following the war, Grey Owl became a pioneering conservationist, environmentalist author, and highly regarded Canadian Indian. In 1937, dressed in traditional Ojibwa apparel, he lectured to an audience at Buckingham Palace that included King George VI and his family. He was exposed as a fraud shortly after his death in April 1938, although his legacy as an environmentalist continues to be celebrated, and rightfully so.[43]

The second notable man to pass himself off as Indian was Sylvester Clark Long, or Buffalo Child Long Lance, born in North Carolina. There is considerable debate as to whether he did in fact have some Indian blood and was mixed white, black, and Indian. Nevertheless, at an early age he passed himself off as Indian; he spoke some Cherokee, appeared in Wild West shows, and attended the Carlisle Indian Industrial School in Pennsylvania as a half Cherokee. He briefly attended West Point military academy before enlisting in the 237th Battalion, CEF, in 1916. He was wounded twice and returned to Canada in 1919 with the rank of brevet sergeant. He was adopted by the Blackfoot Confederacy, and in his acclaimed autobiography *Long Lance* (1928) he represented himself as a full-blooded Blackfoot. He was exposed in 1929 and three years later was found dead in Los Angeles from a gun-shot wound. His death was ruled suicide.[44]

While debate and confusion reigned throughout 1917 and 1918 regarding the two separate registrations, the *MSA* and the *War Regulations against*

Idleness, a shift in policy occurred in the recruitment and military employment of Indians. As Allied forces expanded, including the CEF, there was an
increasing demand for service and support units both in England and in the
rear echelons of the Western Front.

In Canada, not one battalion raised after July 1916 reached full strength,
and all were broken up to reinforce existing units at the front. Moreover, in
February 1918 the entire 5th Division was disseminated across the four divisions of the Canadian Corps. Lieutenant General Arthur Currie obdurately
refused to cut Canadian brigades to the reduced strength of three battalions
(from four), a mandate imposed on British (and other dominion) divisions.
Currie's resistance, supported by both Borden and the Overseas Ministry,
resulted in swollen fighting battalions and a potent Canadian Corps. By this
time, the Canadian Corps, privileged with unparalleled autonomy (as was
Currie), to the exasperation of Haig and certain British politicians, was almost
equivalent to a British Army. Additional machine gun, mortar, engineer, and
auxiliary units had also been added during Currie's dramatic February over-
haul.[45] By May 1918, the Canadian Corps totalled 123,000 men, a strength
increased to as many as 148,000 when augmented by British artillery and support units—which were attached when the corps was used as a spearhead formation during the last hundred days.[46]

The powerful combat capacity of the Canadian Corps was not overlooked
by Haig and paid dividends during the Allied offensives of the last hundred
days, during which the Canadians (and Australians and New Zealanders) were
used as lead formations. This striking power, derived from the relative autonomy of the Canadian (and Australian) Corps, was unmistakable during the
stunning breakthrough at Amiens in August 1918, executed by Currie and his
exceptional Australian peer, Lieutenant General Sir John Monash. At Amiens
both dominion corps acted as spearheads to Rawlinson's 4th British Army
and advanced eight miles on the opening day of 8 August. The "open warfare"
of Amiens was followed by the Canadian Corps' smashing of the Drocourt-
Quéant Line and by Currie's brilliantly planned crossing of Canal du Nord
in late September, in the face of mounting casualties. In fact, the casualties
accrued during these battles, and the subsequent Canadian actions at Cambrai, Valenciennes, and Mons, totalled 48,632 (excluding 6,511 sick with influenza)—roughly 20 percent of the total (241,000) Canadian war casualties. This
figure represents 12.8 percent of all casualties (379,000) sustained by the entire

BEF between 8 August and 11 November, despite the fact that the Canadian Corps was only roughly 6.7 percent of its overall ration-strength.[47] This combat clout, however, required manpower for service and support units. During the Great War, every combatant in the Canadian Corps was supported by no fewer than two non-combatants.[48]

The increased demand for non-combatant auxiliary units in the closing two years of the war directly influenced the position of the Indian soldier. Seeking to address the need for auxiliary troops, in January 1917 the deputy minister of militia, Eugene Fiset, pitched a proposal directly to Duncan Campbell Scott: "It is not thought advisable to recruit complete battalions of either Indians or Half-breeds. In Some Provinces, attempts have been made to recruit one or two platoons of Indians, but so far, no large number have enlisted, and the 114th Battalion was unable to complete the companies they set aside for Indians. However, we need men to complete our 500,000, and it might perhaps, be possible to utilize Indians and Half-breeds, either in the Railway Construction or Forestry Battalions, which are being recruited practically all over Canada." Scott immediately lent his support, and that of his agents, "to stimulate recruiting" for railway and forestry battalions among Indian communities, particularly those in British Columbia and northern Ontario and Quebec.[49] Cooke was given jurisdiction to recruit in Ontario and Quebec. This was the result of a logical realization that Indian men in these communities were employed in lumber-related trades; recruitment was fashioned accordingly. While some historians view this use of Indians in secondary roles as a display of racism, in reality it was a pragmatic decision based on the immediate requirements of the Canadian Corps and the larger conglomerate of Allied formations. White Canadians who were engaged in similar timber-related occupations were also targeted during this period of recruitment.

Scott promoted such recruitment to his agents in specifically targeted areas, stressing the non-combatant status of Indian volunteers:

There are a number of battalions now being recruited for Forestry and Railway Construction work. These battalions are not fighting units, but the men are to be used in lumbering operations in Great Britain and France and in the construction of lines of railway to assist in successfully prosecuting the war. I have thought that there might be in your districts a number of Indians and Half-Breeds who would be excellent material for these battalions and who would be willing to enlist. Although they are not required to become active combatants, they will have the same privileges as the soldiers, the same pay, separation allowance, etc. etc.[50]

The recruitment drive to enlist for service battalions was seen by many as a sanctioning by the Ministry of Militia and the DIA of all-Indian units. This, however, was never the intention. The policy concerning homogenous Indian battalions had already been decided: they were not a feasible option. However, when white officers in British Columbia battalions objected to working amongst Indians, permission was given to form Indian companies or platoons, mirroring the arrangements of the 114th and 107th Battalions. While several West Coast battalions followed this course of action, the majority of forestry and construction battalions were fully integrated and made no modifications based on race.[51]

Nevertheless, Scott thanked his British Columbia agents, saying the "recruiting of Indians and halfbreeds throughout the Province of British Columbia is very much appreciated."[52] Although recruiting in British Columbia was successful, the chief inspector of Indian Agencies for the province, T.M. Tyson, reported to Scott that "white men" had been spreading rumours "that the reason for enlisting Indians was to get them all killed off." He added, however, that he was "looking forward to good results later on for the Forestry work." He also mentioned the fact that in the numerous communities that he visited, "quite a number of the Indians were away hunting and trapping."[53]

As a result of this recruitment effort, Indians were well represented in forestry and railway construction battalions, specifically the 6th, 8th, and 10th Canadian Railway Troops and in units of the Canadian Forestry Corps, both in Britain and in France. James Dempsey incorrectly argues that "It was a sad testimony to attitudes of the period that many Indians who enlisted in hope of becoming combat troops were instead recruited by pioneer battalions and units of the Canadian Forestry Corps and Canadian Railway Troops…. This was less of a reflection on their willingness and ability to fight than it was on the discriminatory attitudes of the military bureaucracy."[54] First, the 107th Battalion was remustered as a pioneer battalion only after it was to be broken up to reinforce infantry battalions, and at the insistence of Campbell, who wanted to keep his Indians together under his command. Second, during 1917 recruiting, including that of Indians, was specifically detailed for forestry and railway battalions. Indians were aware of the unit designation they were joining and the tasks they were to perform, and they chose voluntarily to enlist in these support units. Military pragmatism, not racial prejudice, as Dempsey states, was the reason why many Indians served in these units. Scott lauded the loyalty of his Indian soldier labourers: "You have been doing good work with the Construction Battalion. The willingness of the Indians to serve the Empire is very much appreciated, and they have indeed done credit to themselves in the present crisis.... There have been also quite a number of enlistments in the new Forestry and Construction Battalions."[55]

ILLUS. 15. An Indian Soldier of the Forestry Corps, c. 1917-18. *Library and Archives Canada, PA-129639.*

The need for manpower drastically influenced the military position of Indians during 1917 and 1918. Recruitment efforts were undertaken across the country, including in communities with little historical or cultural martial tradition. Specific effort was made to enlist for auxiliary railway and forestry units, to accommodate the immediate needs of the oversized Canadian Corps. In addition, Indians were initially incorporated into the designs of the *MSA*. After a half-hearted effort to register Indians, however, the government relented and excluded Indians from conscription, basing this decision on the interpretation of treaties with the Crown, the resistance of Scott and his agents to aid in registration, and the logical realization of the futility of attempting to enforce the act in inaccessible regions.

Nevertheless, Indians continued to voluntarily enlist in all military occupations, and Scott attempted, through individual returns by agents, to tabulate the number of Indians in uniform and to promote the accomplishments of his ministry in its ongoing efforts of assimilation. For Scott, the military service of Indians simply represented another palpable example of the progress made in this respect; he disregarded the actual motivations of Indian enlistment and allegiance to the Crown. For example, in late 1916 the Oak River, Manitoba, Sioux wrote to the king: "Long ago a war was existing and as our fore-fathers were in it as we are told. Until then we are told that ... we are knew to be loyal to our King and country and poorest people on your side are we Indians. This terrible war of which we are there to help you, for twelve of our young mens have answered dutys calls to fight for King and country.... Well Beloved King with our poor speeches we will kindly shake hands to you." In reply, the king thanked the Sioux for their loyalty and "was pleased to receive it very graciously."[56] The military alliances fostered and treaties signed with the Crown during colonial warfare still resonated with the majority of Canadian Indians.

Chapter Seven

Indian Soldiers

After the war, Duncan Campbell Scott romantically described the impression Germans had of Indian soldiers:

> If singled out by the foe for particular mention, it may be claimed for the Indians, who were depicted by the Germans in warpaint and with feathers, with scalping knives and tomahawks, ready to carry out ... their treacherous and cruel practices. No doubt, the Germans had a wholesome fear of the Canadian methods of fighting, of the efficiency of our sharp-shooters, and the sudden, desperate nature of our trench raids.... As for the Indian himself, there is no doubt that he excelled in the kind of offensive that had been practiced by his ancestors and was native to him.[1]

While Scott certainly embellished the record of his Indian warriors for the purpose of assimilationist propaganda, his assessment contains a certain degree of legitimacy. In reality, Indians *did* excel as snipers and scouts. While the racial perceptions and stereotypes of battalion commanders may have led to their assignment, the record of Indian snipers and scouts illustrates their effectiveness. Indeed, the Germans were consciously aware of Indians in both the Canadian and American Expeditionary Forces, and they adhered to the common and widely disseminated belief that Indians had intrinsic martial abilities.

German perceptions of indigenous peoples were well established before the war. Prior to 1914, Germany had shown a fascination for indigenous peoples, and they were well represented in popular culture. Carl Hagenbeck, founder of the modern zoo, displayed foreign animals and indigenes during European tours and in *Völkerschau* (literally, "People Show") at his popular Tierpark (outside Hamburg), which opened in 1874. From the opening of his park until 1913, he displayed and toured with Samoans, Laplanders, and various African peoples. In 1886 a group of Eskimos from Hopedale, Labrador, and over sixty Indians from Bella Coola, British Columbia, were part of his exhibition. Hagenbeck influenced Geoffroy de Saint-Hilaire's creation of the "human zoo" exhibition in Paris, which operated between 1877 and 1912 and attracted roughly one million visitors per year. The Parisian World's Fairs of 1878 and 1889 presented exhibitions of indigenous peoples from across the globe. Buffalo Bill Cody's Wild West Show—featuring prominent headliners such as Annie Oakley, Métis Gabriel Dumont, and Sioux Chief Sitting Bull—toured Europe, including Germany, between 1887 and 1889.[2] Cody's show also included Australian Aborigines, two of whom served in the 34th Battalion, Australian Imperial Force, during the war.[3] Thomas A. Britten points out that "the German people held a long-standing affinity for Native Americans, one that stretched back to the nineteenth century." He also attaches importance to Wild West shows and to letters and stories sent home to Europe by German immigrants to North America.[4]

The foremost influence on German perceptions of North American Indians and their martial proclivities was that of the German novelist Karl May (1842–1912), described in *Der Spiegel* as having a reputation "greater than that of any other author between Johann Wolfgang von Goethe and Thomas Mann."[5] His works were translated into twenty languages, sold more than 30 million copies, and were read by an estimated 300 million individuals. His four-novel series *Winnetou* (1893–1910), about an Apache chief, describes the Apaches as noble warriors and honourable people, but also includes lengthy passages describing such practices as torture and scalping. The series was received with great acclaim in both Germany and Austria, as were other books discussing Indian history and culture. Between 1912 and 1963 German cinema produced twenty-three films based on May's novels.[6] *Indian Boyhood* (1902) by Dr. Charles Eastman, a Sioux, was translated into German in 1912.[7] In 1920 German veteran Ernst Jünger published his autobiographical account of the war, *In Stahlgewittern* (The Storm of Steel), and made reference to May's works: "Memories of my third grade class and Karl May came back to me, as I was crawling on my stomach through the dew-covered and thorny grass, careful not to make the least noise, for, fifty metres in front of us, was the entrance to the English trench that detached itself like a dark line in the shadow."[8]

During the First World War, select German propaganda sought to reassure soldiers that they were not facing the warriors depicted in May's novels. An article in *Rheinische Zeitung* stated that there were no Indians fighting on the Western Front because they were dying out on account of being "thoroughly degenerated from drink."[9] In contrast, another German propaganda source suggested that the British army was in numerical decline and all replacements from Canada were "Choctaws, Blackfeet, or Ojibwa."[10]

Testimonies from prisoners of war from both sides also offer insight into German perceptions of Indian soldiers during the war. A German taken prisoner during the Battle of Vimy Ridge told Private Andrew McCrindle (24th Battalion) that his superiors warned him "not to be taken prisoner, as the Canadians are all Red Indians who would scalp them."[11] There is no factual evidence supporting the scalping of enemies by Indians during the war. An officer captured by the U.S. 32nd Division during the Battle of Soissons (18–22 July 1918) asked his captors what percentage of the division was Indian. An American officer captured prior to the Battle of Mihiel (12–15 September 1918) was surprised to be asked by interrogators how many "Indians there were opposing the Boches [Germans] in that sector."[12] A captured German document confirmed that during the St. Mihiel campaign additional snipers were detailed to "kill Indians" as they were "greatly superior" to other troops. A confiscated letter from a soldier of the Sixth Jaeger Regiment stated that "the Indians of the Sioux tribe were identified in one of the last attacks. After the war Karl May can write another book about his experiences with the Redskins."[13] Six Nations Mohawk William Foster Lickers, who enlisted in September 1914, was captured during the Second Battle of Ypres. He was tortured and beaten by his prison guards to see if "Indians could feel pain" and was left paralyzed for the remainder of his life.[14]

Canadian and American media played upon German perceptions and stereotypes. *Stars and Stripes*, the official publication of the AEF, published four articles detailing the heroics of the "American Indian against the Prussian Guard."[15] *The Indian School Journal* also circulated a commentary exaggerating Indian bellicosity: "A Sioux soldier was so full of fight that during the last two weeks of action he could not be kept in his dugout long enough to have his wound stripes sewn on his sleeves."[16] In response to the alleged German anxiety over fighting Indian soldiers, certain American regiments suggested the idea of using Indians, wearing traditional dress and appurtenances, to conduct night raids. (The New Zealand Maori Battalion did in fact do this.)[17]

In reality, many Indians did practice their traditional customs. Many wore moccasins, especially snipers and scouts, as they were quieter than boots. Others, like George Strangling Wolf, adhered to the ancient beliefs of the warrior ethos, as was witnessed by Mike Mountain Horse:

Another custom ... in the life of a warrior on the eve of battle was to cut away a small portion of his body as an offering.... In those dark days of 1917 ... George Strangling Wolf, while praying, took a needle out of his "housewife" (a soldier's name for a sewing kit) and inserted it into the skin near his knee. He then took an army knife and sliced off that portion of the flesh which he was holding out taut with the needle. Pointing in the direction of the sun, and still holding the small portion of bloody flesh in his hand, George offered prayer.[18]

Corporal Francis Pegahmagabow also held an ardent belief in Indian customs and the supernatural: "When I was at Rossport, on Lake Superior, in 1914, some of us landed from our vessel to gather blueberries near an Ojibwa camp. An old Indian recognized me, and gave me a tiny medicine-bag to protect me, saying I would shortly go into great danger. The bag was of skin, tightly bound with a leather throng. Sometimes it seemed to be hard as a rock, at other times it appeared to contain nothing. What was really inside I do not know. I wore it in the trenches." He also believed that chewing a dead twig in times of danger offered protection, and he urged his fellow Ojibwa, Levi Nanibush, to follow suit: "Well, I couldn't believe it, but I tried it and it sure enough works alright.... I was not afraid of anything because of what he told me."[19]

There are countless recorded instances of Indian soldiers bellowing war chants and "whoops." Standing-Rock Sioux Charlie Rogers, of the 18th American Infantry Regiment, "who was the match for 20 Huns, leaped over the parapet swinging his old rifle over his head. He let out a yell he had been saving for years, and it was a genuine war-whoop."[20] Mountain Horse relayed a similar anecdote: "I released my pent up feelings in the rendering of my own particular war song.... Though some of my companions assured me that my war whoops had stopped the war for at least a few seconds, I have never been able to ascertain exactly what was Jerry's [Germans] reaction to my outburst."[21] He also mentions that he used Indian war medicines and ceremonies when preparing for battle. Mountain Horse even went so far as to paint Blackfoot Confederacy victory symbols on the captured guns of an entire German battery during the Battle of Amiens, an indication that he felt he was fighting for his Blood nation and the Confederacy rather than for Canada.[22]

The roles and representation of Indians in the CEF reflected the duality of the racial and martial perception of the noble savage. Many recruiters and battalion commanders believed that, given the historical background of Indian culture and military prowess, they had innate abilities to track, scout, and shoot while also possessing a certain degree of "bloodlust." In addition, many believed that Indians had keener eyesight, especially night vision, had better hearing, and could navigate based on instinct. In reality, many Indians filled the roles of snipers and scouts and excelled at both functions, given their civilian experience as hunters and trappers. It might also be reasonably assumed that during training Indian marksmanship was inimitable on the rifle range. All thirty-five Ojibwa recruited from Fort William, in northern Ontario, became snipers, including Private Michael Ackabee, whose image graces the cover of this book.[23] The depiction of Indian snipers has, at times, been baseless and quixotic, yet it has also been corrupted for fear of prejudicial racial profiling. Nevertheless, after a thorough review of the historical record, it can be safely attested that many Indians, for whatever reasons, were exceptional marksmen.

The highest sniper figures recorded in the history of the CEF belonged to two Indians. Corporal Pegahmagabow, who enlisted on 14 August 1914, claimed 378 unofficial kills, which also ranked him the premier sniper of the entire Great War (and, in fact, ever). In March 1917, while recovering from shell shock in England, Pegahmagabow wrote directly to Scott, seeking permission to return to the 1st Battalion:

I cannot return to my duty in France, they won't let me go.... Alex Logan [his agent at Parry Sound] will tell I have been a good boy at home and I am glad to say that I feel just as lively as I was when I first enlisted 7th August 1914 [sic]. There is no reason why they should keep or delay me back here. It isn't because I got wounded on Sept. 24th last, my wound does not bother me at all.... For my part I would sooner fight my human enemy while I am trying to fight my spiritual enemy as well. Give them a tap to let me go back to my hunting Fritz in France. The reality of soldiering is nothing to me, although I had twenty months under shell fire in France, which I found is not half as bad as it is back here in England. Any soldier will contradict my idea between peace and war, chuck him in the clink for me, he is a-pologetic. [I was] awarded a medal [Military Medal] last June. I want another one while I have a chance.[24]

As an aside, according to archival records, most officers, politicians, and medical authorities believed Indians were immune to shell shock, basing this belief on their idea of the noble savage and presumption of intrinsic Indian bloodlust and martial abilities. No documentation, however, confirms any different diagnosis or treatment from that of Euro-Canadian soldiers.[25]

Although Pegahmagabow won the Military Medal three times (one of only thirty-eight Canadians to accomplish this feat), his unofficial tally of 378 kills is disputed and is symptomatic of Duncan Campbell Scott's poetic licence for propaganda purposes. In late 1919 Scott declared that Corporal Francis Pegahmagabow "bears the extraordinary record of having killed 378 of the enemy." In reality, during the presentation of his Military Medal and two bars by the Prince of Wales (future King Edward VIII) in Toronto in August 1919, Pegahmagabow boasted to reporters that he had tallied 378 kills during the war. Eager to show Indian contributions to the war effort, Scott, using newspaper articles and Pegahmagabow's statements, made this number "official" in his department's year-end report for 1919. This figure has since become fact in Canadian history, although it was never corroborated by evidence or by accounts in either the official records of Pegahmagabow's 1st Battalion or by observers.[26] In fairness, unlike most snipers who were accompanied by equally skilled "spotters," Pegahamagabow chose to hunt alone, and his war record and decorations are evidence of his skill and bravery.

Arguably second to Pegahmagabow was Lance Corporal Henry "Ducky" Norwest of the 50th Battalion, of Cree ancestry from Edmonton, Alberta, who accumulated 115 kills. The former rancher, trapper, and rodeo performer earned the Military Medal with bar, making him one of 838 Canadians to be awarded this double honour. Norwest was killed on 18 August 1918 during the Battle of Amiens. That same day, his commanding officer issued a tribute: "I doubt if anyone in the Canadian Corps or in the whole British Army had a finer record than he.... His Indian blood possibly helped him in his work, possibly inherited his patience and cunning from his hunting forebears ... his example an inspiration." According to the memoirs of the 50th Battalion, "Our famous sniper ... Henry Norwest carried out his terrible duty superbly because he believed his special skill gave him no choice but to fulfil his indispensable mission." On his grave stone, his friends inscribed, "It must have been a damned good sniper that got Norwest."[27] According to a German prisoner of war, his reputation and fame were also known to them, and they feared him.[28]

ILLUS. 16. Ojibwa Sniper Corporal Francis Pegahmagabow, MM with Two Bars. *Woodland Cultural Centre.*

The records of other Indians supported beliefs in their exceptional skill as marksmen. Mississauga Lance Corporal Johnson Paudash (21st Battalion), Hiawatha Band, Keene, Ontario, amassed eighty-eight kills and won the Military Medal. A trio of Indian snipers from the 8th Battalion recorded impressive numbers. Lance Corporal John Ballendine, a Cree from Battleford,

Saskatchewan, finished the war with fifty-eight. Private Philip McDonald, a Mohawk from Akwesasne, was credited with forty before he was killed on 3 January 1916. Lastly, Private Patrick Riel, grandson to Louis Riel, accumulated thirty-eight. He was killed eleven days after McDonald.[29] Other notable snipers were Mississauga brothers Pete and Sampson Comego (Alderville, Ontario), Ojibwa private Roderick Cameron (English River, Ontario) and George Stonefish, a Delaware from the Moravian of the Thames, Ontario. Sampson Comego was killed on 10 November 1915, but in his short period of service he tallied twenty-eight kills. These are but a few accounts recorded in the annuals of the CEF.[30]

While it is easy to fall prey to the noble savage ideal, the archival record does indicate that Indians excelled as snipers and scouts. This should be viewed as a result of their livelihood as hunters and trappers; it also bears witness to the fact that, given their realities of life during this time period, they possessed a greater skill at arms, by tradition or by necessity, than the average Canadian. The achievements and honours of Pegahmagabow, Norwest, and the aforementioned soldiers should be viewed apart from racial identification; they were simply skilled Canadian Indian marksmen who volunteered their talents accordingly. By extension, their commanders, with or without prejudice, which in effect has no bearing, recognized their skills and provided them with a suitable military occupation. The ultimate goal was, after all, to kill Germans and win the war. The topic of Indian snipers has been the subject of debate and, in a sense, mythology. While the record of Pegahmagabow is open to question (though his deserved respect and accolades are not), the historical testimony of Canadian snipers indicates that Indians were certainly among those worthy of recognition and honour.

In addition to serving as snipers and scouts, Canadian Indians were employed in every other branch of the combat arms and auxiliary formations except for the Royal Tank Corps. Albert Cochrane and Edward Lavallee, both from Saskatchewan, joined the Royal Naval Canadian Volunteer Reserve, and Kenneth McDonald of the Yukon joined the Royal Navy.[31] Three members of the defunct 114th Battalion, lieutenants James David Moses, Oliver Milton Martin (both Mohawks from Six Nations), and Mohawk John Randolph Stacey, from Kahnawake, Quebec, all served as pilots in the Royal Flying Corps/Royal Air Force. Stacey was killed on 8 April 1918, and Moses on 1 August 1918.[32] Martin went on to serve in the Second World War, attaining the rank of brigadier general, the highest position ever attained in the Canadian Forces by an Indian.[33] American general John Pershing's French interpreter was Mohawk William Newell, a graduate of Syracuse University.[34]

Indians served in other campaigns in addition to the Western Front. David Bernardan, a Salish Bella Coola from British Columbia, was one of thirty-eight Canadians of the First Overseas Canadian Pioneer Detail, which operated barges on the Tigris and Euphrates Rivers in Mesopotamia from 1916 onwards.[35] Privates William Thompson and John Munninguay, of the Peguis reserve, Manitoba, served on the Western Front with the 203rd Battalion. Afterwards, they, along with Callihoo William of the Enoch Cree, Alberta, served in the 4,300-man strong Canadian Siberian Expeditionary Force at Vladivostok, from October 1918 to May 1919.[36] Two other Peguis Indians were attached to the Serbian army and served on the Balkan Front from 1916 to 1918.[37]

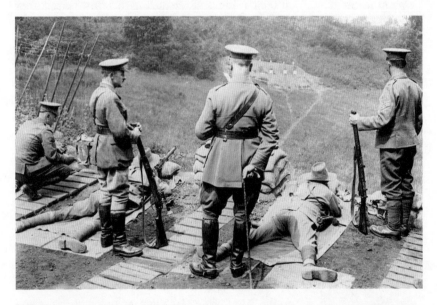

ILLUS. 17. Sniper School, June 1916. Notice the mounted sight on the Canadian-made Ross Rifle (front left). The soldier on the far right is holding a British-made Lee-Enfield. The "jamming" Ross, inferior in rapid-fire, trench-combat conditions, was replaced with the Lee-Enfield in the summer of 1916. Canadian snipers, however, continued to use the Ross because of its superior distance and accuracy, a result of its longer barrel length (by 2.5 inches) and its heavier weight (by 2.5 lbs). *Library and Archives Canada PA-000035.*

In total, at least seventeen Indians were commissioned officers in the CEF during the First World War (0.43 percent of total enlistments). Comparatively, sixty-four American Indians were commissioned in the AEF (0.38 percent). In total, 80 percent of Canadian Indian officers had prior military service in the militia, and all came from professions that required an education, such as law, education, engineering, clerical work, and skilled trades. Simply stated, commissioned Indians were instated based on their level of assimilation. This is not to say, however, that these Indians viewed themselves as assimilated, nor did it mean that they had rejected their Indian culture. Scott personally supported the granting of a commission to Indians on the same criteria as whites. He wrote to Fiset in April 1916 that he would "be glad if the requests of [an] Indian ... desirous of obtaining a commission in the Canadian Army ... can be granted."[38]

Given the requirements for obtaining a commission, including education, social or political connections, the ability to speak *and* write English, and, preferably, prior military service (not to mention that racial prejudices would generally be working against Indians), it is not surprising that most Indians were enrolled as non-commissioned members. Of the total 1914 Indian population of 103,774, 36.8 percent could speak English, 15.9 percent could write English, another 8.2 percent were French speakers, and 1.2 percent could write French. The majority of these literate Indians (70.2 percent) lived east of Manitoba. In addition, Indian reserves in the East were usually closer to urban centres than those in the West.[39] Accordingly, more Indian men were active in the pre-war militia in the East, most notably in southwestern Ontario. This proximity to urban centres also led to an enhanced job market in professions such as those held by Indian officers prior to the war. Of the seventeen known Indian officers, twelve (70.6 percent) came from the provinces of Ontario and Quebec. This proportion equates, exactly, to the number of literate Indians living east of Manitoba. While it has been assumed that racism is responsible for the dearth of Indian officers, this perception is, quite frankly, not factually supported. Simply stated, most Indians did not possess the requirements to receive a commission in the CEF. This, however, does not diminish their abilities as soldiers or their intelligence; it is simply indicative of the social, cultural, and military realities in Canada during and prior to the First World War.

Other anomalies arose from Indian inclusion in Western-society-based militaries. Traditional leadership in many indigenous communities and warrior societies rested with the people themselves. Leaders and war chiefs were appointed, were followed out of respect, and could be replaced at the discretion of the people. Military dress and deportment were foreign to many who joined from remote areas or had little previous contact with whites. Acclimatization to army discipline also proved difficult. Traditionally, there were not the same sharp distinctions between a war chief and warriors as there was between commissioned officers and the ranks. For example, Indian private John Ratt was disciplined for failing to salute an officer. During his hearing he remarked that at home, "when we meet a man there we speak to him one time. No speak anymore to same man all day. Down here me salute everytime [sic] me pass man?"[40] Nevertheless, only two charge parades were recorded in the war diary of Campbell's 107th Battalion in one full year of entries.[41]

It is difficult to objectively discern the degree of adjustment required or the number of hardships faced by Indians, as the majority of information is highly anecdotal. The bulk of documentation was recorded by Indian agents, missionaries, and non-Indian academics and journalists, some with ulterior motives. To what extent this Indian testimony can be trusted as honest is, admittedly, uncertain. Nevertheless, many Indians of the CEF, having come through industrial and residential schooling, were literate, and some did leave personal literary trails. For those who left testimony through secondary sources, it must be assumed that their intentions in speaking and having their stories recorded were relatively benign, and that their accounts are accurate. For example, my great-grandfather William, who enlisted at fifteen years of age in August 1915, was wounded twice, gassed once, and contracted malaria, did not speak about his First World War experiences very often. When he did, however, it was with humility and respect.[42] I assume that his Canadian comrades were the same.

Mike Mountain Horse remarked, "I can readily appreciate the easy adjustment of the white man to the strict disciplinary measures of the army, but to apply the same rules and regulations to young undisciplined natives was quite another matter." He recalled George Strangling Wolf turning out on parade "wearing elk teeth earrings, with an elk teeth necklace to match, and a gaudy red handkerchief around his neck. The crown of his hat was cut away to let in the air, and he was noisily chewing gum, much to the discomfort of the man next to him in line." Mountain Horse also mentions that Private Bumble Bee Crow Chief, a Blood who spoke no English, was struck from battalion strength after he refused to cut his long braids. For the Plains Indians, long hair was symbolic of superiority. When leaving camp, Bumble Bee scolded his fellow Blood Indians (as told in English by Mountain Horse): "Don't be foolish like these white soldiers. I hear they call the war off everyday for mealtime. You boys want to keep on shooting even if you see them sitting down to eat."[43] The records also indicate that many Indians adorned their tents with traditional Native artifacts, and some even wore traditional headdress. The Blackfoot and Blood went so far as to create a word in their languages for Germans, loosely translated as "pointed helmets."[44]

ILLUS. 18. Blood Recruits of the 191st Battalion, Macleod, Alberta, 1916. Left to Right Back Row: George Coming Singer (died overseas, 1919); Joe Crow Chief; Dave Mills; George Strangling Wolf; Mike Foxhead (Blackfoot, died overseas, 1919). Left to Right Front Row: Nick King; Harold Chief Moon; Sergeant-Major Bryan; Joe Mountain Horse; Mike Mountain Horse. *Glenbow Museum Archives, NA-2164-1.*

Two difficulties facing Indian servicemen were their introduction to Western culture and the English language. Many Indians came from remote communities, adhered to their cultural norms and traditions, and had had limited interaction with whites. For example, William Semia, an Ojibwa from northern Ontario, spoke no English when he enlisted in the 52nd Battalion. A fellow Ojibwa taught him rudimentary English during recruit training in

Port Arthur, where he first saw a modern city and, to his disbelief, grocery stores.[45] He went on to become a sergeant and the drill instructor for his battalion. After the war he exclaimed, "Next war me join 1st Battalion, first contingent."[46] John Waymistigoos from the Duck Lake reserve spoke no English but was accepted into the Forestry Depot because he showed proficiency with carpentry tools. Duncan Campbell Scott received reports from across Canada throughout 1916 of "Indians who could not speak a word of English want[ing] to join up, but the fact that they could not understand English was an obstacle that prevented their enlistment."[47]

John Campbell, an Eskimo from the Yukon Territory, made a 3,000-mile journey by trail, canoe, and river-steamer to enlist at Vancouver. He had previously tried to enlist in the Yukon with three Indians. They were all accepted by the recruiting depot and passed the medical exam; however, after complaints from men in the Yukon contingent, they were all summarily released from the unit. No Indian or Eskimo was accepted for service in the Yukon itself prior to conscription.[48] Indians and Eskimos, many of whom came from remote communities and spoke no, or very little, English, were scattered across all formations of the CEF. W.M. Graham, inspector general of Indian Agencies for southern Saskatchewan, received three letters from Indians expressing their loneliness:

"Most of my Indian pals are either Blighty or killed. Two of us Indian boys are left, four of them have paid the price.... I tell you letters are very interesting, especially when your chums are away from you."
—*Elijah Dickson*

"It makes us boys long to get back.... And how proud we feel of the reserve we are doing our duty for." —*John Walker*

"I am quite interested in the news of our reserve. Many is the time I wish I was back in my native country." —*Abel Watech*

Mountain Horse wrote home while in hospital: "I am rather lonely ... I have not talked Blackfoot for over six months."[49]

Newspapers also published excerpts of Indian letters: "I often get very lonesome for my dear children, but my country needs me, so I will do my best for it.... I will die like a good honest soldier if I have to die." The article concluded after the letter by stating, "Countries grow great which produce citizens [although Indians were not citizens] like this Indian hero, and we are told that he is simply characteristic of his fellows."[50] However, letters home from Indians only represent those who could read and write, and they say nothing about those who could not. The latter group may have felt a greater alienation, given that they were less accustomed to white culture, and estrangement from their traditional communities and customs likely augmented the effects of an already strange and traumatizing war.

An interesting facet of Indian service, overlooked by authorities until the spring of 1917, was the censorship of letters written in Indian languages. In September 1917 Duncan Campbell Scott received from the postmaster general "219 letters written in the Indian language by members of the Canadian Expeditionary Force at the front, and which have been transferred to us by the Chief Postal Censor for examination." These letters were written in dialects of Cree, Ojibwa, Sioux, Blackfoot, and the six Iroquois Confederacy languages. With Charles Cooke away recruiting, Indian Affairs did not have the immediate personnel or knowledge to undertake the task of translating and censoring. Letters were, therefore, distributed to local Indian agents for interpretation, causing delays in the actual receipt of letters to the addressees. Ironically, letters written in Cree syllabics were allowed to pass uncensored as Indian Affairs had no personnel with the ability to translate. Nevertheless, the remainder of the letters were translated into English, and none were found to contain reference to any topic requiring censorship. Given the time and effort required for the completion of this task, Scott wrote "a purely personal letter" to the deputy postmaster general, Dr. R.M. Coulter, in May 1917: "I suggested in one of my previous letters to you that I think it hardly necessary to continue the censorship of these letters." Following this communication, Indian Affairs received no more requests to translate and censor Indian letters.[51]

While the inability of Indians to speak English was generally problematic, there was one exception. The American "code-talker" program of Second World War fame had roots in the First World War. In October 1918, E Company, of the 142nd (US) Infantry Regiment, which contained 208 Indians, called on two of its eighty-nine Choctaw soldiers to transmit messages in their Indian language. According to regimental commander Colonel A.W. Bloor, "it was remembered that the regiment possessed ... Indians. They spoke twenty-six different languages and dialects, only four or five of which were ever written. There was hardly one chance in a million that Fritz would be able to translate these dialects and the plan to have these Indians translate telephone messages was adopted. The regiment was fortunate in having two Indian officers who spoke several of the dialects." On 28 October a training school was opened for Indian radio and telegraph operators. During the last two months of the war, various units of the 36th and 41st Divisions employed Indians as telephone operators.[52] It is not known if this practice was adopted by the CEF, although there is evidence to suggest that Cree men might have been used in this function. During the Second World War, both the American and Canadian forces created official code-talker programs.[53]

The lack of understanding of Western military culture did result in unique problems associated with Indian desertion. Records, however, indicate that this practice was no more prevalent among Indians than their white comrades, and the act of desertion should be viewed as a war experience that transcended race. Traditionally, an Indian warrior could leave a war party based on individual prerogative and independent decision. During training or leave in Canada, certain Indians deserted after being dissatisfied with military life or simply did not return to their camps after leave. Similarly, after Indian exemption was granted from the *Military Service Act*, many already enlisted believed that this meant they were free to leave service. There was no uniform policy on Indian desertion, however. In the majority of cases, those who could be found were simply ordered to return to their units and escorted back to their training facilities without confrontation or formal charges being issued. There were cases, however, of charges and altercation.

For example, Blood Indians Jim Only Chief and Laurie Plume deserted in January 1917. They were apprehended and given eighteen months in an Alberta penitentiary before being returned to their unit. They deserted again in May 1918 on stolen horses. Only Chief was given five years in the Edmonton penitentiary, while Plume escaped on his horse to the United States. Upon hearing of the end of the war, he returned to his reserve, only to be arrested for his previous desertion and sentenced to five years' incarceration.[54]

On 7 November 1916 Indian Affairs received a complaint from the chiefs of Kettle Point, Ontario:

> I want to know if an Army Officer or Private from some Company or Regiment have any rights to enter into Indian Reservation to shoot an Indian Private or to force an Indian to go with the overseas. Private

Moses Wolfe was with the Lambton 149 Batt. In training and came home over a month ago and stayed at home on account of sickness, lost his baby and his wife was nearly died. Two Officers drove in ... and having some talk ... [he] refuse to go with them ... one took after him and shoot him on the shoulder and the bullet is in.... We don't want a white man or any other man to enter into our reservation to shoot Indians like beasts. After the War of 1812, the Government set rules for Tecumseh's and Chief Shawnoo's [Tecumseh's cousin who lived at Kettle Point and led local warriors during the War of 1812] Grandsons and Great Grandsons not to be forced to go to war and we are the Grand Children of Tecumseh and Chief Shawnoo. Tecumseh and his Tribe done a big work to save Canada and now we want to know how this shooting affair stands ... we want to have a full understanding of this.

On 25 November local Indian agent Timothy Maxwell wrote Indian Affairs stating that he was "going up to Kettle Point with Chief Jacobs [of Sarnia] ... to find out what we can." He submitted his report on 2 December, which corroborated the story submitted by the chiefs while stating that "there was a trial at Forest over the case." The outcome of the case was that Wolfe was arrested for desertion and taken to London to serve time, after which he was returned to duty. The shooter, Corporal Robert Finegan, was also charged, although the outcome of his trial is not known.[55]

Another problem associated with desertion was the fact that many Indians crossed the U.S.-Canadian border to reside at sister reservations in the United States. This was especially true of Iroquoian deserters. Thompson complained in September 1916 that several of his 114th Battalion "soldiers from Caughnawa [Kahnawake] ... have crossed the line to Malone, N.Y. and to Messina Springs, N.Y., the St. Regis Indians [the New York state portion of Akwesasne] mainly to the latter point." He requested that the "Immigration Department and through it American officials" be tasked with deporting these men "from the U.S. as undesirables." Given the cross-departmental and multi-national effort required to do so, nothing was ever done to apprehend these Indian deserters. Other American Indians who had enlisted in the CEF prior to April 1917 deserted their units, returned to the U.S., and joined American regiments upon hearing of the U.S. entry into the war.[56]

Another factor influencing Indian recruits was the issue of underage enlistment. Many Indians did not know precisely how old they were. The lack of birth registers and the at times perfidious actions on the part of some recruiters within Indian communities led to the enlistment of many underage Indians. This, however, was not unique to Indians; the military accepted underage recruits of all races. For example, my great-grandfather, as mentioned, enlisted with the 20th Battalion in August 1915 at the age of fifteen. His attestation form states age eighteen under the section "Apparent Age." Recruiters simply winked at the official age regulations, since battalions were struggling to fill their manpower quotas.

Nevertheless, chiefs and parents of these underage Indian soldiers frequently wrote to the DIA and Ministry of Militia or directly to the governor general or the king to secure release for their kin. The records indicate that the vast majority were not released, as they had knowingly volunteered, lacked official birth records, or did not submit underage release forms on their own behalf. Many letters from parents or chiefs mention not only that their sons were underage but also treaties promising that Indians would not be called to fight outside of Canada, having been told to "bury their war hatchets."

The chiefs of the Garden River Ojibwa (near Sault Ste. Marie, Ontario), unsuccessfully wrote to Indian Affairs in June 1916 to secure the return of one of their young men, Richard Pine, who,

> made a mistake when he joined not first consulting his guardians as he is not even of age.... He is the Great Grand son of the late Chief Shingwaukoons who Fought in the Battle of Chipewa. A time when Canada had to Struggle for its life a century ago; It was then Promised to the Indians that they never would be again asked to participate in any future trouble that may arise, and that they would only be Protected under the British Flag.... If Canada was to fight for its life again today here in Canada, the Garden River Band will not take to the Bush to Bewail, but die to his heritage which the Great Spirit had aloted to them from the beginning of time.[57]

John and Jane Manitowaba of Parry Island wrote the governor general an articulate four-page letter on 28 December 1916 asking for the release of their underage son Simpson. They argued that not only was he underage, but also they did not consent to his enlistment. John and Jane also reference treaties and prior agreements between Indians and the British Crown, some in exact quotations:

> My [i.e., Jane's] grand-father and his sons and also four of my grand-uncles have fought on the side of the English, One Hundred Years ago or more. And when this war of 1812 ended in a successful issue in favour of British Army defence and valour, those Old Warriors were given promises as rewards for duty by the representatives of the Late Queen Victoria that the English will never call on the Indians and their generations to join in their battles that may arise against nations in the future but to live in peace with all in their country.... They were never rewarded nor their grand-children never rewarded any favour from the Royal Throne of the Grand British Kingdom for the services of those old Indian Warriors that they shared with the British in Canada in their early struggles. And these Indians allied acts were never recognized to the present day nor ever recorded in History as to show any importance on their part that they had done ... each individual of my Tribe in Canada is recognized as a minor only in the eyes of the law.... When the Treaties of Canada with the Indians were made by our Late Queen Mother Victoria the Good through several of Her Gracious Majesty's representatives, there is one particular clause which one of our old Indian Chiefs had expressed Fifty years ago. He quoted this: "If you should get into trouble with the nations, I do not wish to walk out and expose my young men to aid you in any of your wars." The Governor answered in return: "The English never call the Indians out of their country to fight their battles. You are living here and the Queen expects you to live at peace with the white men and your red brothers and with other nations."[58]

While such eloquent and academic prose was not the norm, many Indians who wrote letters were aware of treaty rights, prior allegiance to the British during colonial warfare, and the promises made by British representatives in return for service. For service in the War of 1812, the British promised Indians pensions and 160 acres of land outside of their "own reservations." Aside from the usual gifts of food, blankets, and medals, the British failed to fulfill their promises. Following the deaths of Brock and Tecumseh, larger strategic promises of land and an Indian state were also duly disregarded.

A second letter was written on behalf of the Manitowaba family by the band council the same day, and Simpson himself had written a letter two days prior to the communications of his parents and his council. On 27 January 1917 Jane and John wrote directly to Duncan Campbell Scott, still vying for the release of their son, and included his birth registration and particulars as proof of age. They received a reply on 1 February: "You will understand that this Department cannot interfere in matters which are under the authority of the Department of Militia and Defence.... You will remember the proud record held by the Indians, in loyalty to their country in times of danger.... You should be proud to have your son among those brave men who sacrifice everything to their loyalty and devotion to their country." Simpson was never released from service, despite being underage. He did, however, survive the war.[59]

In keeping with the Iroquoian belief of sovereignty, the letters of family members and of the council regarding the discharge of underage Six Nations soldiers in almost all cases allude to sovereignty and the position of the Six Nations Confederacy as an autonomous ally of both Great Britain and Canada. In August 1916 Lucy Maracle, of the Grand River, wrote the governor general on behalf of her son, stating,

> even if he was of age, it is contrary to the treaty, of Two rows of Wampum belt treaty, and the other belt of one row, a figure of Men, one on each end of the Wampum belt treaty, is the treaty of Allies between the Six Nations Indians, the King must ask the Six Nations Chiefs for help. So they will hold a Council on the subject, and the Chiefs will decide in their Council to help the King in his war. Now this was never done, by the King, to ask the Six Nations Indians for aid.

The mothers of five underage Six Nations boys who had enlisted wrote directly to the king together on 31 January 1917 reiterating the Iroquoian position as equal allies of the Crown. Their letter similarly mentioned the history of that allegiance, and it included photographs of the Silver Covenant Chain and of the Two-Row Wampum Belt. It was deemed by military authorities that all five boys in question were "above the age of 18 years," and as a result they were not discharged from service.[60]

And the Wampum belt Treaty is inserded in here.

Having one row and Two Men standing, one man at each end of the row, holding the Covenent Silver Chain. This signifies the Two Nations. And the first Nation is Mohawks. Oneidas. Onondagas Cayugas, and Senecas, holding one end of the Covenent Silver Chain, and the British Nation holding the other end of the Covenent Silver Chain. Thus the two Nations did Covenented themselves together as Allies, to defend one another in case of war And if the British is in, and if the British needs War help, then the King or Queen will write a letter to the Governor General of Canada to ask the Six Nations Union Lords, now commonly called Chiefs. To ask them to help the British in their War.

Then the Six Nations Union Lords will hold a Council and they shall decide in their Council to help the British of their War. Then the Six Nations Union Lords will address to the Five War Chiefs, to prepare and get ready of their Common Warriors to go and help the British in their War.
And the next Wampum belt Treaty of Two rows in here.

This two rows of Wampum belt Treaty. Signifies the Two saparate Government shall exist. Namely;— the Mohawks. Oneidas. Onondagas. Cayugas, and Senecas, and the British Nation's Government. So the Two saparate Government shall exist and Independently from each other, forever.

ILLUS. 19. Letter from Six Nations Mothers to the King, January 1917. *Library and Archives Canada, RG10 Vol. 6767, File 452-15.*

In a demonstration of allied sovereignty with the Crown, Lieutenant Frederick Loft, a Mohawk, represented the Iroquois Confederacy as a Pine Tree chief in an audience with the king on 21 February 1918. The Confederacy, in an expression of autonomy, had unilaterally declared war on Germany in April 1917 as an ally of both the United States and the British Empire.[61]

British propaganda promoted the war as a joint imperial effort and lauded the national war efforts of its colonies and dominions. According to George Robb, "Visual depictions of the imperial 'family of nations' appeared frequently on war posters and commercial advertisements, though the images typically privileged British people by placing them front and centre, flanked by people from the white dominions, with Indians and Africans in the background." Dominion loyalty was illustrated through propaganda films such as *Sons of the Empire, Canadians on the Western Front, New Zealand Troops in France, A Chinese Labour Contingent,* and *A South African Native Labour Contingent.*[62] A May 1916 Canadian newspaper article remarked that "Hundreds of Indians of military age have enlisted. One sees the brown faces in many a battalion, and in the centres near a reserve scores are in the ranks and in the uniform. It reminds one of the human colour-box in the war as a whole, for the world armies include all shades of flesh, from the whitest of white faces to the blackest of ebony, with all the variegated shades in between."[63]

Blood Indian private George Strangling Wolf was elated to have seen "the Great White King" while in England.[64] By all accounts Indians enjoyed the culture and people of Britain and France, despite the fact that British and French society had ignorant, if not romantic, perceptions of them. Canadian Frank Ferguson recalled in his diary the story of a young boy asking him and his mates who they were. After responding that they were Canadians, the young boy exclaimed, "Strike me pink, Cannydians, and you're white!" Ferguson added, "I suppose he shared the popular idea that all Canadians were redskins." Another Canadian, H.J. Elliot, wrote to his parents amused that the people in Britain "have great ideas about Canada. They imagined we were all wild savages or cowboys that lived in tents, and forests were everywhere, and no farm land." Willard Melvin echoed this British perception in a letter to his father: "A Canadian up here is something of a curio, you can hear people on the street saying, 'There's a Canadian,' like I was a strange animal of some kind!"[65]

Indians, like their white comrades, enjoyed leave in France and England. Private Daniel Pelletier from the Keeseekoose reserve in Saskatchewan remarked, "You could see different places and different people … a chance to see other countries, after all, we had nothing here [in Canada]."[66] Private Mike Foxhead, a nineteen-year-old Blackfoot from Alberta, wrote home to his agent while in England: "Glad to say everything is going on fine and dandy.… I should say this country is very nice. I like it all right.… I am over here at present training. I wanted to do my bit like all other Canadians."[67] Overseas, Indians visited the tourist sights and frequented the bars and brothels. Private John Redbean, an Ojibwa from Manitoba, proudly declared in a letter to his brother shortly after the Battle of Vimy Ridge in 1917, "Whenever I go to England and France I let you know … I always lay with girls such as French, Scotch, Jews and Galacians [sic] too, they are all young girls and they always tease us on the streets whenever we go out for a walk."[68] Others, like Private Joseph DeLaronde, an Ojibwa from Lake Nipigon, Ontario, married "war brides." DeLaronde married the English nurse who tended his wounds while he was convalescing. The couple returned to his reserve after the war. At least two other known Indian soldiers married in England and returned to their communities with their British brides following the war.[69]

The issue of Indians drinking alcohol did not seem to cause any significant problems. For many, the rum ration was their first exposure to alcohol, as, in principle, the *Indian Act* forbade them from buying or possessing alcohol. Ojibwa private Alfred J. Cook, of the St. Peter's reserve, Manitoba, stated that he had always given his ration to a friend and that "I never drank any intoxicating alcohol all the time I was in the army." However, one day after an intense German bombardment, he drank it and recalled that he had to be restrained by his mates from jumping "over the top" to take on the Germans: "I'll say it was fire water. I was really set on fire. I was going to clean up the whole German Army!"[70] While convalescing in England, Pegahmagabow complained in a letter to Scott in March 1917, "My only enemy is right here in England, right here of Whisky. Fire Water, which is about the only thing we could buy out here, which is very toleranent [sic] amusement. I don't want it, to be in such a habit.… I have been a good boy."[71]

A similar concern was voiced by J.W. McLennan, police chief of Kamsack, Saskatchewan, in January 1916: "In this town we have a unit of soldiers [including] several treaty Indians who have enlisted. The object of this letter is to ask your opinion as to whether these men are still to be considered as *Indians* or *British Subjects* as regards procuring Liquor. Several of these Indians have demanded their right, as British Subjects to be allowed their freedom to procure or purchase Intoxicating Liquor." The reply simply stated "that Indians who enlist still retain their status as Indians, and are subject to the provisions of the Indian Act."[72] Four Indians from Walpole Island of the 149th Lambton Battalion training at London, Ontario, "found that the Indian is not being treated as the White man in uniforms, the understanding in the first place we was to be treated in every respect as another Soldier in Canada. We was slighted at in those Public Hotels, turn down because we were Indians. We understood to have the same privileges as any white man in Canada. If we do not get those Privileges we will take the Kings uniforms off and we will live according to the conditions of the British treaty," in other words, exempt from military service. Indian Affairs replied to the local agent, T.A. McCallum: "It may be that they are under the impression that because they have donned the uniform, they would be privileged to obtain liquor from bars on the same conditions as white soldiers. This, of course, is not the case, as it is still an offense under the Indian Act to sell liquor to an Indian even if in uniform.... If these Indians have any complaints as to their treatment in the regiment, they might be submitted to the Department." Once overseas, however, there was no enforcement of the clause preventing Indians from buying or drinking alcohol, and in fact many commanders (succumbing to the stereotype of the "drunken Indian") praised their Indians for their sobriety.[73]

The issue of soldiering as a medium to attain equal rights, including the franchise, was frequently referred to in correspondence directed at Ottawa and London from band councils and individual Indian soldiers and civilians. In January 1916, shortly after official sanction to enlist Indians, Kwawkewlth, British Columbia, Indian agent W.M. Halliday reported to Indian Affairs that his wards expressed that because they "were not voters, and as they had not been consulted either with regard to the taking away of their original heritage, or in the formation of any of our laws they did not feel called upon to take up arms for the flag."[74] The Ontario Committee of Allied Tribes wrote to Borden in November 1917 reminding the patriotic prime minister that "We cannot say that we are fighting for our liberty, freedom and other privileges dear to all nations, for we have none."[75] Conversely, the Indians of the Fort Steele Agency in British Columbia declared to their agent, R.L. Galbraithe, in December 1915 that "they are not in sympathy with the 'Indian Rights Movement.'" This statement was made in an application to secure "Special Game Permits" from

Indian Affairs.[76] In 1913 British Columbia introduced racially stipulated quotas on fishing and hunting licences to favour "white-preference." As a result, many Indians were denied these privileges. Nevertheless, many still participated in these traditional enterprises, while others worked on commercial fishing and sealing vessels and in local canneries.[77]

Many other councils and chiefs wrote to the king or to the Colonial Office requesting the intervention of the British government to secure equal rights, since Indians were fighting directly for the Crown. For example, Ojibwa chief George Fisher questioned the foreign secretary, Sir Edward Grey, over the validity of Indians fighting when "We are not citizens and have no votes, as free men—the Indian Department looks at us as minors in the eyes of the law—and our boys are loyal to the flag.... Sir Sam Hughes, M.P. Minister of Militia of Ottawa should be notified at once—if the Home Government [British] wants his red children to enlist."[78]

A letter to Scott from Private M.E. Steinhauer, of the Saddle Lake Alberta Cree, serves as an example of the countless petitions and letters from councils and individuals across Canada: "I have been wondering since I joined the army whether we are going to get anything out of our country that we are going to fight for.... What I want to find out is, is there a possible chance of us getting our franchise ... after the war is over? I do not think it would be fair not to get anything out of a country that we are fighting for." In July 1916 G.B. Nicholson, chairman of the recruiting committee in the remote community of Chapleau, Ontario (300 kilometres north of Sault Ste. Marie), asked Scott "in connection with the enlistment of Indians for Overseas Service ... whether any inducement can be held out to the Indians in the way of special treatment after the war is over such as giving them the right of the franchise or any special concession on government lands?... A number of Indians enlisting, that question has been put up to me." Scott's reply was in keeping with assimilationist policy and with the refusal of government officials to let Indian war service alter the status quo or be used to promote Indian grievances. Scott stated that he was not aware of any special terms, but "they have exactly the same rights as other soldiers, they have already their share in the Indian reserve lands.... If you mean enfranchisement under the terms of the Indian Act, any Indian who can qualify has now the right to be enfranchised [by relinquishing status] ... probably we might be able to consider individual cases of returned soldiers when the war is over." Indian Affairs superintendent general Arthur Meighen acknowledged that "public interest has recently been attracted to this matter [enfranchisement], owing to the large number of Indians who have enlisted in the Canadian Expeditionary Force."[79] In August 1917 the *New York Times* stated: "The agitation for citizenship is now led by the better educated of the old chiefs of the tribes … who have given their sons freely, and when these young warriors return, their education broadened by contact with the death grapple … it goes without saying that they, too, will expect some voice in the direction of their country's affairs."[80]

A benefit of war service was the interaction between whites and Indians, something not common within the general Canadian populace. On 8 December 1916 Fiset wrote, "No complaints have been received by this Department [Militia] that Indians do not receive as good treatment as others." According to James Dempsey, Indians "got along well with their comrades and after a short time little if any distinctions existed between the Indian and the white soldiers. They entered into sports and pastimes of one kind or another, and took furloughs together." In October 1916 Prime Minster Borden questioned the Ministry of Militia as to whether Indian soldiers were being properly treated.[81] Not only did Indians participate in sporting activities, a few Indian soldiers had been famous athletes prior to enlisting and dominated inter-Allied running competitions. Onondaga private Tom Longboat, from the Six Nations reserve, served as a dispatch runner with the 107th Battalion and won numerous inter-Allied races. He had won the Boston Marathon in 1907 in record time and represented Canada at the 1908 London Olympics. Joseph Keeper of the Norway House Cree ran in the 1912 Stockholm Olympics. During actions at Cambrai in 1917, he was awarded the Military Medal for bravery. Prior to enlisting in December 1916 into the 114th Battalion, Tuscarora Arthur Jamieson of the Six Nations placed eighth in the 1916 Boston Marathon. Both Keeper and Jamieson eventually served as runners with the 107th and participated in, and won, several wartime competitions. The achievements of these soldier-runners were frequently published in Canadian trench newspapers and in the 107th Battalion's routine orders, at the insistence of Lieutenant Colonel Campbell.[82] In addition, Private Alex Decoteau of the Red Pheasant Cree of Saskatchewan placed sixth in the 5,000-metre race at the Stockholm Olympics. He served with the 202nd "Edmonton Sportsmen's" Battalion and the 49th (Edmonton) Battalion and was killed during the Battle of Passchendaele on 30 October 1917 after winning two Allied sports competitions and receiving a gold pocket watch from King George V.[83]

ILLUS. 20. Onondaga Private Tom Longboat of the Six Nations Reserve Buying a "Trench Paper," June 1917. *Library and Archives Canada, PA-001479.*

In addition to their athletic abilities, reports and war diaries indicate that many Indians were well liked for their sense of humour. Thomas A. Britten states that many officers thought their Indian soldiers possessed an "extraordinarily keen sense of humor" and did not seem so "reticent about it."[84] Mountain Horse relates how his fellow Blood, George Coming Singer, became his battalion's "clown" and a favourite of all: "Another new recruit to our battalion was a white man by the name of Kaiser. One morning, at roll call, when his unusual name was called, George Coming Singer, an Indian boy at the other end of the line ... yelled out, 'That's the bird I'd like to get a shot at.'" Although his comrades burst out in laughter, and Coming Singer became somewhat of a treasured member of his battalion, he was punished with latrine duty.[85]

War necessity led to the inclusion of Indians in unprecedented numbers, and their heightened interaction with their fellow countrymen was beneficial to mutual understanding and respect. The exposure of Indian soldiers to those from a conglomeration of Allied nations influenced their perceptions of Canadian society, of whites, and of themselves. For the majority of men who served in the Great War, the camaraderie created by the horrors of trench warfare transcended race. From the historical record available, it appears that the age-old adage of relying on the man beside you in combat, and in turn fighting for him, held true for most men of the Canadian Expeditionary Force, regardless of race, colour, or creed.

For all nations, the sacrifice of the First World War was measured in blood and the staggering number of dead. This was no different for the Indian nations of Canada. They shared equally in the burdens of war, and they still remind the government of their sacrifices for king and country. Indian casualty rates, however, cannot be precisely calculated, since race was generally not recorded on military records. Between December 1918 and February 1919, Scott attempted to discern the exact number of Indians who served in the CEF, and their war particulars and resident Indian status. Based on nominal roles and soldier-specific details submitted by individual agents (or reserves), it is known for certain that at least 4,000 status Indians served in the CEF and that they suffered roughly 1,200 casualties (or a 30 percent casualty rate). For example, 292 men from the Six Nations reserve served overseas (roughly 6.5 percent of the total reserve population, compared to the Euro-Canadian enlistment rate of 5.4 percent of Canada's total population). Of these 292 Six Nations men, thirty-five were killed, fifty-five were wounded, and two were taken prisoner, representing an overall casualty rate of 32 percent. The lesser Indian casualty rate compared to the larger CEF can be attributed to their late inclusion as soldiers, and to the high proportion who served in support units, such as forestry, labour, and pioneer battalions.

The figure of 4,000 represents 35 percent of Indian males of military age, equal to the percentage of Euro-Canadians who enlisted, and comparable to the Euro-Australian percentage of 38.7 (see Table 3).[86] These numbers exclude non-status Indians, Eskimos, and Métis, and are based on the 1914 status-Indian population of 103,774, which increased only slightly during the war years. (The 1917 population was 105,998.) This was a substantial commitment, given that most Indian enlistment occurred after December 1915. It was testimony to the historical and contemporary allegiance of Indians to the British Crown, either directly or via Canada itself. The *Brantford Expositor* proudly claimed that "As in the Revolutionary War and in the War of 1812, so in the Great War the Six Nations stood by their Ancient Treaties with the British Crown.... The blood of the Iroquois warriors of 1776 and 1812 ran true in the veins of their descendants in 1914–1918."[87]

ILLUS. 21. "We shall not sleep": Canadian Dead at the Battle of Mount Sorrel (Hill 62), June 1916. *Library and Archives Canada, PA-000186.*

Category	Canada	Indian
Population, 1914	7,879,000	103,774
Mobilized	629,000	N/A
% Total Population	8.0	N/A
Served in Theatre	422,405	4,000 (estimate)
% Total Population	5.4	3.9
% Mobilized	67.2	N/A
Casualties (including dead)	241,000	1,200 (estimate)
% Moblized	38.3	N/A
% in Theatre	57.1	30.0

TABLE 3. Statistical Comparison of Canadian and Indian Soldiers
Source: Statistics are based on a comparison of the most reliable primary, secondary and government departmental records, including "Return of Indian Enlistments" forms from the Department of Indian Affairs.

In addition to war casualties, the 1918–19 Spanish influenza pandemic devastated indigenous populations, more so than those of their white counterparts. The drastically lower socio-economic standing of Canada's indigenous peoples, their lack of accessibility to heath care, and their well-documented susceptibility to Old World diseases, most notably tuberculosis, were all factors in the higher proportion of sickness and deaths due to the influenza virus. Although global death figures are estimates, recent research concludes that roughly 50 million people died worldwide of the Spanish influenza, compared to a total 10 million war-service deaths or 16 million war-related deaths, including civilian fatalities.

Influenza affected one in six Canadians, resulting in more than 50,000 deaths nationwide (0.62 percent of the total population). By comparison, an estimated 3,500 status Indians died of the disease (3 percent of the total Indian population). The Indian death rate was five times higher than that of the rest of Canada, while tuberculosis rates were twenty times higher than for Euro-Canadians.[88] This says nothing about Eskimo mortality rates. For example, the death rate in Labrador reached 10 percent of the total population and 30 percent of the Eskimo population. The Eskimo villages of Hebron and Okak were literally erased. At Hebron, 86 of the 100 residents died. At Okak, 204 residents from a total of 263 succumbed to the disease by December 1918, and by January every male from Okak was dead. At Sillutalik, the flu killed forty of forty-five residents, while thirteen of eighteen people died at Orlik.[89] A 2008 article for *Emerging Infectious Diseases* outlines, "In various communities of Canada … mortality rates were estimated to be 3–70x higher for indigenous than for non-indigenous populations."[90] Nevertheless, following the war, the Indian population began a slow recovery and by 1939 had increased to 118,406.[91]

While the number of Canadian Indians awarded honours is not officially known, Veterans Affairs states that "at least 50 medals were awarded to aboriginal people in Canada for bravery and heroism."[92] Lieutenants Alexander Smith (Six Nations)[93] and Alexander Brass (File Hills Cree) won the Military Cross, and Pegahmagabow was awarded the Military Medal three times. Enlisting with his brother in April 1916, Private Francis Misinishkotewe, an Ojibwa from Manitoulin Island, Ontario, was awarded the Cross of the Order of St. George (4th Class), the highest Imperial Russian military decoration.[94] Indian Affairs correspondence incorrectly indicates that Private Joseph Francis Monture of the Six Nations was recommended for but did not receive the Victoria Cross.

He was in fact promoted to captain and transferred to the 114th Battalion. No records exist for a soldier of that name in connection to the Victoria Cross, but these occurrences can be linked to Captain Frank Weaver Montour.[95] In addition to casualties and honours, the commitment to the war effort on the home front was shared by all Canadians, including Indians.

Chapter Eight

On the Home Front

In 1917 a mother from the Oneida settlement,[1] outside of London, Ontario, proudly stated, "Yes, I have given four of my boys, and I am sorry that my other children died when they were babies, for I would gladly have given them, too, to fight for England."[2] She had three sons fighting on the Western Front, and the fourth, who enlisted at age fifteen, was discovered as underage in England but was held back for training at Wittley Camp. All had originally enlisted in the 114th Battalion. Her fifth son successfully enlisted at fourteen years of age in 1917 but was released at Halifax prior to embarkation.[3] The enthusiasm for the war effort among Indians was evident on the home front and was felt by women as well as men. Indian women served as nurses and were active in patriotic organizations. For example, Edith Montour of the Six Nations reserve served as a nurse with the U.S. Medical Corps. By 1917 she was stationed in Vittel, France, treating wounded soldiers: "Sometimes we would walk right over to where there had been fighting. It was an awful sight ... whole towns blow[n] up."[4] Fourteen American Indian women served as nurses, and the number of Canadian Indian women is not known.[5]

Indian women also formed patriotic and Red Cross societies on their reserves. They made bandages, knitted various items of clothing, and raised funds by selling traditional crafts. The Canadian Red Cross Society stated that the articles made by Indian women were the finest quality of knitting and sewing they received.[6] The Six Nations Women's Patriotic League, formed in October 1914, produced the greatest yield of needlework of any reserve. In early November the council chiefs granted the league fifty dollars to purchase supplies, and the local patriotic organization in Brantford gave them fifteen dollars' worth of yarn: "This League will do the Indian women good this winter ... they could easily knit one or two hundred dollars worth of yarn. They can do the work, but they cannot get the money and there is prejudice against working through the white people." On 22 November the *Brantford Expositor* celebrated the league's first shipment of one hundred pairs of socks and mitts and one hundred toques and scarves, while also highlighting the general contributions of the community. Similarly, on 29 January 1915 the *Globe* praised the league's efforts.[7]

Although the women continued to produce large quantities of socks and other articles, in February shipments and further knitting were temporarily postponed as the community experienced a minor outbreak of smallpox. In May Mrs. A.M. Garlow, secretary and treasurer of the league, wrote to Scott asking if "we could now send them … now that it [small-pox] has passed away.… It gives me great satisfaction to know that there are some Six Nation blood being shed again." Garlow, the daughter of Chief Josiah Hill, who supported Merritt's 1914–15 proposal for the formation of a Six Nations battalion, added that the community was still divided over the issue of service and patriotic donations to Canada rather than directly to the Crown. Nevertheless, after fumigation shipments were again sent and knitting resumed for the remainder of the war. The league also published and sold a "Descriptive Booklet of the Part Played by the Six Nations Indians in the Great War" in January 1917 to raise funds for supplies and to promote the war effort on the reserve and in surrounding non-Indian communities.[8] The neighbouring Mississauga of the Credit donated $300 to the Patriotic Fund, and the women "assisted the Hagersville branch of the Red Cross both by knitting and making other necessary articles for the men at the front."[9]

ILLUS.22. Members of the File Hills Red Cross Society, 1915. *Library and Archives Canada, C-033262.*

ILLUS.23. Patriotic Concert Poster, File Hills, Saskatchewan, March 1915. *Library and Archives Canada, e010697173.*

Similar patriotic organizations were formed on reserves across Canada. For example, in December 1914 the eighty-eight children of the Fisher River reserve (Manitoba) missionary school wrote to Princess Mary and donated handmade "Christmas gifts to the Sailors and Soldiers who are fighting for the British Empire [and] assure you that our good wishes are greater than the size of our gifts … for our people are poor." The girls from Moosomin's reserve (Battleford, Saskatchewan) school made twelve shirts, which were donated to soldiers through a package and letter to the wife of the governor general. Many other reserves reported that articles of clothing were being made by young girls in order to teach them needlework. This practice was encouraged by Scott and his department. In British Columbia, agent Thomas Deasy reported that the Massett Indians donated two large boxes of handmade curios to be sold at a Red Cross carnival. He also noted that "handiwork" was being done by girls at the missionary schools. [10]

ILLUS. 24. "Canadian Patriotic Indian Chiefs," c. 1915-16. *Library and Archives Canada, PA-030224.*

In addition to women-specific contributions, Indian councils and individuals donated money to war funds and contributed to the agricultural and industrial output of Canada's booming wartime economy and military industrial complex. Mike Mountain Horse proudly stated, "From the outset of this colossal struggle the Red Man demonstrated his loyalty to the British Crown in a very convincing manner. Patriotic and other war funds were generously subscribed to, and various lines of war work participated in at home."[11]

In keeping with Indian Affairs protocol, however, Indian donations to patriotic funds were used as a propaganda tool to increase monetary offerings by all Canadians. In November 1916 the honorary secretary of the Canadian Patriotic Fund, Sir Herbert Ames, received a letter from an Onion Lake, Saskatchewan, Cree, Moo-che-we-in-es, with his contribution of $1.50. Ames wrote to Scott: "We are now looking for every human story we can get to help our campaign for the Canadian Patriotic Fund.... Can you get the story, or could you get him to write a letter, as to why he made the subscription? We can use this to our advantage in the press." Moo-che-we-in-es was persuaded to write a note using Cree syllabics, which was translated into English:

> You asked me to tell you a story about how it came into my mind to pay a little towards "War Money." I heard there was a big war going on over there and I feel like I want to help you in some way and the best I can do is to send a little money for I can't go myself as I am nearly blind. This is to show you I like to help you. I am an Indian. I heard that other Indians were going to give 25 cents each out of their treaty money. I give $1.50 out of the money from the Government for beef I sell the Agency. I am about 50 years old and my wife and two sons are living with me and my son's wife and her child. That is the way I make up that $1.50—25 cents for six. I shake hands to you, Moo-che-we-in-es.

The letter was passed on to Ames, who quickly wrote Scott, "That letter ... is one of the best things I have seen.... If you have anything more as good as this, send it on. We could always utilize advantageously any human story."[12] Moo-che-we-in-es's letter was made into a Patriotic Fund poster that was used across Canada, including reserves.

ILLUS. 25. Moo-che-we-in-es Patriotic Fund Poster, c. 1917. *Library and Archives Canada, C-098670.*

Despite their substantial donations to the Canadian Patriotic Fund, which was designed to aid families of soldiers in hardship, Indian families could not draw on its resources: "The dependants of these Indian soldiers are wards of the Government, and draw living rations from the Government and have no rents to pay, hence since they are a charge on the Government of Canada, and as the Government of Canada is responsible for their maintenance, and for these reasons we cannot recommend that they participate in the distribution of the Patriotic Funds."[13] Immediately after the correspondence concerning Moo-che-we-in-es, Scott wrote Ames in February 1917: "May I hope that you will issue instructions that the dependents of Indian soldiers are to receive the same consideration as whites."[14] Only after Ames and the executive of the Patriotic Fund were made aware of Indian contributions was the policy changed in April 1917, so that "families of Indians who have listed be treated in the same manner as those of other nationalities."[15]

By the end of the war, Indians had donated almost $45,000 to war funds (or forty-three cents per Indian). A further $8,841 was not accepted, as Indian Affairs deemed that certain bands were not in a financial position to make the donations requested out of their monthly funds (see Table 4).[16] By comparison, Canadians donated nearly $50 million to the Patriotic Fund and other war-related charities (or $6.20 per person). This discrepancy should not be taken out of context.

Province	Canadian Patriotic Fund	National Red Cross	Local Patriotic and Red Cross Funds	Other War Funds, including Belgian Relief Fund	TOTAL
Saskatchewan	4,691.00	326.55	11,945.75	24.60	17,257.90
Ontario	6,927.55	697.00	2,759.15	N/A	10,383.70
Alberta	3,143.65	230.10	4,775.65	507.50	8,656.90
British Columbia	447.11	359.25	4,241.00	N/A	5,047.36
Manitoba	811.60	1,029.50	1,178.50	N/A	3,019.60
Quebec	50.00	25.00	100.00	5.00	180.00
TOTAL	16,340.91	2,667.40	25,000.05	537.10	44,454.46

TABLE 4. Indian Patriotic Donations (in dollars)
Source: LAC, RG10, Vol. 6762, File 452-3. Native Contributions to War Funds; Duncan Campbell Scott, *1919 Report of the Deputy Superintendent General of Indian Affairs, Sessional Paper No. 27: The Indians and the Great War* (Ottawa: King's Printer, 1920), 20–25.

Indians joined the CEF in equal per-capita numbers as Euro-Canadians and generally supported the war effort on the home front. These figures are simply indicative of the inferior economic position of Indians within Canadian society.[17]

Canadian Indians also purchased Victory Bonds, although few were in a financial position to do so. The Department of Indian Affairs refused requests by reserves to invest their band funds from Ottawa in Victory Bonds, given that the accumulation of interest would be the same, since all Indian funds belonged to the government. Canadian Victory Bond purchases, however, exceeded $2 billion.[18]

Many Indian communities connected their patriotic donations and agricultural pursuits to military exemption from conscription. The Saskatchewan Onion Lake Cree wrote to Indian Affairs, "All thank you very much for letting us off from conscription. We mean to do all we can for the war by giving all we can afford to the Patriotic Fund and by trying to grow as much grain as we can." The Bella Bella of British Columbia donated $400 "as a show of loyalty to the King." According to their Indian agent, G.E. Darby, "There are many arguments against conscripting Indians but this letter [from the band council] is not intended to set forth but simply to show that although opposed to conscription, they are willing to contribute to patriotic funds, to do all they can in procuring fish for food and anything else that they know how to for the good of the Nation." W.B. Cromlie, the agent at Frog Lake, Saskatchewan, explained to Indian Affairs that his Cree "would rather pay than have any of their men taken to fight. I explained to them that you would be pleased to receive any contribution they might make, but that it would have nothing to do with conscription.... I may say that the application of the Act will no doubt result in more energetic efforts on the part of the Indians this coming year in farm operations."[19]

Despite the contributions of Indian peoples on and off the battlefield, the Canadian government continued its practice of appropriating Indian land when it felt the need. It must be remembered that neither Indian reserves nor band funds belonged to Indians themselves. Ownership and control was vested in the Crown through Indian Affairs. In 1917 Arthur Meighen, Canadian minister of the interior and Indian Affairs, launched the Greater Production Effort program to increase agricultural production on Indian reserves: "We will still leave him enough to trap on, but even if we did not, thirty bushels of wheat to the acre is a lot better than a few squirrels caught by the Indian."[20] Section 90, sub-sections 2 and 3 of the *Indian Act* were altered, under the argument that many reserves were too vast to be completely utilized by the Indians. It was amended so that these lands, if not sold to the government, would be expropriated and leased to whites for agricultural pursuits. In total, 313,398 acres of reserve land were subject to these actions.[21] According to Meighen it was necessary to remove power from "what one may call reactionary or recalcitrant Indian bands to check their own progress by refusing consent to the utilization of their funds or vacant land for their own advantage."[22]

Sub-section 2 of the revision gave the federal government power "to deal with the council of a band who through some delusion or misapprehension acts in a manner contrary to the best interests of the band, and refuses to sanction expenditures which the Governor in Council may consider necessary for the welfare and progress of the band." The need for expenditures to increase agricultural productivity was specifically mentioned, and the *Indian Act* was further amended to make use of "idle" band funds for investment in the Greater Production Effort. The government could dictate the use of reserve land, and band funds, with or without the consent of band councils. Sub-section 3 referred particularly to "large areas of land on Indian reserves [in western Canada] capable of pasturing cattle or producing wheat, and it is desired that all obstacles to the utilization of these lands should, in as far as possible be removed." These changes to the *Indian Act* reinforced those made in 1911 by the minister of the interior and superintendent general of Indian Affairs, Frank Oliver, commonly known as the Oliver Act. His 1911 amendments allowed municipalities or companies to expropriate reserve land, without surrender or consent, for the construction of roads, railways, and other "public works." In addition, the superintendent general was given power to relocate the entire populations of reserves adjacent to a town of 8,000 residents or more and to sell the vacated Indian land.[23] For example, in 1916 the 125 Mi'kmaq of the King's Road reserve (at the Sydney, Nova Scotia, harbour), were forced to relocate against their will. This land surrounding the port was valued for war and commercial shipping.[24]

On 23 April 1918 Meighen issued a statement in the House of Commons concerning his productivity campaign: "We need not waste any time in sympathy for the Indian, for I am pretty sure his interests will be looked after.... The Indian is a ward of the Government still. The presumption of the law is that he has not the capacity to decide what is for his ultimate benefit in the same degree as his guardian, the Government of Canada."[25] Sarah Carter believes that the inspiration for Meighen's program "may have come from the American example, launched in 1917, when the Bureau of Indian Affairs mobilized behind a plan to see that every tillable acre on Indian reservations be intensely cultivated."[26]

The Blood Indians of Alberta serve as a case study for the modifications made to the *Indian Act* for the Greater Production Effort. A 1916 government proposal to sell 90,000 acres had been refused by the Bloods. The head chief filed charges of bribery, fraud, and intimidation against the federal government through the Department of Indian Affairs. Although no legal action was ever taken, the government halted its attempt to seize the land. On 15 February 1918 the government invoked the new amendments and large tracts of land (90,000 acres) were forcibly leased to white farmers; the Indians living on that land were dispossessed. Although the years 1916 and 1917 saw the Blood reserve produce the highest yields of grains and cattle of any in Canada, in 1918 they were deprived of their lands to increase their own production. Wheat farming on the Blood reserve fell from 65,000 bushels in 1917 to 5,000 bushels in 1919. The scheme, however, remained in effect until 1922.[27]

Indian lands were also used directly by the Canadian military. In April 1917 Camp Mohawk was opened by the Imperial Munitions Board (IMB) on the Tyendinaga Mohawk reserve, Ontario, as a training facility for the Royal Flying Corps. After "considerable discussion and explanation," the elected (*Indian Act*) band council agreed to lease the land, provided that the IMB compensate them for all damages to infrastructure and livestock, and that local Indians be given preference for internal jobs. The training school accommodated roughly 900 to 1,000 airmen at any given time throughout 1918. The camp was closed at the end of the war but was again utilized, with Mohawk consent, during the Second World War. Although there were minor disagreements and tensions among Tyendinaga residents, the council, and the IMB, the situation surrounding Camp Mohawk was generally cooperative and indicative of J.R. Miller's observation that Indians were proactive and adopted strategies "to counter attempts to control their lives and eradicate their traditions." A similar situation occurred on the Sarcee reserve in Alberta in 1915, where land was leased for a military facility.[28] Following the First World War, Indian lands were again the object of expropriation under the *Soldier Settlement Act*, designed to aid veterans in establishing agricultural enterprises.

Although Indian lands were confiscated by the Greater Production Effort and for military use, Indian pastoral production increased every subsequent year during the war. This despite the fact that many young men were in uniform, thereby reducing the number of farmers and labourers. The total value of harvested Indian crops increased from $1,856,424 in 1914 to $3,142,016 by 1918. Wheat production improved from 262,726 bushels (on 17,928 acres) in 1914 to 388,731 bushels (on 24,834 acres) in 1917. The value of sold livestock also increased from $307,678 in 1914 to $424,479 in 1918. The total number of farm animals owned by Indians grew from 159,769 to 202,418 over the same time period. Total Indian income from all occupations rose from $6.44 million in 1914 to $9.52 million in 1918 (see Table 5).[29]

According to John Sutton Lutz in his volume *Makuk: A New History of Aboriginal-White Relations* (2010):

> By 1917, the expansion of war industries turned labour surplus into a labour shortage, and Aboriginal People were again drawn into the labour force.... It is apparent that Aboriginal People shared in the increase in wartime employment, from 1914–1919, alongside other Canadians. Yet, despite the rising dollar income, wartime inflation caused real income (constant dollars) to plummet. In the 1920s, real income rose until it hit the prewar levels in 1929–30, then it plummeted again [during the Great Depression].[30]

During the war years, Lutz argues, Indians were "placed in a functional role that Karl Marx referred to as the 'reserve army of the unemployed.' Only in this case, 'reserve' had a double meaning." Just as the need for military manpower had resulted in the eventual inclusion of Indians as soldiers, the demands of wartime agriculture and industry led to Indians' enhanced position in the job market .

In 1918 Indian Affairs reported that "the prevailing wage paid for [Indian] farm labourers and for work in the saw mills and logging camps was higher than at any time previous."[31] Rolf Knight argues in *Indians at Work* (1996), that, as a result, "many semi-commercial Indian farmers began to shift to wage labour, allowing their farms to become subsistence gardens.... This process did not occur overnight.... Nor was it universal. But it had begun before World War I."[32] The comparative tables for the years 1914 and 1918 not only illustrate the dramatic increases in production and wages earned through various occupations, but also reveal regional differences. In British Columbia wages earned through the traditional modes of fishing and hunting/trapping

1914 Province	Farm Products	Beef Sold	Pastoral Wages	Farm Land Rentals	Fishing	Hunting/ Trapping	Other Industries	TOTAL Income
Prince Edward Island	950	N/A	N/A	N/A	2,225	75	3000	6,250
Nova Scotia	17,674	3,528	54,635	230	3,845	8,019	41,820	129,751
New Brunswick	7,169	300	53,325	97	9,565	1,440	14,136	86,032
Quebec	122,112	35,055	234,138	6,992	3,875	115,778	72,002	589,952
Ontario	474,888	26,399	581,364	24,313	105,003	160,462	139,834	1,521,263
Manitoba	119,861	10,220	129,569	245	76,372	459,643	45,060	840,970
Saskatchewan	287,482	92,780	88,513	N/A	74,004	242,174	74,792	859,745
Alberta	153,404	67,144	46,338	14,151	5,720	45,236	87,627	419,620
British Columbia	672,884	72,252	536,410	6,152	337,816	143,714	186,125	1,995,353
TOTAL	1,856,424	307,678	1,724,292	52,180	658,425	1,176,541	664,396	6,439,936

1918 Province	Farm Products	Beef Sold	Pastoral Wages	Farm Land Rentals	Fishing	Hunting/ Trapping	Other Industries	TOTAL Income
Prince Edward Island	2,150	150	550	N/A	950	55	6,500	10,335
Nova Scotia	22,010	5,086	77,810	270	7,735	5,693	33,675	152,570
New Brunswick	8,253	200	36,100	2,600	7,070	1,335	4,425	62,198
Quebec	219,048	36,908	421,848	21,671	9,652	114,692	63,129	899,898
Ontario	960,091	45,545	904,148	62,214	161,488	271,988	106,487	2,834,507
Manitoba	268,797	21,070	109,180	2,656	77,735	136,840	46,825	731,340
Saskatchewan	625,719	124,864	129,681	25,654	30,098	193,040	78,033	1,298,375
Alberta	397,673	118,296	138,680	42,925	5,085	32,741	90,508	915,912
British Columbia	638,305	72,360	408,452	8,309	651,130	278,036	246,365	2,321,587
TOTAL	3,142,016	424,479	2,226,449	166,299	950,943	1,314,429	675,947	9,516,864

TABLE 5. Sources and Values of Indian Income for 1914 and 1918 (in dollars)
Source: Office of Census and Statistics, *The Canada Yearbook, 1914, 1918* (Ottawa: King's Printer, 1915, 1919), 642, 599.

rose significantly. This included work in fish canneries. For example, in 1914 the number of Indian workers, male and female, employed by the Anglo-British Columbia Packing Company was 200 (or 32 percent of the total workforce). By 1917 this figure had risen to 550 (or 42 percent).[33]

Nevertheless, significant Indian participation in the war effort both on and off the battlefield did little to alter governmental policy. As Jonathan Vance asserts, "The dreams of a strong and vibrant pan-Canadian nationalism built on the memory of the Great War were dashed ... in the fact that its rhetoric was too often contradicted by the realities of peacetime. The memory of the war might have been able to work its magic among immigrants, Natives, and French-Canadians if it had been accompanied by some substantive steps towards the society it envisioned. As it was, the myth promised far more than it was able to deliver."[34] Indian veteran Private Daniel Pelletier remarked, "The army treated us all right ... there was no discrimination 'over there' and we were treated good."[35] This relative equality, however, was not manifest in government veteran programs and benefits, and Indians remained wards of the state under the paternalistic *Indian Act*.

Chapter Nine

Peace and Prejudice

Corporal Francis Pegahmagabow returned to his Parry Island reserve in April 1919, after having served as long as any Canadian soldier of the Great War. In the summer of 1919 he met numerous times with his Indian agent, Alexander Logan, to apply for a farming loan under the *Soldier Settlement Act* (*SSA*). He needed Logan's approval for the loan, and each application Pegahmagabow submitted was refused endorsement by his agent. Logan remarked that Pegahmagabow "was disabled and suffered from dementia," and that the site chosen "was most out of the way place for a successful farmer." Although Pegahmagabow wrote directly to Indian Affairs, and to the Soldiers Aid Commission, he received no land, loans, or grants under the *SSA*—certainly not just recompense for a three-time Military Medal winner.[1]

After the war, the government of Canada introduced financial and farm land grant programs for veterans. The first and largest of these initiatives was the *SSA* of 1919 (an amendment to the 1917 act).[2] The *SSA* provided veterans the opportunity to obtain dominion lands at no cost, or to purchase farms and equipment at low interest rates. Essentially, Indians were privy to all benefits of the *SSA*, on par with all other veterans. The act specified, however, that the Department of Indian Affairs was charged with the administration of all benefits, allowances, and pensions for Indians, "thus avoiding the confusion which would inevitably arise if their affairs were administered partly by the Department of Indian Affairs and partly by the Soldier Settlement Board." Although the amendments gave Duncan Campbell Scott "all powers of the Soldier Settlement Board except those of expropriation," applications by Indian veterans were subject to the approval of their individual Indian agents, "who have personal knowledge of the capabilities and needs of Indian returned soldiers."[3] In May 1919 Scott issued all agents with a six-page "guide" pertaining to Indians, the *SSA*, and the duties and power of an agent, stressing that "It must be borne in mind that loans will be made *only to such returned soldiers as have experience in farming or are likely to make success of farming operations.*" For example, Private

Eli Commandant, a Mohawk from the Wahta (Gibson, Muskoka) reserve, applied in 1921 for a wood-sawing machine. Indian Affairs rejected his application, stating that such grants were only made to "bona fide farmers." Interestingly, Eli, who was recruited by Cooke for the 114th in April 1916, was listed as a "farmer" on his attestation papers.[4] Agents were highly selective in order to limit expenditures, and very few Indian applications were endorsed.[5]

As did other governmental policies, the SSA conflicted directly with a 1906 amendment to the Indian Act that stated, "No Indian or non-treaty Indian resident in the provinces of Manitoba, Saskatchewan, Alberta or the Territories shall be held capable of having acquired or acquiring a homestead or pre-emption right under any Act respecting Dominion lands ... in the said provinces and territories."[6] This discrepancy was illuminated when many veterans applied under the SSA to take up farming on their respective reserves. Reserve land could be used personally by any Indian but could not be owned by any Indian, as it remained property of the Crown. Nevertheless, it was "proposed to settle the Indian soldiers as far as possible on reserves belonging to the bands of which they are members ... without the consent of the council of the band."[7] Thus, the small number of Indians who received reserve lands were given a "Certificate of Possession" of little legal value. Indians were also wary of applying for land grants off reserve, having substantiated fears of losing their Indian status and the attached rights guaranteed by treaty and governmental obligations.[8] In this sense, the application of the SSA to Indians was another means of assimilation; it forced Indian veterans and their families off reserve in order to gain the benefits of post-war programs.

While it is known that ten Indians in Ontario and Quebec and six from the prairie provinces received land grants off reserve without losing status, most applicants were denied this right. Only one in ten Indian veterans who applied received loans or land grants on reserve. By 1920 only 160 had received loans. According to Scott, "the needs of an Indian farmer would not perhaps be as extensive as the needs of a white farmer." He maintained that loans should be kept as "low as possible in order not to burden the settler with too large a repayment."[9] Some veterans were denied land as a result of band councils simply ignoring the ministry and refusing the allocation of land to veterans. Personal ownership of land was not customary among most Indian nations; land remained communal because people belonged to Turtle Island (the Earth), not the other way around. Other veterans simply did not apply for fear of overriding band councils and being alienated from their communities.

In fact, the government used the *SSA* to expropriate reserve land. Eastern European immigrants, who came in large numbers at the turn of the century, had been granted most of the fertile Crown land in the prairies. Suitable farm land was required to meet the promises of the *SSA*. An Order in Council (PC 929), ratified on 23 April 1919, granted the Department of Indian Affairs (under the regulations of the *SSA*, 1919) authority to expropriate reserve land "not under cultivation or otherwise properly used" without the consent of the Indians or their councils. Under this law, almost 86,000 acres of reserve land was confiscated and given to white veterans (see Table 6). Due to these circumstances, land claims are ongoing in British Columbia and Alberta.[10]

Indians of Vancouver Island protested to the DIA that parcelling out their lands to white veterans "would be unfair to those of our race who are sleeping in France and Flanders. This is what the Kaiser would have done to us all, whites and Indians, if he had won the war."[11] When an elderly Sioux man was asked in conversation with his agent what should be done with the Kaiser, he replied that he should be "confined to a reservation, given an allotment, and forced to farm." He added that the agent should tell the Kaiser, "Now you lazy bad man, you farm and make your living by farming, rain or no rain; and if you do not make your own living don't come to the Agency whining when you have no food in your stomach, and no money, but stay here on your farm and grow fat till you starve."[12]

After petitioning the government, knowing that the land would be taken without compensation, most bands settled for monetary sums, which were usually equivalent to fair market value. However, even the $1.01 million that was awarded to the Indians for the 85,844 acres was not given directly to the bands; rather, it was held in trust by the DIA, which promised to disperse the money to the various reserves when it saw fit. The 18,223-acre Ochapowace Cree reserve in Saskatchewan was confiscated for $164,160 under protest from the band and the nearby white community. The Cree were forced to relocate to the Sioux reserve at Dundurn. The money was withheld by the DIA, to be used and divided at a later date, and neither the Cree nor the Sioux (traditional enemies) were consulted about their forced co-habitation.[13]

Province	Acres	Paid ($)	Per Acre ($)
Saskatchewan	68,803	831,148	11.91
Alberta	15,887	169,462	10.67
British Columbia	154	12,280	79.74
TOTAL	85,844	1,012,890	11.80

TABLE 6. Reserve Land Sold or Confiscated under the *Soldier Settlement Act*
Source: Fred Gaffen, *Forgotten Soldiers* (Penticton: Theytus Books, 1985), 135.

In conjunction with the Order in Council, an unofficial arrangement was made by the Department of Indian Affairs, in light of the *SSA*, to minimize the amount of land given to Indian veterans on the reserves, since reserve land could be appropriated only if it was not in "proper use."[14] The obvious outcome was that unused reserve land was taken under the *SSA*, leaving little for Indian veterans. It was known by the DIA that Indians were wary of applying for non-reserve land grants. These arrangements reduced the amount of reserve land for Indians, both veterans and non-veterans, while procuring more fertile farm land for non-Indian veterans under the *SSA*; hence, Indian applications for land, loans, and grants subsequently diminished. According to the 1927 *Sixth Report of the Soldier Settlement Board of Canada*, only 224 land grants or loans had been issued to Indian veterans, "most in the Province of Ontario [184 of 224].... The Indians mostly had their locations on the reserves."[15]

Indian veterans also did not receive equal consideration for pensions, disability, or War Veterans' Allowance, despite the promises of Scott in March 1915 that "arrangements will be made with reference to pensions ... Indians who have served in the war would no doubt participate. There could be no discrimination against them."[16] In late 1917 arrangements were made between the Ministry of Militia, the Board of Pension Commissioners, and Indian Affairs whereby responsibility for estates and pensions of Indians killed in the war, and those of Indian veterans, became the sole responsibility of the DIA. Scott wholly endorsed the idea, believing that pensions and any war gratuities should be directly controlled by his department "in order to protect the Indians, by being in a position to see that the money is properly expended, without waste or injudicious purchases.... I may therefore state that all 'Indians', whether treaty or non-treaty, come under the control of this Department." Although many did receive small compensations on a random individual case basis, most were denied on account of being "Indian." This is another example of the confused policy surrounding Indian war service. The ambiguity was obvious during the war in guidelines pertaining to Indian participation, and it was equally evident in repatriation programs during the immediate post-war years. Furthermore, any pension or disability relief to Indian veterans residing on reserve was administered by local agents. A resentful Corporal Pegahmagabow had to ask his agent John Daly to release his veteran funds in allotments, despite the fact that he was short of money and supporting a wife and six children: "He get [sic] it tied up in the bank so I could only get it with his approval. Then when I call for it, he expect me to get down on my knees for it and get sore before he would write me out a cheque."[17] After more than four years at war, and having been awarded three Military Medals and tallying 378 unofficial kills, Pegahmagabow was still, after all, an Indian. Eli Commandant applied for disability pension in 1924. He had received a serious head wound from shrapnel and suffered from dizziness, fainting, as well as shell shock, as verified by two official certificates from his doctor, A.M. Burgess. He was observed by a member of the pension board for one week, after which time it was concluded that Eli had no "medical condition present."[18]

No cognate policy existed among the DIA, the Ministry of Militia, or Veterans Affairs relating to pensions and monetary allocations until 1936. Under the *War Veterans Allowance Act*, only enfranchised Indians living off reserve were officially entitled to the same benefits as non-Indian veterans: "Returned Indian soldiers are subject to the provisions of the Indian Act and are in the same position as they were before enlisting," said Scott,[19] therefore, the allowances of forty dollars per month for a single and seventy dollars per month for a married veteran accorded by the act were not available to non-enfranchised Indian veterans—the vast majority.[20]

Under the current policies very few Indians enjoyed the franchise. A 1918 amendment, 122 A (1), to the *Indian Act* stated, "An Indian who holds no land in a reserve, does not reside on a reserve, and does not follow the Indian mode of life ... and satisfies the Superintendent General that he is self-supporting and fit to be enfranchised, and surrenders all claims whatsoever to any interest in the lands of the band to which he belongs ... the Governor-General may order that such an Indian be enfranchised."[21] Any application for enfranchisement also had to be accompanied by an endorsement from a clergyman, priest, notary public, or justice of the peace, as well as an Indian agent, that the applicant was "of good moral character, temperate in habits and of sufficient intelligence." The endorser also had to "report of the earning capacity of the individual Indian." To become enfranchised the applicant needed to be willing to denounce his Indian culture and heritage and become assimilated. By 1921 only 227 Indians, all from Ontario (212 from the Six Nations reserve), had been enfranchised under the new legislation. Furthermore, in 1920 the DIA passed an involuntary enfranchisement provision for "individual Indians or a band of Indians without the necessity of obtaining their consent ... where it was found upon investigation that the continuance of wardship was no longer in the interests of the public."[22]

In April 1936 Ojibwa private Thomas Peltier wrote to C.G. Power, the minister of pensions and national health. Peltier had been twice wounded in France and discharged as medically unfit, and he was receiving a twenty-four-dollar-a-month pension while supporting a wife and six children (all between three months and eleven years). Peltier explained, "I was not qualified for veteran's allowance because I was an Indian and residing on an Indian Reserve, the very same place from where I enlisted when the country needed my services. For this reason I cannot see why I should not get some help when I really need it.... If we are wards of the Indian Department there should be some arrangements made by the Pension Board and the Indian Department for the welfare of all Indian soldiers who are in need of help."[23] After canvassing Indian agents for other similar examples, Indian Affairs acknowledged the fact that Peltier's case was not an anomaly. In May 1936 H.W. McGill, the deputy superintendent general of Indian Affairs, issued a circular to all Indian agents stating, "The Department of Pensions & National Health has agreed to make the payment of veteran's relief allowances ... to Indians residing on Reserves. Hitherto, these payments have been made ... only to those residing off Reserves."[24] Given that this period marked the height of the Great Depression, this change in policy diffused, slightly, the already numerous economic hardships faced by Indian veterans—eighteen years after the end of the war.

The same discriminatory policy extended to the Royal Canadian Legion and the Last Post Fund (LPF), established in 1909 to prevent veterans of Her Majesty's forces from being buried in a pauper's grave without recognition, and to provide modest financial aid for struggling veterans. In 1926 Indian Affairs bluntly stated, "No special provision is made by [the Fund].... The only time that this Fund will assume the obligation is when a returned Indian soldier dies away from a reserve.... Indian soldiers must not look to the Last Post Fund for any assistance, nor is this Department prepared to carry out arrangements made by the officers of the Fund." No provisions were ever made, including during the war, by Indian or Veterans Affairs, "for the burial of the deceased Indian soldiers, and the only assistance given is the regular grant which may be made from band funds."[25]

Finally, in February 1936 J.C.G. Herwig of the Canadian Legion Dominion Headquarters informed the Department of Indian Affairs and the Ministry of Pensions and National Health that "we are strongly of the opinion that Indian returned soldiers are entitled to the same consideration as others." As such, the following resolution was passed regarding the position of Indian veterans: "That the Indian War Veteran be placed on the same footing and receive the same benefits as his other Canadian comrades especially in regard to the Last Post Fund, Pensioners' relief, and Veterans' Allowances, and that the Canadian Legion, B.E.S.L. [British Empire Service League], do everything in their power to bring this about." This decision no doubt influenced the May 1936 Ministry of Pensions and National Health resolution to award veteran Indians official government pensions, as previously mentioned. Furthermore, it was agreed in March 1936 that Indian Affairs would repay the LPF for the cost of any military burial of a deceased Indian veteran and provide proper headstones to those who had been previously buried without a marker. This prompted the secretary of the LPF to thank Indian Affairs because "Indians appreciate the respect of interment of their ex-soldier dead under the auspices of some such Society as this who desire to do all that humanly can be done to perpetuate the services and sacrifices of our Warrior Dead.... I must say that the Indians and that the family of the deceased appreciate very much any mark which is given to honour the deceased member of the family." The letter also acerbically remarked that the previous burials of Indian soldiers by Indian Affairs had been "conducted very economically but the most regrettable part of it to us is, that no Headstone or Marker was provided and in consequence the deceased goes down to an unknown grave."[26]

Given these changes in policy concerning Indian soldiers, it is obvious that many Canadians acknowledged the valuable participation of Indians during the war and advocated for their equality. Ronald Haycock asserts of Canadians that

> They began to explore the Indian in closer detail, to see the miniscule
> evils of the white man's own creation and to develop an attitude that

wanted a humane improvement in the administration of Indians and the conception of him. The focus became clearer again with the holocaust of war. The Indian was made to appear [in the media] as if he responded with equal alacrity as did other Canadians—indeed more so. In the reader's mind he was again performing a definite role. As in the days when his forebears by their military value were playing active parts and thereby forcing attention, so he did in this war. It is likely, however, that Canadians were ready to look willingly this time, for the literature indicates the stage was set. War brought it into place faster.... Social interest, awareness of the "whole" Indian, a desire for reform and active government sympathy were replacing paternalism, Social Darwinism and noble savage concepts of the beginning of the century.... The Indian became once more a power. He came to be of importance as he was during his part in the fur trade or as a military force.... During the Great Wars he had offered his service to the nation. Now he offered his condition at a time when Canadians wanted to better it—now he offered his culture at a time Canadians wanted to tolerate and preserve it as a worthy contribution to the national life.[27]

In 1921 W. Everard Edmonds, secretary of the Historical Society of Alberta, wrote an article, "Canada's Red Army," for the widely distributed *Canadian Magazine of Politics, Science, Art and Literature* that was also printed by several newspapers:

Indications are not wanting that a race that has slept for centuries is now awakening to life.... This is one of the results of the War. The Indian feels that he has done a man's work, and he will never again be content to stand aside, uttering no word in matters that directly concern him. The spirit of unrest has taken hold of him and is expressing itself in various forms of race consciousness.... That our Indians deserve full citizenship can be doubted by no one who recalls the splendid part they played in the greatest struggle of all time ... more than 4,000 enlisted for active service with the Canadian Expeditionary Force, while there were probably many cases of Indian enlistment that were not reported.... If then, the Indian desires the full privileges of Canadian citizenship, shall we not grant him what he asks? We have long regarded him as a child, but it was no child's part he played in the War.[28]

Haycock, however, contends that only in the 1960s, during a time of sweeping social awareness and political and racial consciousness, did journalists again discuss the cause of the Indian. Enfranchisement was finally granted to Indians in 1960. Although the war may have briefly brought awareness to whites, and perhaps to the government, it did not bring equality or cultural recognition. As Indian sacrifice and participation in the war faded from memory, little attention was given to their social, political, or cultural position within Canada until reassessment in the aftermath of the Second World War.[29]

The war did, however, spawn the creation of a Canadian pan-Indian organization. In addition, veterans influenced the political administration within individual Indian communities. For example, Pegahmagabow became chief of his Parry Island band in 1921, a position he held until 1925, at which point he became band councillor until 1936. Mike Mountain Horse also served on his band council. The most decisive example of change initiated by veterans occurred at the Six Nations of the Grand River. John Moses argues, "As with groups of Great War veterans elsewhere across the country who felt a disconnect between the magnitude of their wartime sacrifices overseas and the political, economic and social prospects to which they returned in peacetime, so too did Six Nations veterans of the Great War return to an environment that they found unresponsive to their needs and aspirations." Moses asserts that the forced implementation by Indian Affairs of an elected band council on the reserve, as opposed to the traditional Longhouse chiefs, was facilitated and made easier by the demands of veterans and of Lieutenant Colonel Andrew T. Thompson (commanding officer of the 114th): "Newly returned Six Nations veterans of the Great War constituted an elite body at the forefront of this movement for profound political change ... this new system was an appropriate reward for their wartime service."[30] In fact, the local Indian agent wrote to Scott in July 1918 predicting the same: "If the Indian soldiers were only home from the front with their influence against the present system, I believe it would be an opportune time to have the system changed to an elected council. The law-abiding Indians have no confidence whatever in the [Longhouse] council or its decisions and are disgusted with the present display of lack of patriotism and duties."[31]

In 1923 Thompson was appointed by the federal government to investigate the political organizations of the Six Nations reserve after a series of confrontations involving rival factions, the RCMP, and a Longhouse group led by Cayuga chief Deskaheh (Levi General). Completed in November 1923, Thompson's report suggested the establishment of an elected band council under the *Indian Act*. In support of his veteran soldiers, he argued, "The separatist party [Deskaheh and supporters], if I may so describe it, is exceptionally strong in the Council of Chiefs, in fact it is completely dominant there. Its members maintain ... that not being British subjects they are not bound by Canadian law, and ... the Indian Act does not apply to the Six Nations Indians." Without consulting Six Nations' representatives, the government, through the use of the RCMP, forcefully deposed the hereditary Longhouse Council and, though voter participation was exceedingly small because the election was boycotted by traditional Iroquois, a new council was elected in October 1924.[32] Nevertheless, in 1924 a group of Iroquois, led by Deskaheh, travelled to Geneva and presented a petition to the League of Nations on 4 November, unsuccessfully pressing the claim of Iroquois Confederacy sovereignty under Article 17 of the League's covenant. Deskaheh had previously petitioned the king and the Colonial Office during a trip to London in 1921, and he travelled throughout Europe from 1923 to 1925 soliciting the support of European nations.[33] These political divisions between supporters of the elective *Indian Act* system and those who maintain the Longhouse underlie the violence and political fissures that currently exist on many Iroquois/Mohawk reserves.

On a larger scale, Indian veterans were instrumental in the creation of the first nationwide Indian political organization—the League of Indians of Canada. Six Nations Mohawk Frederick Loft, a lieutenant in the Canadian Forestry Corps during the war, drew up the principles of the organization in December 1918, following its first meeting on the Six Nations reserve:

> Not in vain did our young men die in a strange land; not in vain are our Indian bones mingled with the soil of a foreign land for the first time since the world began; not in vain did the Indian father and mothers see their sons march away to face what to them were unknown dangers. The unseen tears of Indian mothers in many isolated reserves have watered the seeds from which may spring those desires and

ILLUS. 26. Mohawk Lieutenant Frederick O. Loft, c. 1917–18. *Library and Archives Canada, PA-007439.*

efforts and aspirations which will enable us to reach the stage when we will take our place side by side with the white people, doing our share of productive work and gladly shouldering the responsibility of citizens in this, our country.[34]

The constitution of the League of Indians also included passages concerning denouncement of the residential school system, equality in post-war veteran programs, and the creation of an accommodating Canadian-British-Indian political forum. Clearly, Loft and other Indian veteran members, including Pegahmagabow, associated Indian participation in the war with the principles of self-determination and equality as citizens of Canada: "The principal aim of the League ... is equality for the Indian as a citizen—equality, that is, in the two-fold meaning of privilege and responsibility; and to achieve this objective, our first emphasis must be upon improved educational and health care programs."[35] They also believed that a unified Indian stance, through a political organization, could challenge the government and the *Indian Act*. According to Loft, "We must be heard as a nation."[36] Edmonds noted in 1921 that "mighty movements are stirring and one knows not what the next hour may bring forth.... Tribes far removed from each other, unknown to each other and hitherto uninterested in each other, are now corresponding and exchanging opinions.... The formation of a National Indian League is one way in which the Red Man has expressed his new found manhood."[37]

Indian Affairs immediately tried to undermine Loft's authority by attempting to force enfranchisement upon him under the 1920 provision. Enfranchisement would remove his Indian status and hopefully eliminate "troublemakers and educated Indians from the ranks as a whole." Scott also contemplated issuing criminal charges against Loft for attempting to raise money for land claim issues.[38] Viewing the league as a threat, the DIA also amended the *Indian Act* to state that bands were prohibited from donating funds to Indian political organizations. Nevertheless, the League of Indians of Canada held its second meeting in Sault Ste. Marie, Ontario, in September 1919. Annual meetings were held in other provinces over the next four years. In 1927, to further reduce the ability of Indians to form structured resistance, the *Indian Act* was amended to make it illegal for status Indians to organize politically, or to retain legal counsel in forwarding claims against the government.[39] By the early 1930s the league had splintered into smaller Indian political organizations, such as the

League of Indians of Western Canada, the Indian Association of Alberta, and the Union of Saskatchewan Indians.[40] Although the founding League of Indians of Canada had few tangible accomplishments, it set a precedent for future national Indian assemblies, and it showed Indian Affairs that Indians had the education, motivation, and aptitude to challenge governmental policies.

Arthur Marwick asserts in his seminal work *War and Social Change in the Twentieth Century* (1974), that "in modern war there is a greater participation on the part of larger underprivileged groups in society, who tend correspondingly to benefit, or at least develop a new self-consciousness ... a strengthened market position and hence higher material standards for such groups; it also engenders a new sense of status, usually leading to a dropping of former

ILLUS. 27. Stoneys at Armistice Day Celebration, High River, Alberta, 1918. Left to Right Back Row: Bessie Hanna; Paul Amos; Paul Daniels; Red Cloud; Phil Weinard. Left to Right Front Row: Peter Ear; Peter Bearspaw; Mrs. H. Baines; David Bearspaw; Enoch Rider; Moses Wesley. *Glenbow Musuem Archives, NA-1395-1.*

sectional or class barriers."[41] In the case of Canadian Indians and First World War participation, Marwick's declaration can be summarily dismissed.

Following the war, with their service no longer required, Indian soldiers returned to the position of unwanted peoples and did not receive equitable treatment as veterans. While a new-found self-worth was realized by individual Indian veterans and specific communities, war contributions did not generally influence political campaigning or organizations. Pre-war cultural and social stratums had not been altered, and Indian lobbying, in certain instances involving veterans, did little to change political and socio-economic realities. Indians accrued little direct benefit from service, aside from military pay or the fulfilment of individual motivations for enlistment. The inclusion of Indians in the CEF was a pragmatic decision on the part of the Canadian government, one based on the necessity for manpower to meet national war aims and in response to requests from British authorities. This inclusion was not intended to transcend contemporary social, political, or cultural norms within Canadian society.

Conclusion

Duncan Campbell Scott remarked in 1919 that "The Indians deserve well of Canada, and the end of the war should mark the beginning of a new era for them."[1] Instead of ushering in a new era for Indians, the Department of Indian Affairs continued to dominate most aspects of Indian life, and little change materialized during the interwar decades. The Great Depression compounded the deteriorating socio-economic condition of Indian communities. Indians remained wards of the Crown, under the paternalistic jurisdiction of Indian Affairs. By its actions and policies, the government of Canada evidently thought Indians worthy enough to fight and die for Canada when needed, but not worthy enough to enjoy the privileges and rights of Canadian citizens.

The pragmatic realization of the need for manpower, combined with the October 1915 requests of the imperial government, determined the inclusion of Indians during the First World War. Inclusion, however, remained dependent on the capricious attitudes and policies of the Canadian government directly, or on those policies as interpreted by Scott and Indian Affairs. Participation was predicated on racial considerations, prior policy (such as the 1904 *Militia Act*), past exclusionist practice (seen during the Boer War), and the calculated recognition of imperial and Canadian-specific war needs. Had the war been short, as initially expected, and limited in the requirements for men and materials, Indians would have remained subjugated spectators.

The First World War, however, was a global conflict that encompassed the terrain and populations of peoples that belonged, willingly or otherwise, to established European empires; thus, indigenous peoples inevitably became involved. The unprecedented mobilization of men between 1914 and 1918 was, in contemporary understanding, absolute. Nevertheless, racial considerations and realizations, including probable outcomes, influenced the decisions pertaining to the use of indigenous men in a military capacity by all nations, including Canada. All facets of their military service were carefully weighed and applied so as not to upset the existing racial, social, and political realities of established societies, while at the same time satisfying the demands of imperial and national war aims.

As such, the military inclusion of Indians was a continuation of past, official or unofficial, policies and practices. Since the War of 1812, historical tradition dictated that Indians were used only when and where they were required. Their exclusion during the Boer War adheres to this approach, as does their omission in the 1904 *Militia Act*. Their use during the First World War was no exception to this principle; however, never before had they been called upon in such magnitude. The evolution of Indian participation was gradual and paralleled increasing Canadian contributions and casualties, as well as the amplification of the war in its entirety.

The period from August 1914 to December 1915 can generally be characterized by limited or restrictive policies toward service. Canadian commitments were still in relative infancy, and no CEF unit was active on the Western Front until the 1st Division in March 1915 (aside from the Princess Patricia's Canadian Light Infantry Battalion in February). The following stage of war, from December 1915 to the close of 1916, saw restrictive policies relaxed and replaced by official authorization, which allowed for the enlistment of Indians. This change in policy satisfied both the October 1915 British requests for Indian inclusion and the increasing need for manpower within a growing CEF that was now sustaining heavy casualties. During the final period of the war, from 1917 to the armistice, Canadian authorities took an active role in the recruitment of Indians, and they were initially included in conscription designs. Conscription, however, led to a reassessment of their rights based on treaties, and Indians were eventually excluded from mandatory service.

Indian inclusion was based on calculated racial considerations and was crafted so as not to undermine the contemporary Canadian social and political order. Indians' abilities as soldiers and perceptions of their martial prowess were measured against contemporary racial theories, Social Darwinism, past colonial experiences, and settler-state warfare. These factors, in combination, influenced all aspects of their military participation, including the progression of policy concerning their inclusion, their roles within the CEF, and the refusal of military authorities to endorse an all-Indian battalion.

The elevated and unprecedented participation of Indians during the First World War, however, was a potential catalyst to accelerate their attainment of equal rights. This did not happen. Paternalistic and authoritative policies prevailed, and the recognition of Indian military contributions was fast forgotten. War service, both on and off the battlefield, did not alter their socioeconomic or political realities within Canada, nor did it hasten the attainment of equal rights or enfranchisement. Following the war, veterans were also denied access to most veteran programs.

In late 1917 Arthur Meighen, minster of the interior and superintendent general of Indian Affairs, summarized the relationship between Indians and Canada during the Great War: "It is an inspiring fact that these descendants of the aboriginal inhabitants of a continent so recently appropriated by our own ancestors should voluntarily sacrifice their lives on European battlefields, side by side with men of our own race, for the preservation of the ideals of our civilization, and their staunch devotion forms an eloquent tribute to the beneficent character of British rule over a native people."[2] No better statement represents the negligible impact Indian participation in the war had on the broader social and political realities of Indians within Canada.[3]

Private Harry Ball, of the Piapot Saskatchewan Cree, stated after being wounded, "Of course I was all right after that, but I had to have my leg amputated just below the knee. So you see I am minus one foot now, but I don't grudge the foot. I lost it for my King and Country. I am satisfied that I did my duty."[4] Indians were willing, through the bonding experience of a common war, to enter into Canadian society as equals. Canada, as evidenced by Meighen's declaration, rejected this offer, refusing to acknowledge the shared experience of the First World War and, more importantly, the benefits that could have been derived from it. The sacrifices of Indian soldiers and communities shaped the eras that followed. These experiences challenged notions of Indian identity, as well as their appropriate place in national orders.

Although the Great War ended more than ninety years ago, for the indigenous peoples of Canada the war for cultural, territorial, and socio-economic equality and recognition is still being fought today.

Epilogue

During the Second World War Indian men were asked to participate. The need for manpower once again forced the admittance of Indians into Canadian military formations (see Table 7). Many of the themes and policies regarding their service in the Great War were repeated during the Second World War.

Population 1914	Enlistments 1914–1918	Percent	Population 1939	Enlistments 1939–1945	Percent
103,774	4,000	3.9	118,406	4,250	3.6

TABLE 7. Statistical Comparison of Indians and the World Wars
Source: Office of Census and Statistics, *The Canada Yearbook*, 1914, 1939 (Ottawa: King's Printer, 1915, 1940); Department of Indian Affairs, *Annual Report of the Department of Indian Affairs*, 1919, 1920, 1946, 1947 (Ottawa: King's Printer, 1920, 1921, 1947, 1948).

According to R. Scott Sheffield, 4,250 Indians served during the Second World War from a total 1939 population of 118,406.[1] In terms of percentage, fewer Indians served during the Second World War than during the First World War. Nevertheless, Indians served with distinction. Ojibwa Sergeant Tommy Prince, a member of the joint Canadian/American 1st Special Service Force (the "Devil's Brigade") was awarded the Military Medal and was one of only fifty-nine Canadians to win the American Silver Star. Prince went on to serve in the Korean War. However, like his glorified American Indian counterpart, Ira Hayes (immortalized by the Iwo Jima flag-raising photo and by singer Johnny Cash), Prince died an alcoholic and in squalor.[2] Hayes was one of over 25,000 American Indians to serve in the Second World War out of a total population of 287,970 (8.7 percent).[3]

The individual war memorials throughout Canada and Newfoundland and Labrador are evidence of the impact the world wars had on all communities of the dominions. Cenotaphs also stand in Indian communities and reserves, illustrating Indians' shared efforts in all aspects of the wars. Indian soldiers were not excluded from national honour rolls or dominion and imperial European monuments, such as the Menin Gate in Ypres or the Vimy Memorial in France. Explicit governmental recognition, however, was slower, and bestowed only in the last two decades of the twentieth century, within a general atmosphere of reconciliation among Western societies and international organizations such as the United Nations. On 21 June 2001, on Canadian National Aboriginal Day, the government unveiled the National Aboriginal Veterans Monument in Confederation Park in Ottawa. Schools, military bases, statues, and other landmarks honour select Indian soldiers by bearing their names. For example, in 2006 the headquarters for the 3rd Canadian Ranger Patrol Group was renamed after Pegahmagabow. Tommy Prince has the following honours in his name: a statue, a school, a street, a Canadian Forces base and a separate drill hall, two educational scholarships for indigenous Canadians, and a cadet corps. The honours now bestowed upon Indian veterans are worthy representations of the sacrifices they made in service of king and *Kanata* during both world wars.

Indians continue their long-standing tradition of military service. American Indians are well represented in modern forces. The 4.3 million American Indians make up 1.5 percent of the total U.S. population. Comparatively, Indians represent 1.8 percent of the entire U.S. forces. Currently, over 1,300 indigenous Canadians are serving in the Canadian Forces, representing 2 percent of the total Canadian Forces and 1.7 percent of the regular force.[4] The 2006 census recorded a significantly growing indigenous population of 1.2 million (3.7 percent of the total Canadian population), with 47 percent of that population under the age of twenty-five.[5] Certainly, members of this increasing population will continue to serve, as they have done in the past, both their nations and Canada in our shared Canadian Forces.

NOTES

Notes on Sources

1 See: P. Whitney Lackenbauer and R. Scott Sheffield, "Moving Beyond 'Forgotten': The Historiography on Canadian Native Peoples and the World Wars," in *Aboriginal Peoples and the Canadian Military: Historical Perspectives*, ed. P. Whitney Lackenbauer and Craig Leslie Mantle (Kingston: CDA Press, 2007), 209–232.

2 Fred Gaffen, *Forgotten Soldiers* (Penticton: Theytus Books, 1985); Adrian Hayes, *Pegahmagabow: Legendary Warrior, Forgotten Hero* (Sault Ste. Marie: Fox Meadow Creations, 2003); Janice Summerby, *Native Soldiers, Foreign Battlefields* (Ottawa: Department of Veterans Affairs, 2005).

3 L. James Dempsey, *Warriors of the King: Prairie Indians in World War I* (Regina: University of Regina, 1999).

4 Consult the literature by Lackenbauer, Sheffield, Dempsey, John Moses, Ronald Niezen, Peter Kulchyski, and Sarah Carter.

Preface

1 The policies of the United States in relation to the military service of its Indian populations paralleled many of those of Canada and will be used to highlight elements of the war experience common to all North American Indians. The traditional lands and contemporary reserves of many Indian nations straddled the American-Canadian border. Most Indians did not recognize what, to them, seemed to be an arbitrary demarcation, nor were they obligated to do so under Articles II and III of the 1794 Treaty of Amity, Commerce, and Navigation (the Jay Treaty) negotiated between Britain and the United States in the aftermath of the American Revolution. Article III allows "the Indians dwelling on either side of the said Boundary Line, freely to pass and repass by Land, or Inland Navigation, into the respective Territories and Countries of the Two Parties, on the Continent of America ... and to navigate all the Lakes, Rivers, and waters thereof, and freely to carry on trade and commerce with each other."

2 Vine Deloria Jr., *Custer Died for Your Sins: An Indian Manifesto* (New York: Macmillan, 1969).

3 J.R. Miller, introduction to *Aboriginal Peoples of Canada: A Short Introduction*, ed. Paul Robert Magocsi (Toronto: University of Toronto Press, 2002), 7–8.

4 Métis were not afforded legal distinction until a vague clause was introduced in Section 35 of the 1982 *Constitution Act*.

Introduction

1   Roberta J. Forsberg, *The Chief Mountain: The Story of Canon Middleton* (Whittier, CA: 1964), 32; L. James Dempsey, *Warriors of the King: Prairie Indians in World War I* (Regina: University of Regina, 1999), 54.

2   Dempsey, *Warriors*, 54.

3   Ibid., 53–54.

4   The twenty-four-hour clock was not yet in use at this time. It was first introduced by the BEF/CEF in late 1917. It was not widely used until the 1930s.

5   Jonathan F. Vance, *Death So Noble: Memory, Meaning, and the First World War* (Vancouver: University of British Columbia Press, 1997), 247.

6   Dempsey, *Warriors*, 54–55. According to a February 2010 report, the rates of tuberculosis among First Nations are 31 times higher, and those of Inuit 185 times higher, than Canadian-born, non-indigenous peoples. Bryn Weese, Parliamentary Bureau, "Rates of TB Skyrocket among Inuit, First Nations," CNews, 10 March 2010.

7   Mike Mountain Horse, *My People, The Bloods* (Calgary: Glenbow-Alberta Institute, 1979), vi–ix.

8   Ibid., 140–142.

9   Library and Archives Canada (LAC), RG10, Vol. 6765, Reel C-8510, File 452-9. List of Indians Killed and Wounded Overseas.

10 The thirteen Canadian/Newfoundland First World War Memorials in France and Belgium are as follows. In Belgium: Courtrai—The Royal Newfoundland Regiment in the Battle of Lys, October 1918; Hill 62—The Canadian Divisions in the defence of the Ypres Salient, April–August 1916; Passchendaele—The capture of Crest Farm by the Canadian Corps and the Battle of Passchendaele, October–November 1917; St. Julien—The Canadian First Division during the first gas attack at Ypres, April 1915. In France: Beaumont-Hamel—The Newfoundland Regiment, the Battle of the Somme on 1 July 1916; Bourlon Wood—The crossing of the Canal du Nord, capture of Bourlon Wood and the rupture of the final positions of the Hindenburg Line by the Canadian Corps, 27 September 1918; Courcelette—The Canadian Corps during the Battle of the Somme, September-November 1916; Dury—The capture of the Drocourt-Queant Switch and the breaking of the Hindenburg Line by the Canadian Corps, 2 September 1918; Gueudecourt—The Newfoundland Regiment during the Battle of the Somme, 12 October 1916; Le Quesnel—The attack by the Canadian Corps on 8 August 1918 during the Battle of Amiens, which drove the Germans back some 13 kilometres; Masnieres—The Newfoundland Regiment during the Battle of Cambrai, 20 November 1917; Monchy-le-Preux—The Newfoundland Regiment during the Battle of Arras, 14 April 1917; Vimy—The capture of Vimy Ridge by the Canadian Corps, 9–12 April 1917.

11 Duncan Campbell Scott, *1919 Report of the Deputy Superintendent General for Indian Affairs: The Indians and the Great War—House of Commons Sessional Paper No. 27* (Ottawa: King's Printer, 1920), 13.

12 LAC, RG10, Vol. 6767, File 452-17. Return of Indian Enlistments, 1917; LAC, RG10, Vol. 6771, File 452-29. Return of Indian Enlistments, 1919; Duncan Campbell Scott, *1919 Report*, 13.

13 See C.E. Callwell, *Small Wars: Their Principles and Practice* (Lincoln: University of Nebraska Press, 1996). Relative in the sense the Crimean War (1853–1856), the Franco-Prussian War (1870–1871), and the Balkan Wars (1912–1913), never became general European wars.

14   Tim Cook, *At the Sharp End: Canadians Fighting the Great War 1914-1916, Vol. 1* (Toronto: Penguin Group, 2007), 10.

15   John L. Tobias, "Protection, Civilization, Assimilation," in *Sweet Promises: A Reader on Indian-White Relations in Canada*, ed. J.R. Miller (Toronto: University of Toronto Press, 1991), 127–144.

16   Hew Strachan, *The First World War Volume I: To Arms* (Oxford: Oxford University Press, 2001), 497. See also Richard S. Fogarty, *Race and War in France: Colonial Subjects in the French Army, 1914-1918* (Baltimore: The Johns Hopkins University Press, 2008).

17   Linda Tuhiwai Smith, "Colonizing Knowledges," in *The Indigenous Experience: Global Perspectives*, ed. Roger C.A. Maaka and Chris Andersen (Toronto: Canadian Scholars' Press, 2006), 97.

18   R. Scott Sheffield, "Indifference, Difference and Assimilation: Aboriginal People in Canadian Military Practice, 1900-1945" in *Aboriginal Peoples and the Canadian Military: Historical Perspectives*, ed. P. Whitney Lackenbauer and Craig Leslie Mantle (Kingston: Canadian Defence Academy Press, 2007), 58.

19   The term first appeared in John Dryden's heroic play, *The Conquest of Granada* (1672). It came to prominence after 1851 following Charles Dickens's use of the term as the title of a satirical essay printed in the weekly magazine *Household Words*.

20   George Robb, *British Culture and the First World War* (London: Palgrave, 2004), chapter 1.

21   Duncan Campbell Scott, "The Canadian Indians and the Great War," in *Canada in the Great War Vol. III: Guarding the Channel Ports* (Toronto: United Publishers, 1919), 287.

22   Dempsey, *Warriors*, 1. The Assiniboine are closely related to the Sioux and have a reserve in Saskatchewan and another in Alberta (Stoney-Nakota). "Counting coup" refers to winning prestige in battle through acts of bravery; the most prestigious acts included touching an enemy warrior with the hand or a coup stick and then escaping unharmed. Coups were recorded on the coup stick or by feathers in a headdress.

Chapter One

1   Thomas More, *Utopia* (Wheeling, IL: Harlan Davidson, 1949), 38.

2   While this system was practiced by many First Nations, such as the Algonquian and Iroquois, it was most prevalent among the Haudenosaunee (Five/Six Nations Iroquois Confederacy). While the term *Iroquois* has come to represent these nations, there were many other Iroquoian peoples, often enemies of the Haudenosaunee, such as the Huron, Cherokee, Tionontati (Petun/Tobacco), Erie, Wenro, Nottoway, Susquehannock, and Tuscarora (the sixth nation of the Confederacy as of 1722).

3   J.R. Miller, *Skyscrapers Hide the Heavens: A History of Indian-White Relations in Canada* (Toronto: University of Toronto Press, 2000), 7–14.

4   Donald E. Graves, "His Majesty's Aboriginal Allies: The Contribution of the Indigenous Peoples of North America to the Defence of Canada during the War of 1812," in *Aboriginal Peoples and the Canadian Military: Historical Perspectives*, ed. P. Whitney Lackenbauer and Craig Leslie Mantle (Kingston: CDA Press, 2007), 32.

5   See Lawrence H. Keeley, *War Before Civilization: The Myth of the Peaceful Savage* (Oxford: Oxford University Press, 1996). Through archaeological evidence and oral histories, Keeley argues that only 13 percent of First Nations did not engage in war with their neighbours at least once a year. A mass grave of over 500 men, women, and children who had been scalped and mutilated was found at Crow Creek, South Dakota, and it was dated to the year 1325. Based on housing postmoulds and charcoal remains

(all the houses were burned), the village contained roughly 800 people, which means the casualty rate was roughly 63 percent. Women were least represented in the body count, likely because they were taken as captives. Also see George R. Milner, *The Moundbuilders: Ancient Peoples of Eastern North America* (London: Thames and Hudson, 2004).

6   Maurice Tugwell and John Thompson, *The Legacy of Oka* (Toronto: Mackenzie Institute, 1991), 5.

7   Miller, *Skyscrapers*, 76.

8   Ibid., 28.

9   H.P. Biggar, ed., *The Voyages of Jacques Cartier* (Ottawa: King's Printer, 1924), 64–65. To make matters worse, Cartier kidnapped Domagaya and Taignoagny, both sons of Donnacona, the chief of the Stadacona (Quebec City) St. Lawrence Iroquois, and brought them back to France. However, they returned with Cartier on his second voyage in 1535.

10   Miller, *Skyscrapers*, 31.

11   At contact the only metal known to the eastern Indians of Canada was copper from the vicinity of Lake Superior; it was dispersed throughout North America and used only for limited utilitarian and decorative purposes, given its soft metallic properties.

12   See Richard Middleton, *Pontiac's War: Its Causes, Course and Consequences* (London: Routledge, 2007). The Royal Proclamation is viewed by Canadian Indians as their Magna Carta. It is used in modern-day land claim submissions and is their proof of recognition as sovereign nations. However, the British rescinded the proclamation in November 1768. Fearing a revolution, which inevitably came, the British under William Johnson negotiated a treaty with the Iroquois for Ohio, dubbed the Treaty of Fort Stanwix, in November 1768.

13   Robert S. Allen, *His Majesty's Indian Allies: British Indian Policy in the Defence of Canada, 1774–1815* (Toronto: Dundurn Press, 1992), 15–16.

14   A great deal has been written on the Iroquois Confederacy and its relationship with European powers. The most valuable, but often contradicting, works are: Daniel K. Richter, *The Ordeal of the Longhouse: The Peoples of the Iroquois League in the Era of European Colonialism* (Chapel Hill: The University of North Carolina Press, 1992); Daniel K. Richter and James H. Merrell, eds., *Beyond the Covenant Chain: The Iroquois and Their Neighbors in Indian North America, 1600–1800* (Syracuse: Syracuse University Press, 1987); Daniel P. Barr, *Unconquered: The Iroquois League at War in Colonial America* (London: Praeger, 2006); Timothy J. Shannon, *Iroquois Diplomacy on the Early American Frontier* (New York: Penguin Books, 2008); David L. Preston, *The Texture of Contact: European and Indian Settler Communities on the Frontiers of Iroquoia, 1667–1783* (Lincoln: University of Nebraska Press, 2009); Francis Jennings, ed., *The History and Culture of Iroquois Diplomacy: An Interdisciplinary Guide to the Treaties of the Six Nations and Their League* (Syracuse: Syracuse University Press, 1985); Richard Aquila, *The Iroquois Restoration: Iroquois Diplomacy on the Colonial Frontier, 1701–1754* (Detroit: Wayne State University Press, 1983).

15   For a brilliant account of Johnson, see Fintan O'Toole, *White Savage: William Johnson and the Invention of America* (London: Faber and Faber, 2005).

16   Canada, or *Kanata*, is a Saint-Lawrence Iroquoian word meaning village or settlement.

17   Miller, *Skyscrapers*, 148.

18   Tobias, "Protection, Civilization, Assimilation," 127–144.

19   Bruce Vandervort, *Indian Wars of Mexico, Canada and the United States 1812–1900* (New York: Routledge, 2006), 178–191.

20   See Joseph Manzione, *I Am Looking to the North for My Life: Sitting Bull 1876–1881* (Salt Lake City: University of Utah Press, 1991); Grant MacEwan, *Sitting Bull: The Years in Canada* (Edmonton: Hurtig, 1973); Ian Anderson, *Sitting Bull's Boss: Above the Medicine Line with James Morrow Walsh* (Surrey: Heritage House, 2000); Gary C. Anderson, *Sitting Bull and the Paradox of Lakota Nationhood* (New York: Longman, 1996). The term *reserve* is used in Canada, and *reservation* in the United States.

21   The North West Mounted Police (NWMP) was not created until 1873.

22   Manzione, *I Am Looking*, 5–8.

23   Indian Affairs existed as a sub-portfolio under various ministries, depending on the period, until 1966 when a sole minister was responsible for Indian Affairs and Northern Development. Two men held this responsibility during the First World War: William J. Roche (1912–1917) and Arthur Meighen (1917–1920). In effect, the superintendent general was nothing more than an official political figurehead, and administration and policy was directed and promulgated by the deputy superintendent general, in this case Duncan Campbell Scott.

24   Miller, *Skyscrapers*, 145–146, 254–255. The United States government also passed numerous similar pieces of legislation: the 1830 *Indian Removal Act*, the 1887 *Dawes Severalty Act*, and the 1934 *Indian Reorganization Act*.

25   J.M. Bumsted, "The West and Louis Riel," in *Interpreting Canada's Past: Volume Two, Post-Confederation*, ed. J.M. Bumsted (Toronto: Oxford University Press, 1993), 67–69.

26   Alexander Morris, *The Treaties of Canada with the Indians of Manitoba and North-West Territories* (Toronto: Belfords, Clarke, 1880); *Indian Affairs, Basic Departmental Data, 2003* (Ottawa: Department of Indian Affairs, 2003), 87–103.

27   Miller, *Skyscrapers*, 254.

28   See Blair Stonechild and Bill Waiser, *Loyal Till Death: Indians and the North-West Rebellion* (Calgary: Fifth House, 1997).

29   Vandervort, *Indian War*, 218–222.

30   "Almighty Voice," *Saskatchewan Indian* 3, 6 (1973): 6.

31   J.R. Miller, *Lethal Legacy: Current Native Controversies in Canada* (Toronto: McClelland and Stewart, 2005), 15.

Chapter Two

1   J.M. Barrie, *Peter and Wendy* (London: Hodder and Stoughton, 1911), 51. *Pickaninny* is a derogatory name referring to black children.

2   Ibid., 51. Diana was the mythological Roman goddess of the hunt, wild animals, wilderness, and chastity. Her Greek equivalent is Artemis.

3   Ibid., 51-52. Barrie actually uses the term *noble savage* once in his work: "It is written that the noble savage must never express surprise in the presence of the white."

4   Ibid., 95-96.

5   Ibid., 114.

6   Ibid., 115. Sand Creek (Colorado): An estimated 100–150 Cheyenne killed, the majority women and children; Marias (Montana): 173 Piegan Blackfeet killed, mostly women and children killed, another 140 captured; Wounded Knee (South Dakota): An estimated 150–170 Lakota Sioux killed and 51 wounded, again the vast majority women and children (of the wounded were four men and 47 women and children).

7 Daiva K. Stasiulis and Nira Yuval-Davis, *Unsettling Settler Societies: Articulations of Gender, Race Ethnicity and Class* (London: Sage, 1995), 20.

8 Miller, *Skyscrapers*, 415n57.

9 Ibid., 75.

10 Darwin did not use the term, borrowed from Spencer's 1864 *Principles of Biology*, until his fifth edition of *Origins* in 1869.

11 Victoria Freeman, "Attitudes toward 'Miscegenation' in Canada, the United States, New Zealand, and Australia, 1860–1914," *Native Studies Review* 16, 1 (2005): 42.

12 Ronald G. Haycock, *The Image of the Indian* (Waterloo: Lutheran University Press, 1971), 21.

13 Paul Crook, *Darwinism, War and History: The Debate over the Biology of War from the 'Origin of Species' to the First World War* (Cambridge: Cambridge University Press, 1994), 25.

14 Mike Hawkins, *Social Darwinism in European and American Thought, 1860–1945: Nature as Model and Nature as Threat*, (Cambridge: Cambridge University Press, 1997), 244.

15 Ibid., 191–240.

16 Freeman, "Attitudes," 47, 52, 55.

17 See Robert S. Tilton, *Pocahontas: The Evolution of an American Narrative* (Cambridge: Cambridge University Press, 1994); J.A. Leo Lemay, *Did Pocahontas Save Captain John Smith?* (Athens: The University of Georgia Press, 1992); Grace Steele Woodward, *Pocahontas* (Norman: University of Oklahoma Press, 1969). Historians doubt her saving of Smith and question his account, which is the only testimony of the event. His account was written in 1616, in a letter to Queen Anne asking her to treat Pocahontas with dignity on her visit to London. He may have simply made up or exaggerated the story for her benefit. There is also no evidence to suggest the two had a love affair. In fact, Smith described her as "a child of tenne years old." (John Smith, *A Description of New England*. London: Humfrey Lownes, 1616). The first to write about such relations was John Davis in his 1803 *Travels in the United States of America*. The details of her marriage to John Rolfe are also not known. It seems likely, based on Rolfe's letters, that it was an arranged marriage for the safety and trading benefits of the settlers. Certainly, upon landing in England, she was initially more of an exhibit than a guest. Nevertheless, Disney perpetuates the myth, which is unfortunately taken as fact.

18 Miller, *Lethal Legacy*, 19.

19 Haycock, *Image of the Indian*, 19.

20 J.R. Miller, *Compact, Contract, Covenant: Aboriginal Treaty-Making in Canada* (Toronto: University of Toronto Press, 2009), 222.

21 James Fenimore Cooper, *The Last of the Mohicans* (New York: H.C. Carey and I. Lea, 1826).

22 Haycock, *Image of the Indian*, 1–2.

23 Dempsey, *Warriors*, 17–18.

24 David Omissi, *The Sepoy and the Raj: The Indian Army, 1860–1940* (London: Macmillan Press, 1994), 10–25; David Killingray and David Omissi, eds., *Guardians of Empire: The Armed Forces of the Colonial Powers c. 1700–1964* (Manchester: Manchester University Press, 1999), 14–15.

25 For animated and well-researched accounts from both sides, see James Donovan, *A Terrible Glory: Custer and the Little Big Horn: The Last Great Battle of the American West* (New York: Little, Brown, 2008); Nathaniel Philbrick, *The Last Stand: Custer, Sitting Bull, and the Battle of the Little Bighorn* (New York: Viking Books, 2010).

26 Armstrong Starkey, *European and Native American Warfare, 1675-1815* (Norman: University of Oklahoma Press, 1998), 19.

27 Cynthia H. Enloe, *Ethnic Soldiers: State Security in a Divided Society* (Markham: Penguin Books, 1980).

28 Tom Holm, "Strong Hearts: Native Service in the U.S. Armed Forces," in *Aboriginal Peoples and Military Participation: Canadian & International Perspectives*, ed. P. Whitney Lackenbauer et al. (Kingston: Canadian Defence Academy Press, 2007), 129-132.

Chapter Three

1 Benjamin Drake, *Life of Tecumseh, and his Brother, The Prophet with a Historical Sketch of the Shawanoe Indians* (Cincinnati: Anderson, Gates and Wright, 1858), 141-142. Harrison eventually commanded the American force at the Battle of the Thames (5 October 1813), during which Tecumseh was killed. He became the ninth president of the United States but died on his thirty-second day in office (4 April 1841).

2 Robert S. Allan, *His Majesty's Indian Allies: British Indian Policy in the Defence of Canada, 1774-1815* (Toronto: Dundurn Press, 1992), 134-137.

3 Robert W. McLachlan, *Medals Awarded to Canadian Indians* (Montreal, 1899); Melvill Allan Jamieson, *Medals Awarded to North American Indian chiefs, 1714-1922 and to Loyal African and Other Chiefs in Various Territories within the British Empire* (London: Spink, 1936).

4 Carl Benn, *Mohawks on the Nile: Natives among the Canadian Voyageurs in Egypt 1884-1885* (Toronto: Dundurn Group, 2008).

5 John Moses, *A Sketch Account of Aboriginal Peoples in the Canadian Military* (Ottawa: National Defence, 2004), 48-54.

6 Laurier LaPierre, *Sir Wilfrid Laurier and the Romance of Canada* (Toronto: Stoddart Publishers, 1996), 266.

7 Robert Page, *The Boer War and Canadian Imperialism* (Ottawa: Canadian Historical Association, 1987), 10.

8 J.L. Granatstein, *Canada's Army: Waging War and Keeping the Peace* (Toronto: University of Toronto Press, 2002), 37.

9 Page, *Boer War*, 11.

10 Ibid., 13.

11 LAC, RG10, Vol. 2837, Reel C-11284, File 171-340. Letter from W. Hamilton Merritt to Governor General, 23 March 1896; Letter from Merritt to Deputy Minister Indian Affairs, James A. Smart, 11 May 1898.

12 Mountain Horse, *My People, The Bloods*, 139-140; Dempsey, *Warriors*, 18.

13 Thomas A. Britten, *American Indians in World War I: At Home and at War* (Albuquerque: University of New Mexico Press, 1997), 102-103; Bruce White, "The American Army and the Indian," in *Ethnic Armies: Polyethnic Armed Forces from the Time of the Hapsburgs to the Age of the Superpowers*, ed. N.F. Dreisziger (Waterloo: Wilfrid Laurier University Press, 1990), 78-79.

14   LAC, RG10, Vol. 2837, Reel C-11284, File 171-340. Composition 37th Haldimand Rifles.

15   LAC, RG10, Vol. 2837, Reel C-11284, File 171-340. Letter from Hill to Cameron, 14 February 1896.

16   P. Whitney Lackenbauer and Katherine McGowan, "Competing Loyalty in a Complex Community: Enlisting the Six Nations in the Canadian Expeditionary Force, 1914–1917," in *Aboriginal Peoples and the Canadian Military: Historical Perspectives*, ed. P. Whitney Lackenbauer et al. (Kingston: Canadian Defence Academy Press, 2007), 97.

17   Captain D.E. Cameron, "The Royal Six Nations Regiment," *The Indian Magazine Brantford* 3, 4 (1896): 1–4.

18   LAC, RG10, Vol. 2837, Reel C-11284, File 171-340. Letter from Reed to Panet, 26 February 1896.

19   LAC, RG10, Vol. 2991, Reel C-11307, File 215-977. Letter from Six Nation Council Chiefs to Queen Victoria, 10 November 1899, 21 December 1899.

20   LAC, RG10, Vol. 2991, Reel C11307, File 215-977. Letter from Scott to Governor General, 8 November 1899.

21   LAC, RG10, Vol. 2991, Reel C11307, File 215-977. Letter from Duck Lake Indian agent to Indian Affairs, 13 January 1900; Various letters pertaining to Indian troop contributions.

22   LAC, RG10, Vol. 2991, Reel C-11307, File 215-977. Indian Affairs Notice to all Superintendents, 22 April 1900; Letter from Chamberlain to Lord Minto, Hill and Cameron, 13 February 1900

23   LAC, RG10, Vol. 2991, Reel C-11307, File 215-977. Indian Affairs Notice to all Superintendents, 22 April 1900.

24   Moses, *Sketch Account*, 61.

25   LAC, RG38, A-1-a, Vol.111. Walter White Personal Records.

26   LAC, RG38, A-1-a, Vol.76. George McLean Personal Records.

27   LAC, RG10, Vol. 2991, Reel C-11307, File 215-977. Land Claim for Joseph Hanaven, 29 October 1930.

28   LAC, RG10, Vol. 2991, Reel C-11307, File 215-977. Indian Donations to the Canadian Patriotic Fund.

29   Granatstein, *Canada's Army*, 45–47.

30   Office of Census and Statistics, *The Canada Yearbook 1914* (Ottawa: King's Printer, 1915). Saskatchewan did not institute cadet training, and, given the high proportion of residential schools and Indians in that province, many Indian boys were excluded from cadet training.

31   G.W.L. Nicholson, *Canadian Expeditionary Force, 1914–1919: Official History of the Canadian Army* (Ottawa: Queen's Printer, 1962), 6–10.

32   LAC, RG24, C-1-a, Vol. 6564-Part I. Revision of the *Militia Act*, 1904.

Chapter Four

1   LAC, RG10, Vol. 6810, File 470-2-3. Memorandum: Duncan Campbell Scott, Residential Schools and the Indian Question, 1920. Scott joined Indian Affairs in 1879 and worked as a clerk of various ranks and positions until 1896. He then served as the chief secretary until 1905, after which time he was posted as the chief clerk and accountant until 1909. From 1909 until his promotion to deputy superintendent general in 1913, he was superintendent of Indian Education. Scott was also an accomplished poet and wrote extensively on the Indian condition. His poetry is filled with his belief in the fatal impact theory and the assimilation of the remaining Indian population. For example, his "The Half-Breed Girl" and "The Onondaga Madonna" deconstruct the process of colonialism and the concept of Indians living in the cultural conflict of the convergence of two distinct societies.

2   Scott, "Canadian Indians," 327–328.

3   Sir Robert Borden, *Special Session of Parliament, August 1914* (Ottawa: King's Printer, 1914).

4   Nicholson, *Canadian Expeditionary Force*, 5.

5   Avner Offer, *The First World War: An Agrarian Interpretation* (Oxford: University of Oxford Press, 1989), chapter 11.

6   External Affairs, *Documents on Canadian External Relations Vol. I, 1909–1918* (Ottawa: Queen's Printer, 1967), 48. Telegram from Perley to Borden, 10 September 1914.

7   Ibid., 47–50. Telegrams between Borden and Perley, 7, 29 September 1914.

8   Office of Census and Statistics, *The Canada Yearbook 1914* (Ottawa: King's Printer, 1915–1920), 60–75; J.L. Granatstein and J. Mackay Hitsman, *Broken Promises: A History of Conscription in Canada* (Toronto: Oxford University Press, 1977), 23–24; Nicholson, Appendix C. The often quoted 1914 population of 7.2 million is taken from the 1911 national census, the last compiled before the war, and is therefore not accurate. By 1919 Canada's population was roughly 8.3 million. The percentage of French-Canadians would not increase over the course of the war. Although they accounted for 30 percent of the total Canadian population, French-Canadians made up only 4 percent of all Canadian volunteers, and recruitment levels in Quebec were the lowest of any province.

9   LAC, RG9III-D-3, Vol. 4911, Reel T-10703. War Diaries: Princess Patricia's Canadian Light Infantry, 1914-1915. The PPCLI was independently raised and funded by Montreal millionaire Captain Andrew Hamilton Gault. The PPCLI was absorbed into the Canadian 3rd Division on 22 December 1915.

10 Driss Maghraoui, "Moroccan Colonial Soldiers: Between Selective Memory and Collective Memory—Beyond Colonialism and Nationalism in North Africa," *Arab Studies Quarterly* 20, 2 (1998): 21–25.

11 Shelby Cullom Davis, *Reservoirs of Men: A History of the Black Troops of French West Africa* (Westport: Negro Universities Press, 1970), 142–143.

12 David Omissi, *Indian Voices of the Great War: Soldiers' Letters, 1914–1918* (London: Macmillan Press, 1999), 2–4.

13 "Canadian Indians and World War One," *Saskatchewan Indian Federated College Journal* 1, 1 (1984): 67.

14 LAC, RG24-c-1-a, Vol. 1221, Part 1 HQ-593-1-7. Hodgins to Hughes, with Reply, 8 August 1914.

15   LAC, RG24-c-1-a, Vol. 1221, Part 1 HQ-593-1-7. Hodgins to P.J. Scott (Indian agent Southampton, Ontario), 23 June 1915; Hodgins to J.E. Armstrong (Petrolia, Ontario) and J.C. Nethercott (Methodist Missionary, Moraviantown, Ontario), 18 October 1915; Major General Eugene Fiset, Surgeon General and Deputy Minister of Militia to Duncan Campbell Scott, 22 October 1915; S. Stewart, Secretary of Militia to W.R. Brown (Indian agent Port Arthur, Ontario), 28 October 1915; D.C. Scott to C. McKay (Prince Albert, Saskatchewan), 9 November 1915; Militia Internal Circular, 8 December 1915; RG10, Vol. 6766, Reel C-8511, File 452-13. List: Military Districts and Number of Indians of Military Age.

16   Lackenbauer and McGowan, "Competing Loyalties," 112n.

17   Dempsey, Warriors, 38-39.

18   Ibid., 39. The assumption in the language is that Indians would only be compelled to fight in the event of war with the United States.

19   LAC, RG10, Vol. 6762, Reel C-8508, File 452-2-1. Letter from Chief F.W. Jacobs and Chief E to Scott, August 1914.

20   LAC, RG10, Vol. 6762, Reel C-8508, File 452-2-1. Letter from Chief F.W. Jacobs and Chief E to Scott, August 1914, with Reply 15 September 1914.

21   LAC, RG10, Vol. 6762, Reel C-8508, File 452-2-1. Letter from Chiefs of Sucker Creek to Indian Agent W. McLeod (Manitowaning, Ontario), 26 August 1914; Letter from Chief James Pahpewash to Indian agent W. McLeod (Manitowaning, Ontario); Indians of Manitoulin Island to McLeod, 7 September 1914; 1 September 1914; Letter from Indian Council of Christian Island to Indian Affairs, 2 September 1914.

22   LAC, RG10, Vol. 6762, Reel C-8508, File 452-2-1. Memorandum Indian Affairs, 19 August 1914; Letter from W.M. Halliday (Indian Agent Alert Bay, B.C.) to J.D. McLean (Secretary DIA), 11 September 1914; Letter from Teddy Yellow Fly (Blackfoot Indians) to D.C. Scott, 23 September 1914; Letter D.C. Scott to W.M. Tait (Pincher Creek, Alberta), 24 March 1915.

23   LAC, RG10, Vol. 6762, Reel C-8508, File 452-2-1. Minutes Oshweken Council House, 15 September 1914; Gordon J. Smith (Indian Office Brantford) to D.C. Scott, 16 September 1914; Reply 21 September 1914; Smith to Scott, 26 October 1914.

24   Scott, "Canadian Indians," 293.

25   Ibid., 223. Scott's statement concerning BC Indian nations is certainly a sweeping generalization and is not entirely accurate. While it is reasonably accurate for the southern coastal and Salishan communities, the nations of the central and northern coast and the Kootenay in the southeast all had long-standing martial traditions.

26   LAC, RG10, Vol. 6766, Reel C-8511, File 452-13. Letter from Deasy to Department of Indian Affairs, 1 September 1914, Reply 10 September 1914.

27   Cook, At the Sharp End, 28-30.

28   Mountain Horse, My People, The Bloods, 139, 144.

29   Dempsey, Warriors, 21.

30   LAC, RG10, Vol. 3180, Reel C-11335, File 452, 124-1a. McLean to Iver Fougner (Indian agent Bella Coola/Bella Bella, BC), 13 October 1914.

31   LAC, RG10, Vol. 3180, Reel C-11335, File 452, 124-1a. Scott to Rev. George Prewer (Principal Chapleau Indian Boarding School, Ontario), 21 January 1915; RG10, Vol. 6762, Reel C-8508, File 452-2-2. Letter DIA to Charlie Tucker (Indian agent Bella Coola, BC), December 1914.

32   Verne De Witt Rowell, "Canadian Indians at the Front," *New York Times Current History* 6, 2 (1917), 291.

33   LAC, RG24, Vol. 1221, File 593-1-7. Departmental Letters: Ministry of Militia and Department of Indian Affairs, 1914–1915.

34   James W. Walker, "Race and Recruitment in World War I: Enlistment of Visible Minorities in the Canadian Expeditionary Force," *Canadian Historical Review* 52, 1 (1989): 4–5.

35   Sheffield, "Indifference, Difference and Assimilation," 61–62.

36   LAC, RG150, Box 2648, 15-25. Personal Records First World War; Six Nations of the Grand River Community Archives.

37   LAC, RG10, Vol. 3180, Reel C-11335, File 452, 124-1a. Indian Office Brantford to Department of Indian Affairs, 19, 28 August 1914.

38   Cook, *At the Sharp End*, 71.

39   Joseph Boyden, *Three Day Road* (Toronto: Penguin Books, 2005).

40   Adrian Hayes, *Pegahmagabow: Legendary Warrior, Forgotten Hero* (Sault Ste. Marie: Fox Meadow Creations, 2006), 8–9, 22–23.

41   LAC, RG10, Vol. 3180, Reel C-11335, File 452, 124-1a. Letter from W.J. Dilworth (Indian agent Blood Agency, Alberta) to D.C. Scott, 21 December 1914; RG10, Reel C-10204, Vol. 4063, File 402890. Correspondence Regarding the Appointment of Glen Campbell as Chief Inspector of Agencies, Reserves and Inspectorates in Manitoba, Saskatchewan, Alberta and the Northwest Territories/ Also Subsequent Work while on Loan to Ministry of Militia and Defence and Death as Lieutenant-Colonel in France; RG150, 1992-93/166, 1434. Service Records Glen Campbell.

42   Dempsey, *Warriors*, 19–24.

43   Lackenbauer and McGowan, "Competing Loyalties," 89–115, 96–97, 113–114n. Merritt was the grandson of William Hamilton Merritt, who had been an early Canadian politician and was the driving force behind the building of the Welland Canal. The younger Merritt served in the 1885 North-West Rebellion, commanded an irregular mounted force during the Boer War and eventually commanded the 1st Cavalry Brigade of the Number Two Militia Division until 1913. He was made honorary chief by the Cayuga in 1886. Merritt was also the president of the Canadian Defence League.

44   Walker, "Race and Recruitment," 3.

Chapter Five

1   On 25 May 1915, Law replaced Harcourt as colonial secretary. He was born in New Brunswick and moved to Glasgow at the age of twelve. He is the only British prime minster to have been born outside of the United Kingdom.

2   House of Lords Records Office/Parliamentary Archives (London, UK), Andrew Bonar Law Papers, BL/55/16. Memorandum: Colonial Office to Governors General and Administrators of British Dominions, Colonies and Protectorates, 8 October 1915; Cabinet Memorandum to the Dominions: The Question of Raising Native Troops for Imperial Service, 18 October 1915 (also contained in Harcourt Papers-445).

3   Bonar Law Papers, BL/52/1. Memorandum, 1 December 1915.

4   LAC, RG10, Vols. 6762-6808. Lists of Native Canadians Killed or Wounded and Settlement, Separation and Pension Claims and Files Concerning Indian Enlistment and Service.

5   Bill Rawling, *Surviving Trench Warfare: Technology and the Canadian Corps 1914-1918* (Toronto: University of Toronto Press, 1992), 218; Cook, *At the Sharp End*, 159, 206. The actions at St. Eloi were spearheaded by the 2nd Canadian Division.

6   J.L. Granatstein and J. Mackay Hitsman, *Broken Promises: A History of Conscription in Canada* (Toronto: Oxford University Press, 1977), 36.

7   External Affairs, *Documents on Canadian External Relations Vol. I, 1909-1918*, 103-104. Telegram from Borden to Perley, 31 December 1915; Letter from Borden to Perley, 4 January 1916.

8   Ibid., 93-94. Telegram from Borden to Perley, 30 October 1915.

9   Michael Bliss, *Right Honourable Men* (New York: Harper Collins, 1994), 81.

10   Alan R. Capon, *His Faults Lie Gently: The Incredible Sam Hughes* (Lindsay, ON: Floyd W. Hall, 1969), 140.

11   LAC, MG27IID23, Vol. 1, File 8. Borden to the Governor General in Council, 22 September 1916.

12   LAC, MG27IID23, Vol. 1, File 8. Ordinance: Overseas Military Forces of Canada.

13   Resolution IX of the 1917 Imperial War Cabinet Conference granted the dominions a greater influence in British foreign and war policy and "an adequate voice in foreign policy and foreign relations and should provide effective arrangements for continuous consultation in all important matters of common Imperial concern."

14   Ronald G. Haycock, "Recruiting, 1914-1916," in *Canadian Military History: Selective Readings*, ed. Marc Milner (Toronto: Irwin Publishing, 1998), 67.

15   Nicholson, *Canadian Expeditionary Force*, Appendix C.

16   LAC, RG24, Vol. 1221, File HQ-593-1-7. Letter from Duncan to Deputy Minster of Militia, Eugene Fiset, 25 October 1915; J.D. McLean to Fiset, 4 December 1915.

17   LAC, RG10, Vol. 6766, Reel 8511, File 452-13. Letter D.C. Scott to W.C. McKay, 9 November 1915; Letter J.D. McLean to A.M. Tyson (Inspector Indian Agencies Vancouver, BC), 1 December 1915; Fiset to Scott, 22 October 1915.

18   LAC, RG10, Vol. 3180, Reel C-11335, File 452, 124-1a. Letter D.C. Scott to Rev. George Prewer (Principal Chapleau Indian Boarding School, Ontario), 21 January 1915.

19   LAC, RG10, Vol. 6766, Reel C-8511, File 452-13. Oshweken Council House Minutes, 24 March 1915; W.J. Smith (Indian agent Brantford) to D.C. Scott, 28 April 1915.

20   Lackenbauer and McGowan, "Competing Loyalties," 101.

21   LAC, RG24-c-1-a, Vol. 1221, File HQ-593-1-7. Letter from Thomas Deasy to D.C. Scott, 22 November 1915; Letter from Donaldson to Hughes, 26 November 1915.

22   Dempsey, *Warriors*, 23.

23   LAC, RG150, 1992-93/166, 1434—First World War Service Records Glen Campbell; RG10, Reel C-10204, Vol. 4063, File 402890. Correspondence Regarding the Appointment of Glen Campbell as Chief Inspector of Agencies, Reserves and Inspectorates in Manitoba, Saskatchewan, Alberta and the Northwest Territories/ Also Subsequent Work while on Loan to Department of Militia and Defence and Death as Lieutenant Colonel in France. Letter from Fiset to Scott, 14 July 1915, Reply 16 July 1915.

24   LAC, RG10, Vol. 3180, Reel C-11335, File 452, 124-1a. Despatches: *The Canadian Gazette*, Dominion of Canada, Message from His Majesty the King, 25 October 1915.

25   LAC, RG24-c-1-a, Vol. 1221, File HQ-593-1-7. Letter from Ministry of Militia to A.G. Chisholm (Lawyer, London, Ontario), 26 November 1917.

26   LAC, RG24-c-1-a, Vol. 1221, File HQ-593-1-7. Letters: Col. L.W. Shannon (OC No. 1 Military District) to Ministry of Militia, 2 December 1915; Letter from MGen. William Logie (OC No. 2 Military District) to Hodgins, 3 December 1915; Letter from Hughes to Donaldson, 4 December 1915; Circular Letter, Department of Militia and Defence to OC Divisions and Districts, Inspector General of Eastern Canada and Inspector General of Western Canada, 10 December 1915; RG10, Vol. 6766, Reel C-8511, File 452-13. Letter J.D. McLean to Deasy, 3 December 1915; McLean to Fiset, 4 December 1915, Reply 9 December 1915.

27   LAC, RG24-c-1-a, Vol. 1221, File HQ-593-1-7. Letter from Hodgins to McKay, 3 January 1916; Gwatkin Memorandum, 6 January 1916.

28   LAC, RG150, Box 5135-5-6. Service Records Albert and Enos Kick.

29   Kick as quoted in Susan Applegate Krouse (original documentation by Joseph K. Dixon), *North American Indians in the Great War* (Lincoln: University of Nebraska Press, 2007), 21. LAC, RG10, Vol. 6765, Reel C-8510, File 452-9. Letter S.R. McVitty (Mount Elgin Industrial Institute) to Indian agent Muncey, Ontario, 13 October 1918.

30   Original spelling and punctuation. LAC, RG10, Vol. 3180, Reel C-11335, File 452, 124-1a. Letter Jennie Kick to Indian Affairs, 13 April 1916; Reply 21 April 1916; *Hordenville Weekly Review*, "Oneida Killed at Front," 28 June 1917.

31   Fred Gaffen, *Cross-Border Warriors: Canadians in American Forces, Americans in Canadian Forces from the Civil War to the Gulf* (Toronto: Dundurn Press, 1995), 14.

32   See Britten, *American Indians;* Russel L. Barsh, "American Indians in the Great War," *Ethnohistory* 38, 3 (1991): 276-303; Michael L. Tate, "From Scout to Doughboy: The National Debate Over Integrating American Indians into the Military, 1891-1918," *Western Historical Quarterly* 17, 4 (1986): 417-437.

33   Susan Applegate Krouse, *North American Indians in the Great War* (Lincoln University of Nebraska Press, 2007).

34   LAC, RG24-c-1-a, Vol. 1221-1, File HQ-593-1-7. Letter from Attorney Charles F. Fitzgerald to Ministry of Militia, 9 August 1919, Reply 12 October 1920.

35   LAC, RG24, Vol. 4380, File 34-7-89-Vol. 1. Letter from Hughes to Baxter, 6 December 1915.

36   LAC, RG10, Vol. 3180, Reel C-11335, File 452,124-1a. Letter Baxter to Williams, 18 December 1915.

37   LAC, RG24, Vol. 4383, File MD2-34-7-109. Various correspondence between Baxter, Logie, Scott and Hodgins; RG10, Vol. 6765, Reel C-8510, File 452-7. Letter from Baxter to Scott, 21 January 1916.

38   LAC, RG24, Vol. 4383, File MD2-34-7-109. Letters from Bn OCs 119th Bn, 161st Bn and 227th Bn to Logie, 4 May, 9 August, and 4 May 1916.

39   LAC, RG10, Vol. 6765, Reel C-8510, File 452-7. Letter from Scott to Logie, 19 January 1916, Reply 21 January 1916; Letter Baxter to Scott, 21 January 1916, Reply 25 January 1916; RG24, Vol. 4383, File MD2-34-7-109. Letter Scott to Logie 19 January 1916, Reply 20 January 1916; Letter Logie to Baxter 22 January 1916; Letter Scott to (No. 2 District Recruiting CO), Maj. George Williams, 31 January 1916; Reply 2 February 1916; Cooke to Scott, Report Ending 14 February 1916; *The Globe Toronto* "96 Indians Join 114th Batt.," 8 February 1916.

40   LAC, RG150, 1992-93/166, 9622. Service Records Andrew T. Thompson.

41   Ibid. Five generations of the Thompson family (of Scottish ancestry) lived at the Ruthven Park estate outside Cayuga from 1845 to 1993, including Andrew Thompson. The 1,500-acre Ruthven Park is now a Canadian National Historic Site.

42 Parliament of Canada, Senators and Members: Andrew Thorburn Thompson. www. parl.gc.ca.

43 Scott, *1919 Report*, 7.

44 LAC, RG24, Vol. 4380, File 34-7-89-Vol. 1. WWI Organization 114th Overseas Battalion; LAC, RG24, Vol. 4383, File MD2-34-7-109. Letter Thompson to Logie, 1 March 1916.

45 LAC, RG24, Vol. 4380, File 34-7-89-Vol. 1. Letter from Scott to Logie, 31 May 1916.

46 LAC, RG10, Volume 6765, Reel C-8510, File 452-7. Letter Thompson to Scott, 13 April 1916.

47 LAC, RG24, Vol. 4383, File MD2-34-7-109. OC 227th Bn to Logie, 4 May 1916.

48 LAC, RG10, Volume 6765, Reel C-8510, File 452-7. Letters Cooke to Scott, February and April 1916; Letter Scott to R.J. Lewis (Indian agent Manitoulin Island District), 30 May 1916; Letter Scott to Logie 31 May 1916.

49 P. Whitney Lackenbauer, *Battle Grounds: The Canadian Military and Aboriginal Lands* (Vancouver: University of British Columbia Press, 2007), 81; J.R. Miller, "Owen Glendower, Hotspur, and Canadian Indian Policy," *Ethnohistory* 37, 4 (1990): 386–391.

50 LAC, RG24-c-1-a, Vol. 12221, File HQ-593-1-7. Transfer Tyendinaga Mohawks, 29 May 1916, 20 June 1916.

51 LAC, RG24, Vol. 4383, File MD2-34-7-109. Report of Indians at Camp Borden, 13 September 1916; Various Correspondence Battalions June-July 1916.

52 LAC, RG9-II-B-10, Vols. 31, 38. Nominal Rolls, 114th Overseas Battalion; LAC, RG24-C-1-a, Vol. 1562, File 1. Pay Sheets, 114th Overseas Battalion.

53 LAC, RG24, Vol. 1562, File HQ 683-173-2. Letter from Thompson to Adjutant General, Ministry of Militia, 25 March 1916.

54 Ibid.

55 LAC, RG24, Vol. 1562, File HQ 683-173-2. Inspection Report, 114th Overseas Battalion, 17 October 1916.

56 Robert was a descendant of the Campbell Clan, members of which were the perpetrators of the Glencoe Massacre (Scotland) on 13 February 1692 during the era of the Glorious Revolution and Jacobinism. Seventy-seven members of the MacDonald Clan, including women and children, were killed (or died as a result of the massacre) by Captain Robert Campbell and his followers.

57 Grant MacEwan, *Fifty Mighty Men* (Saskatoon: Western Producer, 1958), 116–119; Kenneth Stephen Coates, *Dictionary of Canadian Biography—Robert Campbell.* www. biographi.ca.

58 Glen also contracted typhoid at this time.

59 Desmond Morton, *Dictionary of Canadian Biography—Glenlyon Archibald Campbell*, www.biographi.ca; MacEwan, *Fifty Mighty Men*, 116–118.

60 Charles Arkoll Boulton, *Reminiscences of the North-west Rebellions: with a record of the raising of Her Majesty's 100th regiment in Canada, and a chapter on Canadian social and political life* (Toronto: Grip Printing and Publishing, 1886); Chapter 14–Batoche Captured; LAC, RG150, 1992–93/166, 1434—First World War Service Records Glen Campbell.

61 Coates, *Dictionary*. Vandervort, *Indian Wars*, 161–191.

62 According to the town of Gilbert Plains, Manitoba, in 1884 Campbell rode his horse over the Riding Mountains into what is now known as the Gilbert Plains and found only one man, Métis Gilbert Ross, and his wife living in a small cabin. Campbell traded his horse for the cabin and moved in. See O.E.A. Brown, *Settlers of the Plains* (Gilbert Plains, MB: Maple Leaf Press, 1953).

63 MacEwan, *Fifty Mighty Men*, 120–121; Morton, *Dictionary*; Parliament of Canada, Senators and Members—Glenlyon Archibald Campbell. Sifton was the MP for Brandon, Manitoba. He was minister of the interior and superintendent general for Indian Affairs in Laurier's cabinet from 1896 to 1905. He was largely responsible for the influx of eastern Europeans (some 3 million) to western Canada at the turn of the century. He was knighted by King George V on 1 January 1915.

64 Morton, *Dictonary*.

65 *New York Times*, "Branded as Liar in Ottawa House," 18 March 1911.

66 MacEwan, *Fifty Mighty Men*, 121. Another anecdote reportedly has Campbell re-enacting his account of riding a Bull Moose for members of the House of Commons.

67 LAC, RG10, Reel C-10204, Vol. 4063, File 402890. Correspondence Regarding the Appointment of Glen Campbell as Chief Inspector of Agencies, Reserves and Inspectorates in Manitoba, Saskatchewan, Alberta and the Northwest Territories. Also Subsequent Work while on Loan to Department of Militia and Defence and Death as Lieutenant Colonel in France. Saulteaux are a branch of the Ojibwa Nation within the Algonquian language grouping. They are also referred to as Anishinaabe. Harriet Campbell (née Burns) died on 17 May 1910 at the age of forty-four.

68 LAC, RG150, 1992-93/166, 1434—First World War Service Records LCol. Glen Campbell.

69 LAC, RG10, Vol. 6766, Reel C-8511, File 452-13. Letter Campbell to Scott, 3 February 1916; Reply 7 February 1916. In *Warriors of the King*, James Dempsey asserts that perhaps Campbell's initial motivation to recruit underage Indians was simply to increase his battalion's strength. Campbell could also have been using his former position of power within the Ministry of Indian Affairs and the Ministry itself to undermine or intimidate parents, chiefs and band councils into agreeing to this policy.

70 Office of Census and Statistics, *The Canada Yearbook, 1916*, 640.

71 Duncan Campbell Scott, *The Administration of Indian Affairs in Canada* (Ottawa: Canadian Institute of International Affairs, 1931), 17.

72 LAC, RG24-c-1-a, Vol. 1221, File HQ-593-1-7. Letter from OC No. 10 Military District to Militia Council, 3 February 1916.

73 LAC, RG10, Vol. 6766, Reel C-8511, File 452-13. Letter Campbell to Scott, 3 February 1916; Morton, *Dictionary*.

74 Office of Census and Statistics, *The Canada Yearbook 1914*, 640. Statistics for the rest of Canada: PEI 61 percent; NS 62 percent; NB 50 percent; QC 26 percent English, 48 percent French; BC 33 percent.

75 LAC, RG9III-D-3, Vol. 5010, Reel T10859, File 725. War Diaries 107th Canadian Pioneer Battalion; Dempsey, *Warriors*, 25.

76 Dempsey, *Warriors*, 25–27.

77 Steven A. Bell, "The 107th 'Timber Wolf' Battalion at Hill 70," *Canadian Military History* 5, 1 (1996): 78.

78 Glenlyon Campbell, interview with the author, 15 January 2008.

79   LAC, RG9-II-B-10, Vols. 31, 38. Nominal Rolls-114th Overseas Battalion; RG24-C-1-a, Vol. 1562, File 1. Pay Sheets, 114th Overseas Battalion; RG150, 1992-93/166, 1434. Service Records Glen Campbell.

80   LAC, RG24, Vol. 4383, File MD2-34-7-109. Report: Indians at Camp Borden, 13 September 1916; LAC, RG10, Vol. 3181, Reel C-11332, File 452, 124-1a. Report Indian Affairs, 4 November 1916.

81   LAC, RG10, Vol. 6762, Reel C-8508, File 452-2-2. Letter from Office of the Minister of the Interior to Scott, 13 April 1916; Scott to Deputy Minister of the Interior, W.W. Cory, 20 April 1916; Scott to A.P. Sladon, 4 May 1916.

82   LAC, RG10, Vol. 3180, C-11335, File 452, 124-1a. Port Arthur *Evening Chronicle*, 4 November 1915; *Saskatchewan Journal*, 7-14 November 1915; RG10, Vol. 3181, Reel C-11335, File 452, 124-1a. *Brandon Sun*, unknown month or day, 1918; Port Arthur *Daily News-Chronicle*, 2 November 1916; RG10, Vol. 6765, Reel C-8510, File 452-7. *Brantford Expositor*, 10 April 1916.

83   I have always found it ironic that Indian warriors were referred to as "Braves" (i.e., the Atlanta Braves).

84   De Witt Rowell, "Canadian Indians at the Front," 291.

85   For example, these numbers appear in the *Ottawa Citizen*, "Red Men on the Firing Line," 19 November 1916, and the *Regina Leader*, "Indians are doing their bit in the Great War," 18 November 1916.

86   LAC, RG10, Vol. 3181, Reel C-11335, File 452, 124-1a. Report Indian Affairs, 4 November 1916; Letter Scott to Ernest Green, 14 November 1916; Office of Census and Statistics, *The Canadian Yearbook 1915*, 639.

87   Mountain Horse, *My People, The Bloods*, 139.

88   LAC, RG24-c-1-a, Vol. 1221, File HQ-593-1-7. Letter Scott to Fiset, 24 February 1916; RG10, Vol. 6766, Reel C-8511, File 452-13. Letter W. Scott Simpson (Indian Agent Stikine/Tahltan, B.C.), 5 March 1916, Letter Fiset to Scott, 30 March 1916.

89   LAC, RG10, Vol. 3181, Reel C-11335, File 452, 124-1a. *Victoria Daily Times*, "Indians Respond to Call to Arms: Deputy Superintendent General is Visitor Here to Meet Indian Lands Commission," 12 June 1916.

90   LAC, RG24-c-1-a, Vol. 1221, File HQ-593-1-7. Letter Henderson to Hughes, 18 March 1916.

91   LAC, RG24-c-1-a, Vol. 1221, File HQ-593-1-7. Memorandums Graham to Campbell, 30 November, 4 December 1916; Letter Cooke to Militia Council and Scott, 15 December 1916.

92   LAC, RG10, Vol. 6766, Reel C-8511, File 452-13. Letter McCarthy to W.J. Roche (Indian Affairs), 21 August 1916; Letter McCarthy to Scott, 22 October 1916.

93   Dennis and Leslie McLaughlin, *For My Country: Black Canadians on the Field of Honour* (Ottawa: Department of National Defence, 2004), 18–22.

94   Calvin W. Ruck, *The Black Battalion 1916-1920: Canada's Best Kept Military Secret* (Halifax: Nimbus Publishing, 1987), 10.

95   Walker, "Race and Recruitment," 11.

96   The only black to be commissioned was the Reverend William A. White, who was bestowed with the honorary rank of captain, as was customary for military chaplains.

97   John G. Armstrong, "The Unwelcome Sacrifice: A Black Unit in the Canadian Expeditionary Force, 1917–19," in *Ethnic Armies: Polyethnic Armed Forces From the Time of the Habsburgs to the Age of the Superpowers*, ed. N.F. Dreisziger (Waterloo: Wilfrid Laurier University Press), 1990, 186.

98   LAC, RG24-c-1-a, Vol. 1221, File HQ-593-1-7. Various correspondence between Thunderwater, Hodgins, Logie and Fiset, December 1916–January 1917.

99   Walker, "Race and Recruitment," 14.

100   Ibid., 20.

101   Ibid., 23.

102   Armstrong, "Unwelcome Sacrifice," 187–188.

103   See Roy Ito, *We Went to War: The Story of the Japanese Canadians who Served in the First and Second World Wars* (Stittsville, ON: Canada's Wings, 1984).

104   John Herd Thompson, *Ethnic Minorities during Two World Wars* (Ottawa: Canadian Historical Association, Government of Canada, 1991), 5–7.

105   LAC, RG10, Vol. 6766, Reel C-8511, File 452-13. Letter Scott to W.B. Brown (Indian agent Port Arthur, Ontario), 21 March 1916.

106   Jonathan F. Vance, *Death So Noble: Memory, Meaning, and the First World War* (Vancouver: University of British Columbia Press, 1997), 245.

107   LAC, RG10, Vol. 6766, Reel C-8511, File 452-13. Letter W.J. Dilworth (Indian agent Blood Agency, Alberta) to Scott, 17 January 1916; Dempsey, 26. In 1940, the Canadian Tuberculosis Association reported that for every 100 Canadian soldiers to be killed in the Great War, six died of tuberculosis.

108   Dempsey, *Warriors*, 24. The United States' policy towards their Indian soldiers was very similar to that of Canada. They maintained a policy of integration. However, they did have units that were made up primarily of Indians such as the 142nd, 158th and 358th Infantry Regiments.

109   Alan Clark, *The Donkeys* (London: Hutchinson, 1961).

110   Scott, *1919 Report of the Deputy Superintendent General*, 15.

111   LAC, RG9, III-D-3, Vol. 5010, Reel T-10859, File 725—War Diaries 107th Pioneer Battalion; Morton.

112   LAC, RG9, III-D-3, Vol. 5010, Reel T-10859, File 725—War Diaries 107th Pioneer Battalion.

113   The twenty-four-hour clock was at this time in use.

114   LAC, RG9, III-D-3, Vol. 5010, Reel T-10859, File 725—War Diaries 107th Pioneer Battalion; Bell, "The 107th 'Timber Wolf' Battalion at Hill 70," 74–76.

115   LAC, RG9, III-D-3, Vol. 5010, Reel T-10859, File 725—War Diaries 107th Pioneer Battalion; Scott, *1919 Report of the Deputy Superintendent General*, 15. The total number of Canadian casualties at Hill 70, from 15 to 25 August, was 9,198. Six Victoria Crosses were awarded to Canadian soldiers during this action.

116   LAC, RG9, III-D-3, Vol. 5010, Reel T-10859, File 725—War Diaries 107th Pioneer Battalion.

117   LAC, RG150, 1992-93/166, 1434. Service Records Glen Campbell; LAC, RG9III-D-3, Vol. 5010, Reel T10859, File 725. War Diaries-107th Pioneer Battalion. According to his great-grandson Glenlyon, "Glen had kidney problems for quite a few years before he went overseas. He had tried to stop a team of stampeding horses at a parade in Dauphin, was trampled, and never fully recovered. Allegedly, during one operation in Winnipeg, he refused anaesthetic, so he could watch the surgery" (Interview with the author).

118 LAC, RG24-c-1-a, Vol. 1221, File HQ-593-1-7. Memorandum with Ministry of Militia and OCs Military Districts from Gwatkin, 20 December 1916.

Chapter Six

1 John Keegan, *The First World War* (Toronto: Random House, 1998), 257

2 Ian Ousby, *The Road to Verdun* (London: Pimlico, 2003), 4–6; John Keegan, *The First World War* (Toronto: Random House, 2000), 286–299.

3 Erich Maria Remarque, *All Quiet on the Western Front* (New York: Fawcett Crest, 1982), 134–135.

4 At Caporetto, also known as the 12th Battle of the Isonzo, the Italians suffered 10,000 killed, 30,000 wounded, 293,000 taken prisoner, and 400,000 deserters; the Austro-Hungarian and German divisions had only a fraction of these casualties.

5 The net gain of the *Westheer* between November 1917 and March 1918 has been the subject of much debate. See John Hussey, "Debate: The Movement of German Divisions to the Western Front, Winter 1917–1918," *War in History* 4, 2 (1997): 213–220; Tim Travers, "Debate: Reply to John Hussey: The Movement of German Divisions to the Western Front, Winter 1917–1918," *War in History* 5, 3 (1998): 367–370; Giordan Fong, "Debate: The Movement of German Divisions to the Western Front, Winter 1917–1918," *War in History* 7, 2 (2000): 225–235.

6 LAC, RG10, Vol. 6770, Reel C-8514, File 452-26-1. Notes on Registration.

7 LAC, RG10, Vol. 6767, Reel C-8512, File 452-17. Memorandum D.C. Scott to all Indian agents, 22 February 1917.

8 LAC, RG10, Vol. 6766, Reel C-8511, File 452-12. Letter Chiefs of Wanikewin to J.D. McLean, 9 January 1917, Reply 11 January 1917.

9 LAC, RG10, Vol. 6768, Reel C-8512, File 452-20. Letter Chief Keepinais to Scott, 2 July 1917; Petition September 1917.

10 LAC, RG10, Vol. 6766, Reel C-8511, File 452-12. Letter Gadieux to W.R. Brown (Indian agent Port Arthur), January 1917; Brown to Scott, 16 January 1917.

11 Dempsey, *Warriors*, 36–37.

12 LAC, RG10, Vol. 6766, Reel C-8511, File 452-12. Scott to Secretary National Service Board, 22 January 1917; McLean to Chiefs Manitoulin Island, 1 February 1917.

13 Rawling, *Surviving Trench Warfare*, 238–240.

14 Nicholson, *Canadian Expeditionary Force*, Appendix C. In fact, during the first three years of the war, Ottawa allocated only $27,000 to recruitment, most of it in 1917 alone.

15 Walker, "Race and Recruitment," 18.

16 LAC, RG10, Vol. 6768, Reels C-8512, C-8513, Files 452-20-1,2,3. *The Evening Telegram*, 23 September 1918.

17 LAC, RG10, Vol. 6768, Reels C-8512, C-8513 File 452-20-1,2,3. Various correspondence among D.C. Scott, Indian Affairs, chiefs, and agents concerning the Military Service Bill and the *Military Service Act*.

18 LAC, RG10, Vol. 6768, Reel C-8512, File 452-20-1. Petition of the Port Simpson and Kitkatla Bands of Indians to Borden, November 1917; Letter Prince to Scott, 27 November 1917.

19 LAC, RG10, Vol. 6768, Reel C-8512, File 452-20-1. Letter G.M. Campbell (Indian Agent Deseronto/Tyendinaga) to Scott, 24 December 1917.

20   LAC, RG10, Vol. 6768, Reels C-8512, C-8513 File 452-20-1,2,3. Letter Long to Governor General, Borden and Ministries 2 November 1917; Angus to the King, 13 November 1917.

21   Dempsey, *Warriors*, 39.

22   LAC, RG10, Vol. 6768, Reels C-8512, C-8513, Files 452-20-1,2,3. Letter Scott to E.F. Jarvis (acting deputy minister of militia), 22 August 1917; Scott to Newcombe, 1 October 1917.

23   Dempsey, *Warriors*, 37. The Robinson Treaty refers to three distinct treaties signed by Ojibwa groups in the vicinities of Lakes Superior and Huron and the Crown between 7 and 9 September 1850 and 13 October 1854; Treaty Numbers 60, 61, and 72 respectively.

24   LAC, RG10, Vol. 6768, Reels C-8512, C-8513, Files 452-20-1,2,3. Letter McKenzie to Scott, 18 October 1917, with Reply 24 October 1917; Scott to Newcombe, 5 November 1917; Memorandum Scott to all Agents, 5 November 1917.

25   LAC, RG10, Vol. 6768, Reels C-8512, C-8513, Files 452-20-1,2,3. Notice: Military Service Act, 1917 to Hunters, Lumbermen, and Others, 13 November 1917.

26   Dempsey, *Warriors*, 41.

27   LAC, RG10, Vol. 6768, Reels C-8512, C-8513, Files 452-20-1,2,3. Circular Memorandum: Chas. J. Dohorty, Minister of Justice, 15 November 1917; Letter Borden to Newcombe, 19 November 1917; Newcombe to Scott, 7 December 1917.

28   LAC, RG10, Vol. 6768, Reel C-8515, File 452-20 Pt. 2. Memorandums pertaining to Indian Conscription (November 1917 to January 1918).

29   LAC, RG10, Vol. 6768, Reels C-8512, C-8513, Files 452-20-1,2,3. Governor General in Council: Military Service Act Regulations, 17 January 1918. East Indians were granted exemption three weeks later. Blacks were not exempted, as they enjoyed the franchise.

30   LAC, RG10, Vol. 6767, Reel C-8512, File 452-15 Pt. 1. Memorandum of 20 February 1918.

31   LAC, RG10, Vol. 6768, Reels C-8512, C-8513, Files 452-20-1,2,3. Department of Militia and Defence: Status of Indians under the *MSA*, 22 February 1918.

32   Alistair Sweeny, *Government Policy and Saskatchewan Indian Veterans: A Brief History of the Canadian Government's Treatment of Indian Veterans of the Two World Wars* (Saskatchewan: Indian Veterans' Association, 1979), 6–8.

33   Ibid., 9.

34   LAC, RG10, Vol. 6770, Reel C-5814, File 452-24. Letters W.L. O'Connor (Office of the Secretary of State) to Scott, 1, 13 December 1917; RG9III, Vol. 5081. Dominion of Canada, Military Voter's Act, 1917: Directions of Guidance for Voters.

35   James Dempsey, *Aboriginal Soldiers and the First World War* (Ottawa: Library and Archives Canada, 2006), 2–3.

36   Ibid., 3.

37   LAC, RG10, Vol. 6768, Reels C-8512, File 452-20-1. Letter Cooke to McLean, 7 October 1918, Reply 12 October 1918; Scott to H.A. Machin (Director Military Service Branch), 16 April 1918.

38   LAC, RG10, Vol. 6770, Reel C-8514, File 452-26. Canada Registration Board: Regulations, 1918; Letter Scott to Robertson, 7 May 1918, Reply 9 May 1918. Note the word *resident* was used rather than *citizen*.

39   LAC, RG10, Vol. 6770, Reel C-8514, File 452-26. *Brantford Expositor*, "Six Nations' Indians Should Have Registered is Finding," 12 July 1918; Letter Scott to M. MacBride (mayor of Brantford).

40 LAC, RG10, Vol. 6765, Reel C-8510, File 452-7. Letter Cooke to Scott, 28 February 1917. The petition also cited the 17 October 1717 land grant to the Indians by the king of France, similar documents pertaining to establishment of Indian lands at Oka in 1718 and 1735, and agreements made with Sir William Johnson (British superintendent of Indian Affairs 1755-1774) and General Edward Braddock in 1755 during the Seven Years' War. In addition, the petition included a passage on the 200-year-long land dispute at Oka between the Mohawks and the local Seminary of St. Sulpice, which began in 1717. These same documents would be submitted as part of unsuccessful Kanesatake land claims with Indian Affairs in 1975 and 1977, and again in negotiations during the 1990 Oka Crisis. The continued failure of governments to negotiate, or acknowledge, Mohawk grievances at Kanesatake/Oka culminated in 1990 with the seventy-eight-day-long Oka Crisis, which necessitated the deployment of the Canadian Forces, 4,500 strong, to confront armed Mohawk warriors. See Timothy C. Winegard, *Oka: A Convergence of Cultures and the Canadian Forces* (Kingston: CDA Press, 2008).

41 LAC, RG10, Vol. 6771, File 452-27. Privy Council of Canada Regulations PC 815, 4 April 1918; Letter McLean to Council Fort William Band, 22 May 1918; Letter McLean to M. Campbell (Indian agent Tyendinaga/Deseronto), 29 May 1918.

42 Scott, "Canadian Indians," 289-290.

43 See Donald B. Smith, *From the Land of the Shadows: The Making of Grey Owl* (Saskatoon: Western Producer Prairie Books, 1990). This is considered the definitive biography.

44 See Donald B. Smith, *Chief Buffalo Child Long Lance: The Glorious Impostor* (Alberta: Red Deer Press, 2002). Again, this book is deemed to be the definitive biography.

45 As of February 1918, the British reorganization produced divisions of 16,000 men, divided up into three brigades of three battalions each. Under Currie, the Canadian Corps maintained four divisions of 23,000 men, made up of three brigades of four battalions, and also added 100 men to each existing battalion. A British division had three field engineer companies, whereas a Canadian division had nine, plus a pontoon bridging unit. A single machine gun battalion accompanied each British division. Canadian divisions had three times as many. This meant that there was one machine gun for every thirteen men. The British could only boast one for every sixty soldiers. Canadian Corps HQ also benefited. It had 100 more trucks, twice the signallers, and because the 5th Division's artillery brigades remained intact, had many more heavy guns and mortars at its disposal. Currie also knew that the formation of a Canadian Army (what he viewed as two significantly weak corps) might not guarantee Canadian autonomy, as such a big formation could not, in all cases, remain together. He also stressed that there were not enough qualified Canadian officers to fill the estimated positions (an increase of 33 percent), nor were there enough specialized Canadian soldiers to meet the requirements for an army's service and support units.

46 Rawling, *Surviving Trench Warfare*, 241-242. See also Shane B. Schreiber, *Shock Army of the British Empire: The Canadian Corps in the Last 100 Days of the Great War* (St. Catherine's: Vanwell Publishing, 2004).

47 See Schreiber, *Shock Army.*

48 This figure is drawn from Sir Arthur Currie, *Canadian Corps Operations, 1918* (Ottawa: Department of Militia and Defence, 1919).

49 LAC, RG10, Vol. 6766, File 452-13. Letter Fiset to Scott, 11 January 1917, Reply 15 January 1917.

50 LAC, RG10, Vol. 6766, Reel C-8511, File 452-13. Letter Scott to R.S. Gauthier (Indian agent, Maniwaki, Quebec), 22 January 1917.

51   LAC, RG10, Vol. 6766, Reel C-8511, File 452-13. Various correspondence Scott, Indian
     Affairs, BC agents and recruiters, January to April 1917.

52   LAC, RG10, Vol. 6766, Reel C-8511, File 452-13. Letter Scott to H. Graham (Indian
     Commissioner, BC), 14 February 1917.

53   LAC, RG10, Vol. 3181, Reel C-11335, File 452, 124-1a. Letter Tyson to Scott, 19 March
     1917.

54   Dempsey, *Warriors*, 25.

55   LAC, RG10, Vol. 3181, Reel C-11335, File 452, 124-1a. Letter Scott to Sapper W.C. Jacobs
     (6th CRT.), 4 July 1917.

56   LAC, RG10, Vol. 3181, Reel C-11335, File 452, 124-1a. Letter Sioux of Oak River to the
     King, 10 August 1916, Reply 9 January 1917.

Chapter Seven

1   Scott, "Canadian Indians," 285.

2   See Carl Hagenbeck, *Beasts and Men: Being Carl Hagenbeck's Experiences for Half a
     Century among Wild Animals* (London: Longmans, Green, 1912); Nigel Rothfels, *Savages
     and Beasts: The Birth of the Modern Zoo* (Baltimore: The Johns Hopkins University
     Press, 2002). Many of these Bella Coola Indians returned to their communities
     having been converted to Catholicism while in Europe; divisions still persist in their
     communities today.

3   David Huggonson, "Aboriginal Diggers of the 9th Brigade. First AIF," *Journal of the
     Royal Australian Historical Society* 79 (1993): 217.

4   Britten, *American Indians*, 107. My mother (the youngest of six children) and her family
     immigrated to Canada from the Netherlands in 1952. Her oldest siblings, who were
     teenagers during the Second World War in Nazi-occupied Holland, were disappointed
     when they disembarked at Montreal not to see a "country full of Red Indians."

5   Kenneth William Townsend, *World War II and the American Indian* (Albuquerque:
     University of New Mexico Press, 2000), 34.

6   Ibid., 33–35.

7   Britten, *American Indians*, 107–108.

8   Ernst Jünger, *The Storm of Steel* (London: Chatto and Windus, 1929), 5.

9   Britten, *American Indians*, 108.

10   Dempsey, *Warriors*, 63.

11   Ted Barris, *Victory at Vimy: Canada Comes of Age: April 9–12, 1917* (Toronto: Thomas
     Allen, 2007), 185.

12   Dianne Camurat, "The American Indian in the Great War: Real and Imagined"
     (master's thesis, Institut Charles V of the University of Paris VII, 1993), section 1.2.3.

13   Britten, *American Indians*, 109.

14   Lackenbauer and McGowan, "Competing Loyalties," 89–115.

15   Camurat, "American Indians," section 1.1.

16   Britten, *American Indians*, 100–101.

17   Ibid., 109.

18   Mountain Horse, *My People, The Bloods*, 74–75.

19   Hayes, *Pegahmagabow*, 29.

20   Britten, *American Indians*, 101.

21   Mountain Horse, *My People, The Bloods*, 30.

22   Dempsey, *Warriors*, 48, 58.

23   Dempsey, *Aboriginal Soldiers*, 4.

24   LAC, RG10, Vol. 3181, Reel C-11335, File 452, 124-1a. Letter Pegahmagabow to Scott, 8 March 1917. Many doctors believed it impossible for Indians to suffer shell shock because of their upbringing and "innate" stoicism.

25   See Lewis R. Yealland and E. Farquhar Buzzard, *Hysterical Disorders of Warfare* (London: Macmillan, 1918). Yealland gained his MD from the University of Western Ontario in 1912. He believed, like most other Great War physicians, that shell shock was not an illness but a sign of cowardice and a lack of discipline, and he often used electroshock therapy. He was, however, renowned for "curing" shell shock and getting his patients back to the front very quickly. He was a firm believer in auto-suggestion.

26   Hayes, *Pegahmagabow*, 35-43.

27   LAC, RG9III-D-3, Vol. 4941, Reel T10748, File 441. War Diaries 50th Canadian Infantry Battalion. The shy Norwest got his nickname from avoiding or "ducking" women.

28   Dempsey, *Warriors*, 52-53.

29   LAC, RG9III-D-3, Vol. 4918, Reel T10710-10711, File 369. War Diaries 8th Canadian Infantry Battalion.

30   Scott, *1919 Report*, 15, 27.

31   Dempsey, *Warriors*, 61.

32   Scott, *1919 Report*, 16-17.

33   Gaffen, *Forgotten Soldiers*, 24.

34   Barsh, "American Indians in the Great War," 279.

35   Scott, *1919 Report*, 20.

36   Dempsey, *Warriors*, 65-66. See also Timothy C. Winegard, "The Canadian Siberian Expeditionary Force, 1918-1919, and the Complications of Coalition Warfare," *Journal of Slavic Military Studies* 20, 2 (2007): 283-328; Benjamin Isitt, *From Victoria to Vladivostok: Canada's Siberian Expedition, 1917-1919* (Vancouver: University of British Columbia Press, 2010).

37   Scott, *1919 Report*, 19.

38   LAC, RG10, Vol. 3180, Reel C-11335, File 452, 124-1a. Letter Private Oliver Macklin to Scott, 29 March 1916; Scott to Fiset, 18 April 1916.

39   Office of Census and Statistics, *The Canada Yearbook 1914* (Ottawa: King's Printer, 1915-1920), 638-640.

40   Britten, *American Indians*, 113.

41   LAC, RG9IIID3, Vol. 5010, Reel T-10859, File 725. 107th Battalion War Diaries.

42   He served with the 21st Battalion and was wounded by shell fragments, and was subsequently shot and gassed during the Battle of St. Eloi Craters in March 1916. Thereafter, he was released for being underage. He then joined the foreign service branch of the Royal Canadian Naval Volunteer Reserve and served out the remainder of the war on a mine sweeper off of the Ivory Coast of Africa, where he contracted malaria. He also served as a chief petty officer in the Canadian Navy during the Second World War. He died, lucid, in Caledonia, Ontario, when I was ten years old, in 1987. His brother, Claude, won the Distinguished Conduct Medal and the Italian Military Medal (equivalent to the Victoria Cross), and his other brother, Adam, the Russian St. George's Cross. (They both served on the Western Front, the Italian Front and in Northern Russia during the Civil War.) They were all civilian soldiers. I also dedicate this book to these three brothers.

43   Mountain Horse, *My People, The Bloods*, 141–142.

44   Gaffen, *Forgotten Soldiers*, 22.

45   LAC, RG10, Vol. 3181, Reel C-11335, File 452, 124-1a. Port Arthur *News Chronicle*, 14 November 1917.

46   LAC, RG10, Vol. 6771, File 452-29. Service Records.

47   Dempsey, *Warriors*, 26–27.

48   LAC, RG10, Vol. 3180, File 452-124-1A. Service Records; LAC, RG10, Vol. 6771, File 452-30.

49   Dempsey, *Warriors*, 60–61. *Blighty* is slang for England, derived from the Hindustani word *vilayati*, meaning foreigner.

50   LAC, RG10, Vol. 3181, Reel C-11335, File 452, 124-1a. Unknown and undated newspaper article.

51   LAC, RG10, Vol. 6771, Reel C-8515, File 452-35-1. Correspondence between Scott, Coulter, and Indian Agents, April to September 1917.

52   U.S. National Archives RG120, File 301641, MLR: NM91 1241. Letter from A.W. Bloor to CO 36th Infantry Division, 23 January 1919.

53   See William C. Meadows, "North American Indian Code Talkers: Current Developments and Research," in *Aboriginal Peoples and Military Participation: Canadian and International Perspectives*, ed. P. Whitney Lackenbauer et al. (Kingston: Canadian Defence Academy Press, 2007), 161–213.

54   Dempsey, *Warriors*, 68.

55   LAC, RG10, Vol. 3181, Reel C-11335, File 452, 124-1a. Letter Chiefs of Kettle Point to Indian Affairs, 7 November 1916; Maxwell to McLean, 24 November, 2 December 1916; Unknown Newspaper, "Injured Deserter now in Custody," 18 November 1916. This scenario was eerily repeated seventy-nine years later at Kettle and Stoney Point. On 6 September 1995, during the Aboriginal occupation of Canadian Forces Base (CFB) Ipperwash and the Ipperwash Provincial Park, Anthony "Dudley" George was shot in the shoulder by Ken Deane of the Ontario Provincial Police Tactics and Rescue Unit. George subsequently died of his wounds, making him the only Indian killed by a law enforcement agency in a land claims dispute in the twentieth century. In July 1997, Deane was sentenced for criminal negligence to 180 hours of community service. He was killed in a car crash in February 2006. See Peter Edwards, *One Dead Indian: The Premier, the Police, and the Ipperwash Crisis* (Toronto: McClelland and Stewart, 2003).

56   LAC, RG10, Vol. 3181, Reel C-11335, File 452, 124-1a. Letter Thompson to Scott, 22 September 1916; Britten, 59.

57   LAC, RG10, Vol. 6767, Reel C-8512, File 452-15-1. Letter from Garden River Chiefs to Indian Affairs, 2 June 1916.

58   LAC, RG10, Vol. 6767, Reel C-8512, File 452-15-1. Letter from Jane and John Manitowaba to Governor General, 28 December 1916.

59   LAC, RG10, Vol. 6767, Reel C-8512, File 452-15-1. Letter from Simpson Manitowaba to Indian agent Alex Logan, 26 January 1916; Letter from Jane and John Manitowaba to Scott, 27 January 1917, with Reply, 1 February 1917.

60   LAC, RG10, Vol. 6767, Reel C-8512, File 452-15-1. Letter Lucy Maracle to Governor General, 2 August 1916; Letter from Six Nations Mothers to King George V, 31 January 1917, with Reply 16 May 1917.

61   Donald B. Smith, "Fred Loft," in Encyclopedia of North American Indians, ed. Frederick E. Hoxie (New York: Houghton Mifflin Harcourt, 1996), 345. This distinction is not a hereditary title like those of other Iroquoian sachems (chiefs). The title and position in the Great Council of Chiefs was given because of extraordinary abilities and actions. Pine Tree chiefs could not (unlike hereditary chiefs) be dehorned (deposed) by clan mothers, although the council and the people could be told to "be deaf to his voice and advice."

62   Robb, British Culture, 14–15.

63   LAC, RG10, Vol. 3180, Reel C-11335, File 452,124-1a. Unknown Newspaper, "Canadian Indians Showing Their Loyalty in This War," 6 May 1916.

64   Dempsey, Warriors, 58.

65   Tim Cook, Shock Troops: Canadians Fighting the Great War Vol. 2, 1917–1918 (Toronto: Penguin, 2008), 47–48.

66   Dempsey, Warriors, 49.

67   LAC, RG10, Vol. 3181, Reel C-11335, File 452, 124-1a. Undated Letter from Foxhead to E.D. Hardwick.

68   LAC, RG10, Vol. 6771, Reel C-8515, File 452-35-1. Letter from Pastor Donald (Indian agent Griswold Manitoba) to Scott, 18 April 1917.

69   Scott, "Canadian Indians," 289.

70   Gaffen, Forgotten Soldiers, 10.

71   LAC, RG10, Vol. 3181, Reel C-11335, File 452, 124-1a. Letter from Pegahmagabow to Scott, 8 March 1917. In 1956 the last law prohibiting Indians from consuming alcohol was repealed.

72   LAC, RG10, Vol. 3180, Reel C-11335, File 452, 124-1a. Letter from McLennan to Scott, 8 January 1916, with Reply, 15 January 1916.

73   LAC, RG10, Vol. 3180, Reel C-11335, File 452, 124-1a. Letter from Indian Soldiers 149th Battalion to McCallum, 31 May 1916, Letter McCallum to McLean, 6 June 1916, with Replies 13 June 1916; Britten, 112.

74   LAC, RG10, Vol. 6766, Reel C-8511, File 452-13. Letter from Halliday to McLean, 17 January 1916.

75   LAC, RG10, Vol. 6768, Reel C-8513, File 452-20-1,2. Various correspondence concerning conscription and the franchise.

76   LAC, RG10, Vol. 3180, Reel C-11335, File 452, 124-1a. Letter from Galbraithe to Scott, 21 December 1915.

77   John Sutton Lutz, Makuk: A New History of Aboriginal-White Relations (Vancouver: University of British Columbia Press, 2010), 239.

78   LAC, RG24-c-1-a, Vol. 1221-1, File HQ-593-1-7. Letter from Chief Fisher to Grey, 19
      February 1916.

79   LAC, RG10, Vol. 6767, Reel C-8512, File 452-15-1. Letter from Steinhauer to Scott,
      27 August 1916; LAC, RG10, Vol. 3180, Reel C-11335, File 452, 124-1a. Letter from
      Nicholson to Scott, 31 July 1916, with Reply 3 August 1916; Department of Indian
      Affairs, *Annual Report of the DIA, 1917* (Ottawa: King's Printer, 1918), 20.

80   De Witt Rowell, "Canadian Indians at the Front," 291.

81   LAC, RG24-c-1-a, Vol. 1221-1, File HQ-593-1-7. Letter from Fiset to Thunderwater, 8
      December 1916; Letter from Borden to Hodgins, 16 October 1916; Dempsey, *Warriors*,
      49.

82   LAC, RG9, III-D-3, Vol. 5010, Reel T-10859, File 725. War Diaries 107th Battalion; Scott,
      "Canadian Indians," 325–326.

83   Alex Decoteau Heritage Site at http://www.edukits.ca/decoteau/history_timeline2.html

84   Britten, *American Indians*, 111.

85   Mountain Horse, *My People, The Bloods*, 142.

86   LAC, RG10, Vol. 6762-6808. Lists of Native Canadians Killed or Wounded; Scott, *1919
      Report*. It has been accurately counted that roughly 300 Indians died during the war.
      Based on Canadian casualty rates, the total Indian casualties would be roughly 1,200;
      RG10, Vol. 6771, Reel C-8515, File 452-30. Circulars: Scott to all Indian Agents, 16
      December 1918 and 7 February 1919; Lists of Returned Indian Soldiers, 1919–1920.

87   LAC, RG10, Vol. 3181, Reel C-11335, File 452, 124-1a. *Brantford Expositor*, 22 January
      1919.

88   Lisa Sattenspiel and Dawn Herring, "Structural Epidemic Models and the Spread of
      Influenza in the Central Canadian Sub-Arctic," *Human Biology* 10, 1 (1998): 3; Lisa
      Sattenspiel and Dawn Herring,"Death in Winter: Spanish Flu in the Canadian Subarctic,"
      in *The Spanish Influenza Pandemic of 1918-1919: New Perspectives*, 173–190; Maureen
      Lux, "The Bitter Flats: The 1918 Influenza Epidemic in Saskatchewan," *Saskatchewan
      History* 49, 1 (1997): 3–13; Maureen Lux, "The Impact of the Spanish Influenza Pandemic
      in Saskatchewan, 1918–1919" (MA thesis, University of Saskatchewan, 1989).

89   Jenny Higgins, "The 1918 Spanish Flu," *Newfoundland and Labrador Heritage Web Site*,
      2007, http://www.heritage.nf.ca/law/flu.html.

90   John F. Brundage and G. Dennis Shanks, "Deaths from Bacterial Pneumonia during
      1918–19 Influenza Pandemic," *Emerging Infectious Diseases* 14, 8 (2008): 1193–1199.

91   Dominion Bureau of Statistics, *The Canada Year Book 1940* (Ottawa: King's Printer,
      1941), 1062.

92   Veterans Affairs Canada, at http://www.vac-acc.gc.ca/pdf/cr/pi-sheets/Aboriginal-pi-e.
      pdf.

93   Smith is the father of Harold J. Smith, better known as Jay Silverheels, who played the
      character of Tonto in the Lone Ranger television series (1949–1957). Tonto means "fool"
      or "dumb" in Spanish, Italian, and Portuguese.

94   Gaffen, *Forgotten Soldiers*, 111–112.

95   LAC, RG10, Vol. 3181, Reel C-11335, File 452, 124-1a. Letter Indian Affairs to Charles
      McGibbon (Indian agent, Brantford), 15 October 1916, with Reply, 3 November 1916.

Chapter Eight

1 The Oneida of the Thames insist that they are not on a reserve because they purchased their lands from the Crown and private holders in the 1840s. As such, certain components of the *Indian Act* have never been applied to them. Nevertheless, the majority support an elected council, although voter participation is less than 40 percent. Because they purchased their lands, which were never "reserved" to them under treaty, they generally prefer the term "Oneida Settlement" as opposed to "reserve." They are, however, recognized by the government as the "Oneida 41 Indian Reserve."

2 De Witt Rowell, "Canadian Indians at the Front," 292.

3 LAC, Schuyler, Personal War Records.

4 Janice Summerby, *Native Soldiers, Foreign Battlefields* (Ottawa: Department of Veterans Affairs, 2005), 17-19.

5 Barsh, "American Indians in the Great War," 280. The number, however, would have been very small, since traditionally war was the business of men.

6 Department of Indian Affairs, *Annual Report of the DIA, 1917* (Ottawa: King's Printer, 1918), 18.

7 LAC, RG10, Vol. 6763, File 452-5-1. Letter from Mrs. M.A. Brown, Brantford, to Scott, 23 November 1914; *Brantford Expositor*, "Six Nation Indian Women's Patriotic League," 22 November 1914; *Globe*, "Canadian Indians are Doing Their Share," 29 January 1915.

8 LAC, RG10, Vol. 6763, File 452-5-1. Letter from Garlow to Scott, 16 May 1915, with Reply 22 May 1915; Account Voucher Indian Affairs/A.M. Garlow, 15 December 1916.

9 LAC, RG10, Vol 6771, File 452-29. Letter from H. Van Loon, Indian agent Hagersville, to Scott, 13 January 1919.

10 LAC, RG10, Vol. 6763, File 452-5-1. Letter from Fisher River School Children to Princess Mary, December 1914; Letter from Belle A. Maple (Moosomin's reserve) to the Duchess of Connaught, 29 March 1915; Letter from Deasy to Scott, 26 May 1916.

11 Mountain Horse, *My People, The Bloods*, 139.

12 LAC, RG10, Vol. 6762, File 452-2. Letter from Ames to Scott, November 1916; Letter from Moo-che-we-in-es to Scott, 4 December 1916; Letter from Ames to Scott, 15 December 1916.

13 LAC, RG10, Vol. 6762, File 452-2. Correspondence: Indian Affairs and Patriotic Fund, 1917.

14 LAC, RG10, Vol. 6762, File 452-2. Letter from Scott to Ames, 28 February 1917.

15 LAC, RG10, Vol. 6762, File 452-2. Correspondence: Indian Affairs and Patriotic Fund, 1917. It should be noted that donating to the fund was not a requirement to receive benefits.

16 LAC, RG10, Vol. 6762, File 452-3. Native Contributions to War Funds; Duncan Campbell Scott, *1919 Report of the Deputy Superintendent General of Indian Affairs, Sessional Paper No. 27: The Indians and the Great War* (Ottawa: King's Printer, 1920), 20-25.

17 See Philip H. Morris, *The Canadian Patriotic Fund: A Record of its Activities from 1914-1919* (Ottawa: The Mortimer Co., 1920).

18 LAC, RG10, Vol. 6770, File 452-23. Victory Bond Contributions. American Indians purchased $25 million worth of Liberty Bonds during the war.

19   LAC, RG10, Vol. 6762, Reel C-8508, File 452-2 Pt 3. Letter from G.E. Darby, Bella Bella, to Indian Affairs, 18 January 1918; Letter from W.B. Cromlie, Frog Lake, to Indian Affairs, 19 January 1918; Letter from W. Sibbald, Onion Lake, to Scott, 11 February 1918.

20   S.D. Grant, "Indian Affairs under Duncan Campbell Scott: The Plains Cree of Saskatchewan 1913–1931," *Journal of Canadian Studies* 18, 3 (1983): 30.

21   Department of Indian Affairs, *Annual Report of the DIA, 1918* (Ottawa: King's Printer, 1919), 10, 18–20; Brian A. Titley, *A Narrow Vision: Duncan Campbell Scott and the Administration of Indian Affairs in Canada* (Vancouver: University of British Columbia Press, 1986), 40–41.

22   Sarah Carter, "'An Infamous Proposal:' Prairie Indian Reserve Land and Soldier Settlement after World War I," *Manitoba History* 37 (1999): 13.

23   DIA, *Annual Report, 1918*, 19; James Dempsey, "The Indians and World War One," *Alberta History* 31, 3 (1983): 5–6.

24   Miller, *Skyscrapers*, 312.

25   Brian A. Titley, *A Narrow Vision: Duncan Campbell Scott and the Administration of Indian Affairs in Canada* (Vancouver: University of British Columbia Press, 1986), 41.

26   Carter, "Infamous Proposal," 12.

27   Dempsey, "The Indians in World War One," 5–7.

28   Lackenbauer, *Battle Grounds*, 39–82, 264. This practice would again occur during the Second World War with enduring ramifications, most notably at Stoney Point Reserve, Ontario. In 1942 the *War Measures Act* was used to expropriate this land for the creation of a military training facility. The eighteen Ojibwa/Potawatomi families were relocated to neighbouring Kettle Point reserve to the indignation of all concerned. They were never fully integrated into the Kettle Point community and lived as "refugees" until the reclamation of the land (CFB Ipperwash and the Ipperwash Provincial Park) by force during the now infamous 1995 Ipperwash Crisis.

29   Office of Census and Statistics, *The Canada Yearbooks, 1914–1918*.

30   Lutz, *Makuk*, 104, 226.

31   Ibid., 104.

32   Rolf Knight, *Indians at Work: An Informal History of Native Labour in British Columbia, 1848–1930* (Vancouver: New Star Books, 1996), 175.

33   Lutz, *Makuk*, 207.

34   Vance, *Death So Noble*, 258.

35   Dempsey, *Warriors*, 51.

Chapter Nine

1   Hayes, *Pegahmagabow*, 44–46.

2   LAC, RG10, Vol. 6770, Reel C-8514, File 452-22. SSB Form No. 25: Loan Regulation of the Soldier Settlement Board of Canada, 1918–1919.

3   LAC, RG10, Vol. 11154, Reel C-V-8, File 34. *Soldier Settlement Act*, 1919.

4   Wahta Band Council, *A History of the Wahta Mohawk Community* (Wahta, ON: Joan Holmes and Associates, 2002), 106–108.

5   LAC, RG10, Vol. 11154, Reel C-V-8, File 34. Memorandum Scott to all Indian Agents, 6 May 1919.

6   LAC, RG10, Vol. 4048, File 357. *Indian Act.*

7   Scott, *1919 Report*, 28–29.

8   Dempsey, "The Indians and World War One," 8.

9   Carter, "An Infamous Proposal," 9-21.

10   R. Scott Sheffield, *A Search for Equity: A Study of the Treatment Afforded to First Nations Veterans and Dependants of the Second World War and the Korean Conflict* (Ottawa: Department of Indian Affairs, April 2001), 6; Gaffen, *Forgotten Soldiers*, 135.

11   Carter, "An Infamous Proposal," 16.

12   Britten, *American Indians*, 185–186.

13   Dempsey, *Warriors*, 77.

14   "Canadian Indians and World War One," *Saskatchewan Indian Federated College Journal* 1, 1 (1984): 71.

15   Gaffen, *Forgotten Soldiers*, 36.

16   LAC, RG10, Vol. 3180, Reel C-11335, File 452, 124-1a. Scott to F. Peters, 18th Battalion, 11 March 1915.

17   Hayes, *Pegahmagabow*, 61–63.

18   Wahta Band Council, *History*, 108.

19   LAC, RG10, Vol. 3181, Reel C-11335, File 452, 124-1a. Scott to Officer in Charge of Estates, Ministry of Militia, 8 November 1917.

20   LAC, RG10, Vol. 3181, Reel C-11335, File 452, 124-1a. The Secretary Board of Pension Commissioners for Canada to Scott, 11 December 1917, with Reply 12 December 1917.

21   Scott, *1919 Report*, 31.

22   Ibid., 31.

23   LAC, RG10, Vol. 6771, Reel C-8515, File 452-40. Peltier to Power, 20 April 1936. Peltier's Indian agent attested that Peltier's annual income was roughly $400.

24   LAC, RG10, Vol. 6772, Reel C-8516, File 452-40. Circular: McGill to all Indian agents, 12 May 1936.

25   LAC, RG10, Vol. 6771, Reel C-8515, File 452-37. Letter J.D. MacLean to Brantford Indian agent, 23 July 1926.

26   LAC, RG10, Vol. 6771, Reel C-8515, File 452-37. Herwig to the Department of Indian Affairs and the Ministry of Pensions and National Health (Dr. R.E. Wodehouse), 8 February 1936; Secretary of the Last Post Fund to MacLean, 19 January 1936.

27   Haycock, *The Image of the Indian*, 90–91.

28   W. Everard Edmonds, "Canada's Red Army," *Canadian Magazine of Politics, Science, Art and Literature* 54, 5 (1921): 340–342.

29   See R. Scott Sheffield, *"The Red Man's On the Warpath": The Image of the "Indian" and the Second World War* (Vancouver: University of British Columbia Press, 2004).

30   John Moses, "The Return of the Native: Six Nations Veterans and Political Change at the Grand River Reserve, 1917–1924," in *Aboriginal Peoples and the Canadian Military: Historical Perspectives*, 117–128. See Moses for details concerning veterans and political reform on the Six Nations.

31   LAC, RG10, Vol. 6770, File 452-26, Pt. 1. Letter from Brantford Indian agent to Scott, 5 July 1918.

32   For excellent accounts of the various political groups and factions see: Scott R. Trevithick, "Conflicting Outlooks: The Background to the 1924 Deposing of the Six Nations Hereditary Council" (master's thesis, University of Calgary, 1998); Six Nations Hereditary Longhouse Council, *The Redman's Appeal for Justice: The Position of the Six Nations that they Constitute an Independent State* (Oshweken, ON: Six Nations of the Grand River, 1924); Andrew T. Thompson, *Report by Col. Andrew T. Thompson Commissioned to Investigate and Enquire into the Affairs of the Six Nations Indians, 1923* (Ottawa: King's Printer, 1924); Ronald Niezen, "Recognizing Indigenism: Canadian Unity and the International Movement of Indigenous Peoples," *Comparative Studies in Society and History* 42, 1 (2000): 119–148.

33   Townsend, *World War II and the American Indian*, 118.

34   LAC, RG10, Vol. 3211, File 527, 787. Various Correspondence on Loft and the League of Indians of Canada, 1919–1935.

35   Grant, "Indian Affairs under Duncan Campbell Scott," 34.

36   Peter Kulchyski, "A Considerable Unrest: F.O. Loft and the League of Indians," *Native Studies Review* 4 (1988): 101.

37   Edmonds, "Canada's Red Army," 340–342.

38   Kulchyski, "Considerable Unrest," 106–107.

39   LAC, RG10, Vol. 3211, File 527, 787. Various Correspondence on Loft and the League of Indians of Canada, 1919–1935.

40   Hayes, *Pegahmagabow*, 49–51. In 1920 American Indians formed the political organization American Indians of the World War (AIWW).

41   See Arthur Marwick, *War and Social Change in the Twentieth Century: A Comparative Study of Britain, France, Germany, Russia and the United States* (London: Palgrave Macmillan, 1974).

Conclusion

1   Scott, "Canadian Indians," 19.

2   Department of Indian Affairs, *Annual Report of the DIA, 1917* (Ottawa: King's Printer, 1918), 17.

3   For example, the residential school system was not abolished until the 1960s, despite government knowledge of the sexual and physical abuse and rampant disease within the schools. The first institutions were running by the 1840s, and the last vestige of the program ceased in 1996 with the closing of White-Calf College in Saskatchewan. In 1919, 389 schools were operational nationwide (the majority in the Western provinces), accommodating 12,413 Indian children. Between 1894 and 1908 mortality rates in Western Canadian schools ranged from 35 percent to 60 percent over a five-year period (five years after entry 35 percent to 60 percent of children had died), according to a 1909 report by Indian Affairs medical superintendent Dr. Peter Bryce. These statistics were made public in 1922, after Bryce, no longer attached to Indian Affairs, published his findings. Similarly, another report of 1922 concluded that 50 percent of children in Western schools had tuberculosis. In 2005, a $1.9 billion compensation package was announced by the federal government, and on 11 June 2008 Prime Minister Stephen Harper issued a formal apology to residential school victims and families on behalf of the government and people of Canada.

4   Dempsey, *Warriors*, 46.

Epilogue

1   Sheffield, "Indifference, Difference and Assimilation," 71.

2   See P. Whitney Lackenbauer, "A Hell of a Warrior: Remembering the Life of Sergeant Thomas George Prince," in *Intrepid Warriors: Perspectives on Canadian Military Leadership*, ed. Bernd Horn (St. Catharines: Vanwell, 2007), 95-138. Ira Hayes was photographed raising the flag at Iwo Jima. He died at age thirty-two of alcoholism and exposure in a remote desert in Arizona. He was the subject of the 1961 movie *The Outsider* and the inspiration for Johnny Cash's 1964 title "The Ballad of Ira Hayes." Hayes was also recently portrayed in Clint Eastwood's 2006 *Flags of Our Fathers*. Prince was portrayed in the 1968 movie *The Devil's Brigade*. Prince died in 1977 at the age of sixty-two in a Salvation Army hostel in Winnipeg, Manitoba.

3   Gaffen, *Forgotten Soldiers*, 76.

4   Lieutenant General Andrew B. Leslie, foreword to *Aboriginal Peoples and Military Participation: Canadian and International Perspectives*, ed. P. Whitney Lackenbauer et al. (Kingston: Canadian Defence Academy Press, 2007), vii; Grazia Scoppio, "Diversity Best Practices in Military Organizations in Canada, Australia, the United Kingdom, and the United States," *Canadian Military Journal* 9, 3 (2009): 26.

5   Statistics Canada, 2006 Census. www.statcan.gc.ca.

Selected Bibliography

Manuscript, Archival, and Library Collections

Andrew Bonar Law Papers, House of Lords Record Office/Parliamentary Archives, London, UK, Volumes: BL/50–BL/64

Lewis Vernon Harcourt Papers, Bodleian Library, Oxford, UK, Volumes: 443–557

Library and Archives Canada (LAC), Ottawa, Canada

Manuscript Group (MG):
26H: Robert Borden/Arthur Currie Papers
27IID23: Sam Hughes Family Collection
30E100: Arthur Currie Papers
30E133: Andrew McNaughton Papers

Record Groups (RG):
9: Department of Militia and Defence, Canadian Expeditionary Force and Ministry of the Overseas Military Forces of Canada
10: Department of Indian Affairs
24: Ministry of Militia and Defence
27: Department of Labour
150: Ministry of the Overseas Military Forces of Canada

National Archives (NA) United Kingdom, Kew-London, UK, Records of the Colonial Office (CO) and War Office (WO).

United States National Archives and Records Administration (Washington, DC, and College Park, Maryland)

75: Bureau of Indian Affairs
120: US Army

Walter Hume Long Papers, British Library, London, UK, Volumes: 62404, 62421–62424, 62437

Other Sources

Allen, Robert S. *His Majesty's Indian Allies: British Indian Policy in the Defence of Canada, 1774–1815.* Toronto: Dundurn Press, 1992.

"Almighty Voice." *Saskatchewan Indian* 3, 6 (1973): 1–6.

Anderson, Gary C. *Sitting Bull and the Paradox of Lakota Nationhood.* New York: Longman, 1996.

Anderson, Ian. *Sitting Bull's Boss: Above the Medicine Line with James Morrow Walsh.* Surrey: Heritage House, 2000.

Aquila, Richard. *The Iroquois Restoration: Iroquois Diplomacy on the Colonial Frontier, 1701–1754.* Detroit: Wayne State University Press, 1983.

Armitage, Andrew. *Comparing the Policy of Aboriginal Assimilation: Australia, Canada and New Zealand.* Vancouver: University of British Columbia Press, 1995.

Armstrong, John G. "The Unwelcome Sacrifice: A Black Unit in the Canadian Expeditionary Force, 1917–1919." In *Ethnic Armies: Polyethnic Armed Forces from the Time of the Hapsburgs to the Age of the Superpowers,* edited by N.F. Dreisziger, 178–197. Waterloo: Wilfrid Laurier University Press, 1990.

Backhouse, Constance. *Colour-Coded: A Legal History of Racism in Canada.* Toronto: University of Toronto Press, 1999.

Barr, Daniel P. *Unconquered: The Iroquois League at War in Colonial America.* London: Praeger Books, 2006.

Barrie, J.M. *Peter Pan.* Toronto: Bantam Classic, 1985.

Barris, Ted. *Victory at Vimy: Canada Comes of Age, April 9–12, 1917.* Toronto: Thomas Allen Publishers, 2007.

Barsh, Russel Lawrence. "American Indians in the Great War." *Ethnohistory* 38, 3 (1991): 276–303.

Bell, Steven A. "The 107th 'Timber Wolf' Battalion at Hill 70." *Canadian Military History* 5, 1 (1996): 73–78.

Benn, Carl. *The Iroquois in the War of 1812.* Toronto: University of Toronto Press, 1998.

—. *Mohawks on the Nile: Natives among the Canadian Voyageurs in Egypt 1884–1885.* Toronto: Dundurn Group, 2008.

Bernstein, Alison R. *American Indians and World War II.* Norman: University of Oklahoma Press, 1991.

Berton, Pierre. *Vimy.* Toronto: Penguin Books, 1986.

Biggar, H.P., ed. *The Voyages of Jacques Cartier including Cartier's Narratives of 1534.* Ottawa: King's Printer, 1924.

Bliss, Michael. *Right Honourable Men.* New York: Harper Collins, 1994.

Borden, Robert. *Canada in the Commonwealth: From Conflict to Co-operation.* Oxford: Clarendon Press, 1929.

—. *Special Session of Parliament, August 1914.* Ottawa: King's Printer, 1914.

Boulton, Charles. *I Fought Riel: A Military Memoir.* Toronto: James Lorimer Publishers, 1985.

—. *Reminiscences of the North-west Rebellions: With a Record of the Raising of Her Majesty's 100th Regiment in Canada, and a Chapter on Canadian Social and Political Life.* Toronto: Grip Printing and Publishing, 1886.

Boyden, Joseph. *Three Day Road.* Toronto: Penguin Books, 2005.

Britten, Thomas A. *American Indians in World War I: At Home and at War.* Albuquerque: University of New Mexico Press, 1997.

Brown, Ian Malcolm. *British Logistics on the Western Front: 1914–1918.* Toronto: Preager, 1998.

Brown, O.E.A. *Settlers of the Plains.* Gilbert Plains, MB: Maple Leaf Press, 1953.

Brundage, John F., and G. Dennis Shanks. "Death from Bacterial Pneumonia during 1918–19 Influenza Pandemic." *Emerging Infectious Diseases* 14, 8 (2008): 1193–1199.

Bumsted, J.M. "The West and Louis Riel." In *Interpreting Canada's Past, Vol. 2: Post-Confederation*, edited by J.M. Bumsted, 64–74. Toronto: Oxford University Press, 1993.

Calamai, Peter. "Beothuk Mystery." *McMaster University Science Writer* (2005): 1–4.

Callwell, C.E. *Small Wars: Their Principles and Practice*. Lincoln: University of Nebraska Press, Reprint 1996.

Cameron, Captain D.E. "Royal Six Nations Regiment." *The Indian Magazine, Brantford* 3, 4 (1896): 1–4.

Camurat, Dianne. "The American Indian in the Great War: Real and Imagined." Master's thesis, Institut Charles V of the University of Paris VII, 1993.

"Canadian Indians and World War One." *Saskatchewan Indian Federated College Journal* 1, 1 (1984): 65–72.

Cannadine, David. *Ornamentalism: How the British Saw their Empire*. London: Penguin Books, 2001.

Capon, Alan R. *His Faults Lie Gently: The Incredible Sam Hughes*. Lindsay, ON: Floyd W. Hall, 1969.

Carter, Sarah. "'An Infamous Proposal': Prairie Indian Reserve Land and Soldier Settlement after World War I." *Manitoba History* 37 (1999): 9–21.

Cell, Gillian T. *English Enterprise in Newfoundland 1577–1660*. Toronto: Toronto University Press, 1969.

Clark, Alan. *The Donkeys*. London: Hutchinson, 1961.

Colonial Office. *The Colonial Office Lists for 1914–1919*. London: Waterlow and Sons, 1914–1919.

Cook, Tim. *At the Sharp End: Canadians Fighting the Great War 1914–1916, Vol. 1*. Toronto: Penguin Group Canada, 2007.

—. *Shock Troops: Canadians Fighting the Great War 1917–1918, Vol. 2*. Toronto: Penguin Group Canada, 2008.

Cooper, James Fenimore. *The Last of the Mohicans*. New York: H.C. Carey and I. Lea, 1826.

Crook, Paul. *Darwinism, War and History: The Debate over the Biology of War from the 'Origin of Species' to the First World War*. Cambridge: Cambridge University Press, 1994.

Currie, Arthur. *Canadian Corps Operations, 1918*. Ottawa: Department of Militia and Defence, 1919.

Daunton, Martin, and Rick Halpern, eds. *Empire and Others: British Encounters with Indigenous Peoples, 1600–1850*. Philadelphia: University of Pennsylvania Press, 1999.

Davis, Shelby Cullom. *Reservoirs of Men: A History of the Black Troops of French West Africa*. Westport: Negro Universities Press, 1970.

Dawson, Robert MacGregor. *The Development of Dominion Status 1900–1936*. London: Oxford University Press, 1937.

De Witt Rowell, Verne, "Canadian Indians at the Front." *New York Times Current History* 6, 2 (1917): 290–292.

Deloria Jr., Vine. *Custer Died for Your Sins: An Indian Manifesto*. Norman: University of Oklahoma Press, 1988.

Dempsey, James. *Aboriginal Soldiers and the First World War*. Ottawa: National Library and Archives of Canada, 2006.

—. "The Indians and World War One." *Alberta History* 31, 3 (1983): 1–8.

—. "Persistence of a Warrior Ethic Among the Plains Indians." *Alberta History* 36, 1 (1988): 1–10.

—. *Warriors of the King: Prairie Indians in World War I*. Regina: Canadian Plains Research Center, 1999.

Department of External Affairs. *Documents on Canadian External Relations, Vol. I: 1909–1918*. Ottawa: Queen's Printer, 1967.

Department of Indian Affairs. *Annual Reports of the Department of Indian Affairs (1900–1940)*. Ottawa: King's Printer, 1901–1941.

—. *Basic Departmental Data, 2003*. Ottawa: Department of Indians Affairs, 2003.

—. *Indians of Ontario: An Historical Review*. Ottawa: Department of Citizenship and Immigration, Indian Affairs Branch, 1962.

Donovan, James. *A Terrible Glory: Custer and the Little Bighorn*. New York: Little Brown, 2008.

Drake, Benjamin. *Life of Tecumseh, and his Brother, The Prophet with a Historical Sketch of the Shawanoe Indians*. Cincinnati: Anderson, Gates and Wright, 1858.

Edmonds, W. Everard. "Canada's Red Army." *Canadian Magazine of Politics, Science, Art and Literature* 54, 4 (1921): 340–342.

Edwards, Peter. *One Dead Indian: The Premier, the Police, and the Ipperwash Crisis*. Toronto: McClelland and Stewart, 2003.

Enloe, Cynthia H. *Ethnic Soldiers: State Security in Divided Societies*. Markham: Penguin Books, 1980.

Evans, Julie, Patricia Grimshaw, David Philips, and Shurlee Swain. *Equal Subjects, Unequal Rights: Indigenous Peoples in British Settler Colonies, 1830–1910*. Manchester: Manchester University Press, 2003.

Ferguson, Niall. *The Pity of War: Explaining World War I*. London: Penguin Press, 1998.

Fogarty, Richard S. *Race and War in France: Colonial Subjects in the French Army, 1914–1918*. Baltimore: The Johns Hopkins University Press, 2008.

Fong, Giordan. "Debate: The Movement of German Divisions to the Western Front, Winter 1917–1918," *War in History* 7, 2 (2000): 225–235.

Forsberg, Roberta J. *The Chief Mountain: The Story of Canon Middleton*. Whittier, CA, 1964.

Foster, Hamar. "Indigenous Peoples and the Law: The Colonial Legacy in Australia, Canada, New Zealand and the United States." In *Asia Pacific Legal Developments*, edited by D. Johnston and D. Ferguson, 466–500. Vancouver: University of British Columbia Press, 1998.

Fournier, Suzanne, and Ernie Crey. "Killing the Indian in the Child: Four Centuries of Church-Run Schools." In *The Indigenous Experience: Global Perspectives*, edited by Roger C.A. Maaka and Chris Andersen, 141–149. Toronto: Canadian Scholars' Press, 2006.

Fowler Jr., William M. *Empires at War: The Seven Years' War and the Struggle for North America, 1754–1763*. Toronto: Douglas and McIntyre, 2005.

Fox, J.E.J. "From Pleasantville to Englebeimer." *Veteran Magazine* 7, 1 (1928): 69–70.

Franco, Jere' Bishop. *Crossing the Pond: The Native American Effort in World War II*. Denton: University of North Texas Press, 1999.

Freeman, Victoria. "Attitudes toward 'Miscegenation' in Canada, the United States, New Zealand, and Australia, 1860–1914." *Native Studies Review* 16, 1 (2005): 41–69.

Fuller, J.G. *Troop Morale and Popular Culture in the British and Dominion Armies 1914–1918*. Oxford: Clarendon Press, 1990.

Gaffen, Fred. *Cross-Border Warriors: Canadians in American Forces, Americans in Canadian Forces from the Civil War to the Gulf*. Toronto: Dundurn Press, 1995.

—. *Forgotten Soldiers*. Penticton: Theytus Books, 1985.

Gallishaw, John. *Trenching at Gallipoli: The Personal Narrative of a Newfoundlander with the Ill-fated Dardanelles Expedition*. New York: The Century, 1916.

Goldfrank, Esther Schiff. *Changing Configurations in the Social Organization of the Blackfoot Tribe during the Reserve Period*. New York: J.J. Augustin, 1945.

Goldie, Terry. *Fear and Temptation: The Image of the Indigene in Canadian, Australian, and New Zealand Literatures*. Kingston: McGill-Queen's University Press, 1989.

Government of Canada. *Canadian Soldiers Active Military Services Act, 1916*. Ottawa: Government Printing Bureau, 1916.

—. *Soldier Settlement Act, 1917, S.C. 1917, C.21*. Ottawa: Government Printing Bureau, 1917.

—. *Soldier Settlement Act, 1919–1923*. Ottawa: Government Printing Bureau, 1919–1923.

Granatstein, J.L. *Canada's Army: Waging War and Keeping the Peace*. Toronto: University of Toronto Press, 2002.

Granatstein, J.L., and J. Mackay Hitsman. *Broken Promises: A History of Conscription in Canada*. Toronto: Oxford University Press, 1977.

Grant, S.D. "Indian Affairs under Duncan Campbell Scott: The Plains Cree of Saskatchewan 1913–1931." *Journal of Canadian Studies* 18, 3 (1983): 21–39.

Hagenbeck, Carl. *Beasts and Men: Being Carl Hagenbeck's Experiences for Half a Century among Wild Animals*. London: Longmans, Green, 1912.

Hawkins, Mike. *Social Darwinism in European and American Thought, 1860–1945: Nature as a Model and Nature as a Threat*. Cambridge: Cambridge University Press, 1997.

Haycock, Ronald G. *The Image of the Indian*. Waterloo: Lutheran University Press, 1971.

—. "Recruiting, 1914–1916." In *Canadian Military History: Selected Readings*, edited by Marc Milner, 57-81. Toronto: Irwin, 1998.

—. *Sam Hughes: The Public Career of a Controversial Canadian*. Waterloo: Wilfrid Laurier University Press, 1986.

Hayes, Adrian. *Pegahmagabow: Legendary Warrior, Forgotten Hero*. Sault Ste. Marie: Fox Meadow Creations, 2006.

Higgins, Jenny. "The 1918 Spanish Flu." *Newfoundland and Labrador Heritage Web Site*, 2007, http://www.heritage.nf.ca/law/flu.html.

Holm, Tom. "Strong Hearts: Native Service in the U.S. Armed Forces." In *Aboriginal Peoples and Military Participation: Canadian and International Perspectives*, edited by P. Whitney Lackenbauer et al., 127–152. Kingston: Canadian Defence Academy Press, 2007.

Hopkins, A.G. "Back to the Future: From National History to Imperial History." *Past and Present* 164 (1999): 198–243.

Howley, James P. *The Beothuks or Red Indians: The Aboriginal Inhabitants of Newfoundland.* Cambridge: Cambridge University Press, 1915.

Huggonson, David. "Aboriginal Diggers of the 9th Brigade. First AIF." *Journal of the Royal Australian Historical Society* 79 (1993): 214–223.

Humphries, Mark Osborne, ed. *The Selected Papers of Sir Arthur Currie, 1917–1933.* Waterloo: LCMSDS Press, 2008.

Hunt, George T. *The Wars of the Iroquois: A Study in Intertribal Trade Relations.* Madison: University of Wisconsin Press, 1960.

Hussey, John. "Debate: The Movement of German Divisions to the Western Front, Winter 1917–1918." *War in History* 4, 2 (1997): 213–220.

Huttenback, Robert A. *Racism and Empire: White Settlers and Colored Immigrants in the British Self-Governing Colonies, 1830–1910.* Ithaca, NY: Cornell University Press, 1976.

Hyam, Ronald. *Britain's Declining Empire: The Road to Decolonisation, 1918–1968.* Cambridge: Cambridge University Press, 2006.

Isitt, Benjamin. *From Victoria to Vladivostok: Canada's Siberian Expedition, 1917–1919.* Vancouver: University of British Columbia Press, 2010.

Ito, Roy. *We Went to War: The Story of the Japanese Canadians who Served during the First and Second World Wars.* Stittsville, ON: Canada's Wings, 1984.

Jamieson, Melvill Allan. *Medals Awarded to North American Indian Chiefs, 1714–1922 and to Loyal African and Other Chiefs in Various Territories within the British Empire.* London: Spink, 1936.

Jennings, Francis, ed. *The History and Culture of Iroquois Diplomacy: An Interdisciplinary Guide to the Treaties of the Six Nations and Their League.* Syracuse: Syracuse University Press, 1985.

Jünger, Ernst. *The Storm of Steel.* London: Chatto and Windus, 1929.

Keegan, John. *The First World War.* New York: Random House, 2000.

Keeley, Lawrence H. *War before Civilization: The Myth of the Peaceful Savage.* Oxford: Oxford University Press, 1996.

Kiernan, V.G. *Colonial Empires and Armies, 1815–1960.* Stroud: Sutton Publishing, 1998.

Killingray, David, and David Omissi, eds. *Guardians of Empire: The Armed Forces of the Colonial Powers c. 1700–1964.* Manchester: Manchester University Press, 1999.

Knight, Rolf. *Indians at Work: An Informal History of Native Labour in British Columbia, 1848–1930.* Vancouver: New Star Books, 1996.

Krouse, Susan Applegate (original documentation by Joseph K. Dixon). *North American Indians in the Great War.* Lincoln: University of Nebraska Press, 2007.

Kulchyski, Peter. "A Considerable Unrest: F.O. Loft and the League of Indians." *Native Studies Review* 4 (1988): 95–113.

—. "Primitive Subversions: Totalization and Resistance in Native Canadian Politics." *Cultural Critique* 21 (1992): 171–195.

Lacey, Amy. "John Shiwak: An Eskimo Patriot." *Them Days—Stories of Early Labrador* 17, 1 (1991).

Lackenbauer, P. Whitney. *Battle Grounds: The Canadian Military and Aboriginal Lands.* Vancouver: University of British Columbia Press, 2007.

—. "A Hell of a Warrior: Remembering the Life of Sergeant Thomas George Prince." In *Intrepid Warriors: Perspectives on Canadian Army Leadership,* edited by Bernd Horn, 95–138. St. Catharines, ON: Vanwell Publishing, 2007.

Lackenbauer, P. Whitney, and Katherine McGowan. "Competing Loyalties in a Complex Community: Enlisting the Six Nations in the Canadian Expeditionary Force, 1914–1917." In *Aboriginal Peoples and the Canadian Military: Historical Perspectives,* edited by P. Whitney Lackenbauer et al., 89–115. Kingston: Canadian Defence Academy Press, 2007.

LaPierre, Laurier. *Sir Wilfrid Laurier and the Romance of Canada.* Toronto: Stoddart Publishers, 1996.

Lemay, J.A. Leo. *Did Pocahontas Save Captain John Smith?* Athens: University of Georgia Press, 1992.

Leslie, Andrew B. Foreword to *Aboriginal Peoples and Military Participation: Canadian and International Perspectives,* edited by P. Whitney Lackenbauer et al., vii. Kingston: Canadian Defence Academy Press, 2007.

Lewis-Maybury, David. "Indigenous Peoples." In *The Indigenous Experience: Global Perspectives,* edited by Roger C.A. Maaka and Chris Andersen, 17–29. Toronto: Canadian Scholars' Press, 2006.

Lind, Frank. *The Letters of Mayo Lind.* St. John's: Robinson, 1919.

Lutz, John Sutton. *Makuk: A New History of Aboriginal-White Relations.* Vancouver: University of British Columbia Press, 2010.

Lux, Maureen. "The Bitter Flats: The 1918 Influenza Epidemic in Saskatchewan." *Saskatchewan History* 49, 1 (1997): 3–13.

—. "The Impact of the Spanish Influenza Pandemic in Saskatchewan, 1918–1919." MA thesis, University of Saskatchewan, 1989.

Maaka, Roger, and Augie Fleras. *The Politics of Indigeneity: Challenging the State in Canada and Aotearoa New Zealand.* Dunedin: University of Otago Press, 2005.

MacEwan, Grant. *Fifty Mighty Men.* Saskatoon: Western Producer, 1958.

—. *Sitting Bull: The Years in Canada.* Edmonton: Hurtig Publishers, 1973.

MacFarlane, John, and John Moses. "Different Drummers: Aboriginal Culture and the Canadian Armed Forces, 1939–2002." *Canadian Military Journal* 6, 1 (2005): 25–32.

McGhee, Robert. "Contact between Native North Americans and the Medieval Norse: A Review of Evidence." *American Antiquity* 49, 1 (1984): 4–26.

McLachlan, Robert W. *Medals Awarded to Canadian Indians.* Reprinted from *The Gazette.* Montreal: 1899.

McLaughlin, Dennis. *Fighting for Canada: Chinese and Japanese Canadians in Military Service.* Ottawa: Department of National Defence, 2003.

McLaughlin, Dennis, and Leslie McLaughlin. *For My Country: Black Canadians on the Field of Honour*. Ottawa: Department of National Defence, 2004.

McLeod, Donald Wayne. "The Canadian Indian and World War One: Historical Background and Participation." Master's thesis, Royal Military College of Canada, 1979.

MacMillan, Margaret. *Paris 1919*. New York: Random House, 2003.

Maghraoui, Driss. "Moroccan Colonial Soldiers: Between Selective Memory and Collective Memory—Beyond Colonialism and Nationalism in North Africa." *Arab Studies Quarterly* 20, 2 (1998): 21–42.

Manzione, Joseph. *I Am Looking to the North for My Life: Sitting Bull 1876–1881*. Salt Lake City: University of Utah Press, 1991.

Marshall, Ingeborg. *A History and Ethnography of the Beothuk*. Montreal: McGill-Queen's University Press, 1996.

—. "An Unpublished Map Made by John Cartwright between 1768 and 1773 Showing Beothuck Indian Settlements and Artifacts and Allowing a New Population Estimate." *Ethnohistory* 24, 3 (1977): 223–249.

Marwick, Arthur. *War and Social Change in the Twentieth Century: A Comparative Study of Britain, France, Germany, Russia and the United States*. London: Palgrave Macmillan, 1974.

Meadows, William C. "North American Indian Code Talkers: Current Developments and Research." In *Aboriginal Peoples and Military Participation: Canadian and International Perspectives*, edited by P. Whitney Lackenbauer et al., 161–214. Kingston: Canadian Defence Academy Press, 2007.

Middleton, Richard. *Pontiac's War: Its Causes, Course and Consequences*. London: Routledge, 2007.

Miller, J.R. *Compact, Contract, Covenant: Aboriginal Treaty-Making in Canada*. Toronto: University of Toronto Press, 2009.

—. Introduction to *Aboriginal Peoples of Canada: A Short Introduction*, edited by Paul Robert Magocsi, 3–37. Toronto: University of Toronto Press, 2002.

—. *Lethal Legacy: Current Native Controversies in Canada*. Toronto: McClelland and Stewart, 2004.

—. "Owen Glendower, Hotspur, and Canadian Indian Policy." *Ethnohistory* 37, 4 (1990): 386–391.

—. *Skyscrapers Hide the Heavens: A History of Indian-White Relations in Canada*. Toronto: University Press, 2001.

Milloy, John S. *A National Crime: The Canadian Government and the Residential School System 1879–1986*. Winnipeg: University of Manitoba Press, 1999.

Milner, George R. *The Moundbuilders: Ancient Peoples of Eastern North America*. London: Thames and Hudson, 2004.

Ministry of Militia. *Canadian Expeditionary Force Units: Instructions Governing Organization and Administration*. Ottawa: Government Printing Bureau, 1916.

More, Thomas. *Utopia*. Wheeling, IL: Harlan Davidson, 1949.

Morris, Alexander. *The Treaties of Canada with the Indians of Manitoba and North-West Territories*. Toronto: Belfords, Clarke, 1880.

Morris, Philip H. *The Canadian Patriotic Fund: A Record of its Activities from 1914–1919.* Ottawa: The Mortimer Co., 1920.

Morrow Jr., John H. *The Great War: An Imperial History.* London: Routledge, 2004.

Morton, Desmond. *Silent Battle: Canadian Prisoners of War in Germany 1914–1918.* Toronto: Lester Publishing, 1992.

Morton, Desmond, and J.L. Granatstein. *Marching to Armageddon.* Toronto: Lester and Orpen Dennys, 1989.

Moses, John. "Aboriginal Participation in Canadian Military Service: Historic and Contemporary Contexts." *Canadian Army Journal* 3, 3 (2000): 43–47.

—. "The Return of the Native: Six Nations Veterans and Political Change at the Grand River Reserve, 1917–1924." In *Aboriginal Peoples and the Canadian Military: Historical Perspectives,* edited by P. Whitney Lackenbauer et al., 117–128. Kingston: Canadian Defence Academy Press, 2007.

—. *A Sketch Account of Aboriginal Peoples in the Canadian Military.* Ottawa: Department of National Defence, 2004.

Mountain Horse, Mike. *My People, The Bloods.* Calgary: Glenbow-Alberta Institute and Blood Tribal Council, 1979.

Nichols, Roger L. *Indians in the United States and Canada: A Comparative History.* Lincoln: University of Nebraska Press, 1998.

Nicholson, G.W.L. *Canadian Expeditionary Force 1914–1919: Official History of the Canadian Army.* Ottawa: Queen's Printer, 1962.

—. *The Fighting Newfoundlander: A History of The Royal Newfoundland Regiment.* London: Thomas Nelson Printers, 1964.

Niezen, Ronald. "Recognizing Indigenism: Canadian Unity and the International Movement of Indigenous Peoples." *Comparative Studies in Society and History* 42, 1 (2000): 119–148.

Noon, John A. *Law and Government of the Grand River Iroquois.* New York: Viking Fund, 1949.

O'Brien, Mike. "Out of a Clear Sky: The Mobilization of the Newfoundland Regiment, 1914–1915." *Newfoundland and Labrador Studies* 22, 2 (2007): 401–427.

O'Connor, P.S. "The Recruitment of Maori Soldiers, 1914–1918." *Political Science* 19, 2 (1967): 48–83.

Offer, Avner. *The First World War: An Agrarian Interpretation.* Oxford: Oxford University Press, 1989.

Office of Census and Statistics. *The Canada Yearbook, 1914–1919, 1939–1940.* Ottawa: King's Printer, 1915–1920, 1940–1941.

Omissi, David. *Indian Voices of the Great War: Soldiers' Letters, 1914–1918.* London: Macmillan Press, 1999.

—. *The Sepoy and the Raj: The Indian Army, 1860–1940.* London: Macmillan Press, 1994.

O'Toole, Fintan. *White Savage: William Johnson and the Invention of America.* London: Faber and Faber, 2005.

Ousby, Ian. *The Road to Verdun.* London: Random House, 2003.

Page, Robert. *The Boer War and Canadian Imperialism.* Ottawa: Canadian Historical Association, 1987.

Philbrick, Nathaniel. *The Last Stand: Custer, Sitting Bull, and the Battle of the Little Bighorn.* New York: Viking Books, 2010.

Pope, Peter E. *The Many Landfalls of John Cabot.* Toronto: University of Toronto Press, 1997.

Porch, Douglas. *Wars of Empire.* London: Cassell, 2000.

Preston, David L. *The Texture of Contact: European and Indian Settler Communities on the Frontiers of Iroquoia, 1667–1783.* Lincoln: University of Nebraska Press, 2009.

Rawling, Bill. *Surviving Trench Warfare: Technology and the Canadian Corps, 1914–1918.* Toronto: University of Toronto Press, 1992.

Ray, Arthur J. "Constructing and Reconstructing Native History: A Comparative Look at the Impact of Aboriginal and Treaty Rights Claims in North America and Australia." *Native Studies Review* 16, 1 (2005): 15–39.

Remarque, Erich Maria. *All Quiet on the Western Front.* New York: Fawcett Crest, 1982.

Renouf, M.A.P. "Prehistory of Newfoundland Hunter-Gatherers: Extinctions or Adaptations?" *World Archaeology* 30, 3 (1998): 403–420.

Richter, Daniel K. *The Ordeal of the Longhouse: The Peoples of the Iroquois League in the Era of European Colonization.* Chapel Hill: University of North Carolina Press, 1992.

Richter, Daniel K., and James H. Merrell, eds. *Beyond the Covenant Chain: The Iroquois and Their Neighbors in Indian North America, 1600–1800.* Syracuse: Syracuse University Press, 1987.

Robb, George. *British Culture and the First World War.* New York: Palgrave, 2002.

Rothfels, Nigel. *Savages and Beasts: The Birth of the Modern Zoo.* Baltimore: The Johns Hopkins University Press, 2002.

Royal Commission on Aboriginal Peoples. *Treaty Making in the Spirit of Co-existence: An Alternative to Extinguishment.* Ottawa: Canada Communication Group, 1993.

Ruck, Calvin W. *The Black Battalion: 1916–1920, Canada's Best Kept Military Secret.* Halifax: Nimbus Publishing, 1987.

Sattenspiel, Lisa, and Dawn Herring. "Structural Epidemic Models and the Spread of Influenza in the Central Canadian Sub-Arctic." *Human Biology* 70, 1 (1998): 91–115.

—. "Death in Winter: Spanish Flu in the Canadian Subarctic," in *The Spanish Influenza Pandemic of 1918–1919: New Perspectives,* 173–190.

Schreiber, Shane B. *Shock Army of the British Empire: The Canadian Corps in the Last Hundred Days of the Great War.* St. Catharines, ON: Vanwell Publishing, 2004.

Scoppio, Grazia. "Diversity Best Practices in Military Organizations in Canada, Australia, the United Kingdom and the United States." *Canadian Military Journal* 9, 3 (2009): 17–30.

Scott, Duncan Campbell. *The Administration of Indian Affairs in Canada.* Ottawa: Canadian Institute of International Affairs, 1931.

—. "The Canadian Indians and the Great War." In *Canada in the Great War, Vol. III: Guarding the Channel Ports,* 327–328. Toronto: United Publishers, 1919.

—. *1919 Report of the Deputy Superintendent General of Indian Affairs, Sessional Paper No. 27: The Indians and the Great War.* Ottawa: King's Printer, 1920.

Shannon, Timothy J. *Iroquois Diplomacy on the Early American Frontier.* New York: Penguin Books, 2008.

Sheffield, R. Scott. "Indifference, Difference and Assimilation: Aboriginal People in Canadian Military Practice, 1900–1945." In *Aboriginal Peoples and the Canadian Military: Historical Perspectives*, edited by P. Whitney Lackenbauer et al., 57–71. Kingston: Canadian Defence Academy Press, 2007.

—. "'Of Pure European Descent and of the White Race' Recruitment Policy and Aboriginal Canadians, 1939–1945." *Canadian Military History* 5, 1 (1996): 8–15.

—. *"The Red Man's on the Warpath": The Image of the "Indian" and the Second World War.* Vancouver: University of British Columbia Press, 2004.

—. *A Search for Equity: A Study of the Treatment Accorded to First Nations Veterans and Dependants of the Second World War and the Korean Conflict.* Ottawa: Department of Indian Affairs and Northern Development, 2001.

Six Nations Hereditary Longhouse Council. *The Redman's Appeal for Justice: The Position of the Six Nations that they Constitute an Independent State.* Oshweken, ON: Six Nations of the Grand River, 1924.

Smith, Donald B. *Chief Buffalo Child Long Lance: The Glorious Impostor.* Calgary: Red Deer Press, 2002.

—. "Fred Loft." In *Encyclopedia of North American Indians,* edited by Frederick E. Hoxie, 135. New York: Houghton Mifflin Harcourt, 1996.

—. *From the Land of the Shadows: The Making of Grey Owl.* Saskatoon: Western Producer Prairie Books, 1990.

Smith, Linda Tuhiwai. "Colonizing Knowledges." In *The Indigenous Experience: Global Perspectives,* edited by Roger C.A. Maaka and Chris Andersen, 91–110. Toronto: Canadian Scholars' Press, 2006.

Speck, Frank G. *Beothuk and Micmac.* New York: Museum of American Indian Heye Foundation, 1922.

Stacey, A.J., and Jean Edwards Stacey. *Memoirs of a Blue Puttee: The Newfoundland Regiment in World War One.* St. John's: DRC Publishers, 2002.

Stacey, C.P. *Introduction to the Study of Military History for Canadian Students.* Ottawa: Directorate of Training CF, 1972.

Starkey, Armstrong. *European and Native American Warfare, 1675–1815.* Norman: University of Oklahoma Press, 1998.

Stasiulis, Daiva K., and Nira Yuval-Davis. *Unsettling Settler Societies: Articulations of Gender, Race, Ethnicity and Class.* London: Sage, 1995.

Stevenson, Michael D. "The Mobilization of Native Canadians during the Second World War." *Journal of the Canadian Historical Association New Series* 7 (1996): 205–226.

Stonechild, Blair, and Bill Waiser. *Loyal Till Death: Indians and the North-West Rebellion.* Calgary: Fifth House, 1997.

Strachan, Hew. *The First World War, Volume 1: To Arms.* Oxford: Oxford University Press, 2001.

Streets, Heather, ed. *Martial Races and Masculinity in the British Army, 1857–1914.* Manchester: Manchester University Press, 2006.

Summerby, Janice. *Native Soldiers—Foreign Battlefields.* Ottawa: Department of Veterans Affairs, 2005.

Sweeny, Alistair. *Government Policy and Saskatchewan Indian Veterans: A Brief History of the Canadian Government's Treatment of Indian Veterans of the Two World Wars*. Saskatoon: Tyler, Wright and Daniel, 1979.

Tait, R.H. *Newfoundland: A Summary of the History and Development of Britain's Oldest Colony from 1497 to 1939*. Nyack, NY: Harrington Press, 1939.

—. *The Trail of the Caribou: The Royal Newfoundland Regiment 1914–1918*. Boston: Newfoundland Publishing, 1933.

Tate, Michael L. "From Scout to Doughboy: The National Debate over Integrating American Indians into the Military, 1891–1918." *Western Historical Quarterly* 17, 4 (1986): 417–437.

Thompson, Andrew T. *Report by Col. Andrew T. Thompson Commissioned to Investigate and Enquire into the Affairs of the Six Nations Indians, 1923*. Ottawa: King's Printer, 1924.

Thompson, John Herd. *Ethnic Minorities during Two World Wars*. Ottawa: Canadian Historical Association, Government of Canada, 1991.

—. *The Harvests of War: The Prairie West 1914–1918*. Toronto: McClelland and Stewart, 1978.

Tilton, Robert S. *Pocahontas: The Evolution of an American Narrative*. Cambridge: Cambridge University Press, 1994.

Titley, Brian A. *A Narrow Vision: Duncan Campbell Scott and the Administration of Indian Affairs in Canada*. Vancouver: University of British Columbia Press, 1986.

Tobias, John L. "Protection, Civilization, Assimilation." In *Sweet Promises: A Reader on Indian-White Relations in Canada*, edited by J.R. Miller, 127–144. Toronto: University of Toronto Press, 1991.

Townsend, Kenneth William. *World War II and the American Indian*. Albuquerque: University of New Mexico Press, 2000.

Travers, Tim. "Debate: Reply to John Hussey: The Movement of German Divisions to the Western Front, Winter 1917–1918." *War in History* 5, 3 (1998): 367–370.

Treager, Edward. *The Aryan Maori*. Wellington: G. Didsbury Government Printer, 1885.

Trevithick, Scott R. "Conflicting Outlooks: The Background to the 1924 Deposing of the Six Nations Hereditary Council." Master's thesis, University of Calgary, 1998.

Tugwell, Maurice, and John Thompson. *The Legacy of Oka*. Toronto: Mackenzie Institute, 1991.

Upton, L.F.S. "The Extermination of the Beothucks of Newfoundland." *The Canadian Historical Review* 58, 2 (1977): 133–153.

Vance, Jonathan F. *Death So Noble: Memory, Meaning, and the First World War*. Vancouver: University of British Columbia Press, 1997.

Vandervort, Bruce. *Indian Wars of Canada, Mexico and the United States: 1812–1900*. New York: Routledge, 2006.

Wahta Band Council. *A History of the Wahta Mohawk Community*. Wahta, ON: Joan Holmes and Associates, 2002.

Walker, James W. "Race and Recruitment in World War I: Enlistment of Visible Minorities in the Canadian Expeditionary Force." *Canadian Historical Review* 70, 1 (1989): 1–26.

White, Bruce. "The American Army and the Indian." In *Ethnic Armies: Polyethnic Armed Forces from the Time of the Hapsburgs to the Age of the Superpowers*, edited by N.F. Dreisziger, 69–88. Waterloo: Wilfrid Laurier University Press, 1990.

Wilson, Barbara. *Ontario and the First World War, 1914–1918: A Collection of Documents*. Toronto: Champlain Society, 1977.

Winegard, Timothy C. "The Canadian Siberian Expeditionary Force, 1918–1919, and the Complications of Coalition Warfare." *Journal of Slavic Military Studies* 20, 2 (2007): 283–328.

—. "An Introduction to Charles A. Cooke within the Context of Aboriginal Identity." *Ontario History* 102, 1 (2010): 78–80.

—. *Oka: A Convergence of Cultures and the Canadian Forces*. Kingston: Canadian Defence Academy Press, 2008.

Woodward, Grace Steele. *Pocahontas*. Norman: University of Oklahoma Press, 1969.

Yealland, Lewis R., and E. Farquhar Buzzard. *Hysterical Disorders of Warfare*. London: Macmillan, 1918.

INDEX